AQA Sociology

Exclusively endorsed by AQA

AS

Circe Newbold
Mark Peace
Liz Swain
Michael Wright

Consultant
Patrick McNeill

 Nelson Thornes

Published in 2008 by:
Nelson Thornes Ltd
Delta Place
27 Bath Road
CHELTENHAM
GL53 7TH
United Kingdom

12 / 10 9 8 7 6 5 4 3

A catalogue record for this book is available from the British Library

ISBN 978 0 7487 9830 8

Cover photograph by Photolibrary

Illustrations include artwork drawn by Angela Knowles, Harry Venning and Wearset Ltd

Page make-up by Wearset Ltd, Tyne and Wear

Printed in China

Acknowledgements

The authors and publisher would like to thank the following for permission to reproduce photographs and other copyright material:

p3: Alamy / Images of Africa Photobank; p11: Alamy / Creatas / JUPITERIMAGES; p13: Alamy / Sally and Richard Greenhill; p15: Alamy / David Levenson; p22: Getty Images; p23: Getty Images Europe; p26: Alamy / David Crausby; p29: Alamy / Photofusion Picture Library; pp33, 42: Alamy / Joshua Roper; p47: Alamy / David Lyons; pp49, 226: Alamy / Design Pics Inc; p52: Alamy / Arnis Altens; p55: Alamy / Huw Jones; p59: Alamy / PCL; pp61, 114: Getty Images / Popperfoto; p66: Getty Images / Time & Life Pictures; p68: Radius Images / Alamy; p69: ColorBlind; p70: Alamy / TP Photography Stock; p77: Alamy / Jack Picone; p78: Alamy / Mike Goldwater; p84: Alamy / Ian Thraves; p89: Alamy / Catherine Paffey; p91: Alamy / Roger Cracknell 17/ Europe; p93: Alamy / Keith Leighton; p98: Alamy / David Hoffman Photo Library; p102: Alamy / Photofusion Picture Library; p109: Alamy / Roger Bamber; p112: Alamy / Jennie Hart; pp115, 154, 159: Getty Images; p121: Alamy / Peter Titmuss; p126: Alamy / BananaStock / JUPITERIMAGES; p131: Alamy / Bob Handelman; p132: Alamy /Janine Wiedel / Photolibrary; p141: Alamy / Mike Abrahams; p145: Alamy / Mira; p151: Alamy / Stock Connection Distribution; p177: Alamy / Liz Boyd; p178: Alamy / Philip Scalia; p180: Alamy / George S de Blonsky; p186: Alamy / David Hoffman Photo Library; pp186, 194: Alamy / Andrew Butterton; p198: Alamy / Frans Lemmens; p202: Alamy / Vario Images GmbH & Co. KG; p204: Doctor Stock / Richard Pasley; p219: Alamy / Aflo Foto Agency; p221: Alamy / Jamie Simpson; p224: Alamy / Gaja Snover; p234: Alamy / Janine Wiedel Photolibrary; p236: Alamy / Duncan Hale-Sutton; p242: Alamy / Christopher Pillitz; p244: Alamy / David Levenson; p246: Alamy / B.A.E. Inc.; p250: Alamy / Image Source Black

Contents

AQA introduction

Nelson Thornes has worked in partnership with AQA to ensure this book and the accompanying online resources offer you the best support for your GCSE course.

All resources have been approved by senior AQA examiners so you can feel assured that they closely match the specification for this subject and provide you with everything you need to prepare successfully for your exams.

These print and online resources together **unlock blended learning**; this means that the links between the activities in the book and the activities online blend together to maximise your understanding of a topic and help you achieve your potential.

These online resources are available on **kerboodle!** which can be accessed via the internet at **http://www.kerboodle.com/live**, anytime, anywhere. If your school or college subscribes to this service you will be provided with your own personal login details. Once logged in, access your course and locate the required activity.

For more information and help visit **http://www.kerboodle.com**

Icons in this book indicate where there is material online related to that topic. The following icons are used:

💡 Learning activity

These resources include a variety of interactive and non-interactive activities to support your learning.

✓ Progress tracking

These resources include a variety of tests that you can use to check your knowledge on particular topics (Test yourself) and a range of resources that enable you to analyse and understand examination questions (On your marks…).

🔎 Research support

These resources include WebQuests, in which you are assigned a task and provided with a range of web links to use as source material for research.

How to use this book

This book covers the specification for your course and is arranged in a sequence approved by AQA.

The book content is divided into six topics matched to the six topics of the AQA Sociology AS specification – Culture and Identity; Families and Households; Wealth, Poverty and Welfare; Education; Health and Sociological Methods. Each topic introduction contains a table mapping the topic content to the specification so you can see at a glance where to find the information you need. Topics are then further divided into chapters, each with its own summary, and then sections, making them clear and easy to use.

The features in this book include:

Learning objectives

At the beginning of each section you will find a list of learning objectives that contain targets linked to the requirements of the specification.

Key terms

Terms that you will need to be able to define and understand.

Hint

Hints to aid your understanding of the topics.

Links

This highlights any key areas where topics relate to one another.

Research study

Summaries of important sociological research studies to enhance your knowledge and understanding of a topic.

Summary questions

Short questions that test your understanding of the subject and allow you to apply the skills you develop to different scenarios. The final question in each set is designed to be more challenging and to require more thought.

Nelson Thornes is responsible for the solution(s) given and they may not constitute the only possible solution(s). Answers are supplied free at www.nelsonthornes.com/sociology_answers.

AQA Examiner's tip

Hints from AQA examiners to help you with your study and to prepare for your exam.

AQA Examination-style questions

Questions in the style that you can expect in your exam. The Sociological Methods questions are tested in the Education and Health sections.

AQA examination questions are reproduced by permission of the Assessment and Qualifications Alliance.

Chapter summary

A bulleted list at the end of each chapter summarising the content in an easy-to-follow way.

■ Web links in the book

As Nelson Thornes is not responsible for third party content online, there may be some changes to this material that are beyond our control. In order for us to ensure that the links referred to in the book are as up-to-date and stable as possible, the websites are usually homepages with supporting instructions on how to reach the relevant pages if necessary.

Please let us know at **kerboodle@nelsonthornes.com** if you find a link that doesn't work and we will do our best to redirect the link, or to find an alternative site.

Sociology AS introduction

Introduction for students

Studying sociology will not change your life but it should change the way you look at life, at people and at society, both in this country and worldwide.

The key point to understand about sociology is that it has a particular way of looking at society and social life; in fact it has several ways of doing this, but they have one thing in common – they do not take anything at face value. Sociology is a social science and, like all good science, good sociology is based on logical arguments that are based on good evidence. As far as possible, sociology takes an objective look at the social world, avoiding the personal and moral preferences, values and prejudices that lie behind 'common sense' and the political slants that can underlie press journalism and, arguably, much of the output of TV stations. Of course, it is not as simple as that; your studies will show you how questions of 'bias' and 'objectivity' are hotly debated by sociologists but it remains true that good science aims, as far as possible, to minimise bias and to maintain objectivity.

The sociologist Peter Berger said this in his book *Invitation to Sociology* which was first published in 1963. 'The sociologist', he wrote, 'is someone concerned with understanding society in a disciplined way'. He also wrote: 'the sociologist … is a person intensively, endlessly, shamelessly interested in the doings of men'. (NB Yes, he wrote 'men': that is a good example of how what is taken for granted at one period of history is challenged in another period. No sociologist today would use the word 'men' to mean 'men and women'. Feminist perspectives have put us right about that.)

More recently, the same message comes across from Nick Abercrombie in his book *Sociology*, published in 2004. This would be a good book for you to dip into after you have been studying sociology for a few weeks. The ideas in it are not easy but it is quite short and it is very clearly written. It gives a good picture of what sociology is like at the beginning of the 21st century.

Abercrombie is particularly good when he is writing about the difference between sociology and common sense. He makes the point that 'Because we take our everyday world for granted – it is simply there – we do not typically question it or ask why it takes the form that it does'. But sociology does ask these questions and that means it challenges our 'common sense'.

It questions the assumptions on which our everyday lives are based. It asks questions that some people find uncomfortable and suggests answers that some people, especially people in authority, feel threatened by. As a result, says Abercrombie, it can 'make people angry or surprised or intrigued or transformed – or even reassured'.

He concludes that sociology 'tries to identify and solve the puzzles that the everyday world throws up and, in doing so, provides the way of giving a different meaning to the cosy everyday world around us'.

Studying sociology at AS level

The AQA specification gives your school or college quite a lot of choice about which topics in sociology you will study. But, whatever they are, you should aim to bring this questioning attitude to bear. So, for example, when you are looking at what sociologists have had to say about families and households, you will learn about the research that has been done, the concepts that have been developed and used, and the theories that have been produced in an attempt to describe and explain what a family is, why there are families, how people live in families, how family life affects people's lives, how the wider society affects life in families and, in particular, how the family has changed and continues to change. You will find that some research findings contradict others, that different sociologists approach their subject matter in different ways, and that they arrive at different conclusions. What I hope you will find is that some of the research and some of the conclusions make you 'angry or surprised or intrigued or transformed – or even reassured'. If your study of sociology gives 'a different meaning to the cosy everyday world' around you, it will have succeeded. If it leaves you with the same views and the same perspective on life as you had when you started the course, then it will have failed.

So, when you are reading what sociologists have found in their research and you think about the conclusions that have been drawn from it, you should ask questions such as:

- How does he or she know that?
- What is their evidence?
- How did they do the research? What were the research methods?
- Is there any sort of bias in the work?
- Do the conclusions really follow from the evidence?

- What have other sociologists had to say about the same topic?

If you go into more detail in your studies of a particular piece of research, you could ask:

- Why did the researcher choose to study this topic?
- Who paid for it to be done?
- Could the topic have been researched in some other way?
- What other conclusions might have been drawn from the same evidence?

Taking the exam

In the end, you will take the AS exam and you will want to get the best result you can. Of course, you must show that you have the necessary knowledge and understanding of what sociologists have said about the topics that the examiner asks questions about. But I promise you that the really high grades go to candidates who, in addition to showing what they know, also show that they have thought about their sociology, have weighed up the arguments and the evidence, and can express themselves and their conclusions in a considered response to the question set.

■ Introduction for teachers

Sociology at this level can be said to have two main aims:

1 to give all students some understanding of contemporary society and social life
2 to prepare a minority of students to study sociology at degree level.

Balancing these aims is not easy but it is what both the revised specification and this textbook aim to achieve.

The revised specification

The team that produced the revised specification worked within certain constraints, but also with some opportunities.

The most obvious constraints were the revised AS/A-level qualification criteria from QCA, which required a move from six units to four, and the revised AS/A-level subject criteria for sociology, which can be found on the QCA website.

The opportunities were that, while the revised subject criteria are not radically different from the previous version, there are some important changes of emphasis. The section on 'Aims' starts as follows:

The study of A level sociology should focus on contemporary society. Studying sociology should foster the development of critical and reflective thinking with a respect for social diversity. It should provide an awareness of the importance of social structure and social action in explaining social issues. Students should be encouraged to develop their own sociological awareness through active engagement with the contemporary social world.

The subject criteria also include phrases such as 'active involvement in the research process', 'personal identity, roles and responsibilities within society', and 'lifelong interest in social issues'.

The AQA revision committee fully supported the aims of the revised subject criteria but was mindful of the need to avoid overdoing the changes so that there would be enough continuity with the current specification to be fair to teachers and students.

A main driver of the revision has therefore been to bring the revised specification up to date in terms of its focus both on contemporary society and on recent developments in sociology. At the same time, it has maintained some degree of continuity with the old specification.

Coursework

The revised subject criteria ruled out coursework for sociology at this level. The AQA revision committee sought to find ways to ensure that the emphasis on sociological methods should not be lost and to encourage teachers to help their students engage in 'active involvement in the research process'. This has been achieved by including research methods in Units 2 and 4 (A2), where the exam paper will include questions both on research methods in their own right, and on research methods as they are applied in contexts. 'Education' and 'Health' were chosen for Unit 2, and 'Crime and Deviance' and 'Stratification and Differentiation' for Unit 4, on the grounds that these topics have rich potential for this 'methods-in-context' approach.

This book

This book has been written by a team of authors consisting of experienced teachers and examiners who have had access to advice and guidance from the senior examining team at AQA. It is endorsed by AQA.

Patrick McNeill

Culture and identity

Introduction

Culture is the way that people live within their society, in relation to shared beliefs, language and traditions. Another part of culture is the artefacts that are left by members of a society. An artefact is any object made by humans. This could be an ornament, a painting or a newspaper. Although there are many definitions, perhaps the best way to understand culture is to see it as the behaviour that is learned by members of a society.

Our personal identity is the things we think are true about ourselves and our beliefs, for example that we are hardworking or that we are not good at sport. Sociologists are particularly interested in the relationship between our sense of personal identity and the culture of the society in which we live.

If we consider beliefs about marriage and family life there is **cultural diversity** within and between cultures and over time. Fifty years ago most people got married before they had children; these marriages were based on monogamy (one man and one woman). This has changed over time – being born outside marriage is no longer seen as shameful.

Socialisation

Socialisation is the process through which we learn from others how to behave within our culture. Without the process of socialisation we would not behave in ways that are recognised as 'human'.

There are two parts to the socialisation process; **primary socialisation** and **secondary socialisation**. These involve different agencies or groups of people.

The topic of culture and identity is particularly interesting for sociology students as it allows the application of a range of sociological theories to contemporary social life. The debate about whether society shapes our behaviour or we shape society through our actions is key to understanding every AS and A2 sociology topic.

To conclude, sociologists are interested in culture as it helps us to understand why people behave in the ways they do. It is important that we recognise that although cultural beliefs and behaviour are diverse we should not assume that the culture of our society is superior to that of other cultures. Sociologists are interested in how we learn our culture and how this shapes our sense of individual and social identity.

Concepts of culture

Values, norms and mores

Learning objectives:

- Understand the nature–nurture debate in sociology.

- Assess the importance of socialisation in shaping behaviour.

- Explain the differences between values, norms, mores and roles.

Key terms

Values: are beliefs about what is good and bad, some values are based on religious beliefs while others may be based on the needs of the social system.

Norms: are guidelines for behaviour in specific social settings.

Mores: are internalised attitudes towards certain social behaviours that are seen as taboo or completely morally unacceptable by members of a culture.

Social roles: are patterns of behaviour that are expected from people holding certain positions in society.

The nature–nurture debate: this debate is about how much of our behaviour is genetic (natural) and how much is learned (cultural). Sociologists would argue that culture is more powerful in shaping our behaviour than nature.

Hint

Think about the journey from home to school or college. You expect drivers to stop at a red light and drive on the left. You do not expect pedestrians to step onto the road. If people did not observe cultural rules for driving and walking this would result in chaos and the journey to school would be dangerous.

We are born into a society that already exists and we begin to learn the culture of our society very early in our lives. Some aspects of human behaviour are genetic, for example our physiological (bodily) need for food. Babies cry when they are hungry and are satisfied when this physical need is met. However, as we get older we learn to respond to the physical need for food in ways that are seen as acceptable in our culture, for example eating at specific times. Our culture acts as a template for shaping how we meet our physiological needs. Language is another example of how we adapt – humans are born with the capacity to use language but there are thousands of different languages in the world today. Non-verbal communication is also influenced by culture. Sitting with legs crossed is often used to communicate someone is relaxed in Britain, but is offensive in Ghana and Turkey. Anything we learn can be understood as cultural and all societies have ways of teaching culture to their members, sometimes through direct instruction in schools or religious institutions. Behaviour that is seen as 'correct' is also taught informally, for example, by smiles or frowns from those we interact with. The media is becoming more and more important in the secondary socialisation process.

Through the socialisation process we learn **values**. Examples of widely held values in contemporary society include the belief that human life is sacred and it is important to work hard at school. We also learn **norms** through the socialisation process. For example, in a job interview it is appropriate to dress smartly and not swear; however, when relaxing with friends we can behave differently. **Mores** are behaviours that are seen as completely unacceptable within a culture, for example incest; if these are broken a strong and swift punishment can be expected. We understand **social roles** – for example a mother is expected to be loving and a judge is expected to be authoritative. We learn these roles through the socialisation process.

The **nature–nurture debate** in sociology is focused on the extent to which our behaviour is shaped by nature or culture.

As a result of the socialisation process and our experience of interacting with others we all develop our own sense of identity. Without the socialisation process social life would be impossible as we would be unable to predict what other people would do. For any society a shared culture that allows us to predict what other people will do is essential. We internalise behaviour patterns and cultural rules through the social relationships we engage in.

Summary questions

1. Identify three behaviours that are different in different cultures.

2. Suggest two ways in which we learn the culture of our society.

3. Using material from this section and elsewhere examine the view that biology (nature) is the strongest influence on human behaviour.

Subcultures

Learning objectives:

■ Understand the concept of subculture.

■ Recognise how subcultures can develop as a response to the way society is structured and organised.

■ Apply Cohen's concept of status frustration to contemporary subcultures.

Key term

Subculture: a culture within a culture where a group develops distinctive norms and values that are different from those of the mainstream culture.

Links

This material links to the topic of Crime and Deviance (A2).

Patrick's (1973) study can be usefully applied to questions on participant observation in the Sociological Methods topic (AS) and the Theory and Methods topic (A2).

Hint

Explain in your own words how Patrick's study can be used to illustrate Cohen's ideas. How were the actions of the young men inverting mainstream norms by the things they did? How might the acts have given them status?

Some groups within a society develop some distinctive norms and values that are different from or opposite to mainstream culture. These groups are known as **subcultures**.

Subcultures can be based around the culture of origin of immigrant groups who retain many of their own cultural traditions. These cultural traditions include clothes, food, religion and language. However, other subcultures can be based on social class and age. Subcultures can emerge as a result of the experiences of people in their society.

Albert Cohen (1955) developed an explanation of delinquent youth subcultures. Cohen tried to explain why young working-class men were more likely to commit crime than other social classes but these crimes seemed to be committed for 'kicks' or fun. Cohen claimed that young working-class men were the group who statistically are least likely to succeed in education and therefore find it most difficult to get well-paid jobs, they were unable the get the status to expect if they were to be regarded as successful. In areas where there were many young working-class men suffering from status frustration there was a strong possibility of a subculture developing. In this subculture some of the norms and values of mainstream society were inverted or 'turned upside down'. This became a way of getting back at a society in which they could not succeed. Some of the norms that might be acted out by a delinquent subculture in school might be rudeness to teachers, outside school the members of the subculture might be violent and commit petty crime and vandalism.

Research study: James Patrick (1973) 'A Glasgow gang observed'

In the late 1950's James Patrick (not his real name) joined a violent Glaswegian gang for four months. One incident he observed illustrated Cohen's ideas well. One day the gang went to a public library and made lots of noise, they then set a waste paper bin on fire before running away.

One example is the way young working-class men in the 1990s adopted the fashion of the wealthy. Burberry clothing used to be regarded as an upper-class brand and by paying the higher prices of the brand working-class men were seen as claiming the status of the wealthy. The negativity surrounding the subculture in the media and the identification of the group as 'chavs' meant that the status gained was short-lived.

Summary questions

4 How does the behaviour of the gang members in Patrick's study illustrate how subcultures develop deviant ways of gaining status?

5 Suggest two reasons for the existence of subcultures in contemporary Britain.

6 Explain why social inequality might lead to subcultures.

High and low culture

Culture and identity

Learning objectives:

- Explain how the concept of culture is sometimes used to refer to particular cultural forms.
- Understand why the concept of high culture is value laden.
- Compare different types of cultural capital.

Link

This material links to the Mass Media topic (A2).

Key terms

Elite: in sociology the elite is a relatively small dominant group within a larger society. The elite enjoy high status and privilege within a society.

Cultural capital: a concept used by the Marxist writer Bourdieu, which refers to the use of language, confidence and social skills. The middle class are seen as having more cultural capital than the working class.

Link

This material links to the Education topic (AS) and the Stratification and Differentiation topic (A2).

A sociological understanding of culture is the institutions, artefacts, values and norms that are present in a particular society; this is the broadest definition of culture. However, there are several common-sense understandings of the term 'culture' and these tend to be used in judgemental ways. In the following sections some of these will be explored.

Some understandings of culture see it as the best and most accomplished artistic works. High culture is associated with the tastes of wealthy and educated people and is often juxtaposed with 'low' culture or 'mass' culture. High culture is valued more highly in our society; it is the cultural tastes of the **elite**.

Hint

Think about the different attitudes to and funding of minority high cultural arts such as opera and popular mass cultural arts such as soap operas. Why does the National Lottery support the National Opera, which does not have large enough audiences to survive without the additional funding? Do different sections of society regard each art form the same? If a person were described to you as 'highly cultured' what sorts of tastes would they have in music, art and literature?

When we think of high culture we might think of Shakespeare, Da Vinci and Verdi. Understanding high culture needs access to a particular kind of education. From a Marxist perspective the ruling class benefit from their culture being seen as superior as they are seen to be more intellectually able to appreciate this type of culture. This division between high and low culture is reinforced through the socialisation process. Agencies of socialisation, such as the education system and the mass media, present some cultural products as more 'worthy' than others.

Cultural capital

Pierre Bourdieu, in his analysis of educational achievement in France in the 1960s, suggested that middle-class success in education is not just a result of economic advantage but also of cultural advantage. Bourdieu argues that through the process of socialisation the children of the wealthy learn to understand and appreciate high culture as this is the type of culture that their parents appreciate. The school curriculum tends to be based on cultural forms that are seen as rare and worthy and a child who is familiar with this culture is more likely to succeed.

Low culture is the counterpart of high culture and is seen as inferior to it. Low culture is associated with the tastes of lower socio-economic groups. Low culture is sometimes called mass culture.

Summary questions

7 Identify two characteristics of high culture.

8 Suggest two reasons why different types of cultural capital might give middle-class children an advantage at school.

9 Explain the ideological functions of the idea that some cultural forms are superior to others.

Mass culture

Learning objectives:

- Understand why the term 'mass culture' is value laden.

- Explain the pessimistic view of mass culture.

- Summarise the proposed link between mass culture and capitalism.

Link

This material links to the Mass Media and Theory and Methods topics (A2).

Key terms

Folk culture: group habits or customs of traditional rural communities. These customs emerge directly from lived experience; examples might be songs such as ballads.

Culture industries: the culture industries are sometimes known as the creative industries and are involved in the manufacture and production of cultural commodities such as music, film, publishing, television and radio.

AQA Examiner's tip

In your responses to 24-mark questions that ask you to 'examine the view' of a particular issue, you must always make criticisms of the view in question. Make lists of criticisms of different theories to help you to do this in the exam.

Hint

Consider the plots of the last five films you have watched. What do they have in common? Listen to the top-selling singles this week – are there more similarities than differences?

Mass culture is a value-laden term and is often used in the same way as low culture. The term is used in a negative way to describe the cultural tastes of the working class. Concerns about the effects of the mass media on culture were raised by the Frankfurt School of sociologists after the Second World War. Adorno, Marcuse and Horkheimer were dismissive of the content of the mass media and its effects on society.

Writing from a Marxist perspective, the Frankfurt School claimed that mass economic production had led to the development of mass society. This was caused by the breakdown of neighbourhoods as people moved from their traditional communities in search of work. With the breakdown of these working-class communities traditional **folk culture** was disappearing. The **culture industries** including the mass media became very important in helping isolated individuals make sense of their world. The culture industries exist within a capitalist system and to make a profit they must appeal to a mass audience. The products of the culture industries have therefore to pitch their products at a level that can be understood by everyone. The production of culture is more and more centralised and the consumption of it leads to an uncritical mass of people who are made passive by unchallenging media output.

Theodor Adorno was a trained classical musician and was one of the members of the Frankfurt School of sociologists. Adorno criticised popular music for offering the working class easy pleasure by producing a simplified type of music in order to make a profit. Although there appears to be a diversity of popular music available to consumers, all popular music is simple in structure and just variations on the same theme. Over time this 'debased' type of culture stops people being able to appreciate more complex musical forms. The cultural commodities circulated by the mass media, made the working classes docile and content and willing to accept life in an unfair social system.

The Frankfurt School was critical of mass culture and the culture industries. They saw the culture industries as central to the capitalist system. Not only are they sources of vast profits for owners, but they also create false needs in the working class through advertising. They saw the culture industries as bad for the working classes as they actually stopped them thinking about important political issues. Finally, they present a distorted, one-dimensional view of society. As a result of the need to appeal to a mass audience cultural forms are simplified; there is a dumbing-down of culture. For example, characters in films are simplified in terms of 'goodies' and 'baddies', themes are 'universal' and stereotypes are common.

Summary questions

10 Identify two characteristics of mass culture.

11 Suggest two reasons for the alleged decline in folk culture.

12 Using examples assess the view that mass culture works to maintain a passive workforce.

Popular culture

Learning objectives:

- Describe why the term 'popular culture' is less judgemental than 'low' or 'mass' culture.

- Understand the importance of style in analysing youth subcultures.

- Explain how youth subcultures can be seen as an expression of working-class resistance.

Key term

Hegemony: the dominant class in any society will attempt to make the ideas that benefit them accepted by everyone. If they can persuade disadvantaged groups to accept the political and moral values of the ruling class then they have achieved hegemony. However, Gramsci points out that there are always pockets of resistance to ruling class hegemony. Youth subcultures can be interpreted as a form of this resistance.

Hint

It is interesting to try to 'read' the meanings of subcultural styles. Take any contemporary subculture such as skaters, EMOs or goths and read the meaning of the clothes they wear and the music they listen to. Are they expressing any resistance to mainstream culture?

AQA Examiner's tip

Always try to apply sociological ideas to contemporary society in your exam answers as this will show that you understand the material.

The term 'popular culture' is less value-laden than the term 'mass culture' but both concepts are used to describe cultural forms enjoyed by many people. Popular culture is commercially produced and includes objects, images, artefacts, literature and music of 'ordinary' people. Examples of popular culture are films, television programmes, magazines, newspapers, etc. Popular culture reflects the norms, values, institutions and artefacts that make up the everyday lives of the majority of people in a society. Popular culture is often contrasted with elitist high culture; it is the culture of the working class rather than the ruling class.

In the 1960s and 1970s a number of civil rights and protest movements emerged in America and Europe. These included student riots in Paris, such as Vietnam protests. The civil rights movement and feminism also emerged at this time. In music, Elvis Presley, the Beatles and Bob Dylan reflected some of the ideas of these new social movements. The music, literature, protests and lifestyles of the young did not bear out the Frankfurt School view of mass culture as making the working class passive and accepting of capitalism. The young were not passive; they were actively challenging mainstream ideas.

Stuart Hall and other writers working at the Centre for Contemporary Cultural Studies (CCCS) in Birmingham led the way in trying to understand popular culture. The CCCS analysed the lives and culture of ordinary people and how class, gender and ethnicity influenced youth and the development of youth subcultures.

The concept of cultural resistance was used to understand how youth subcultures did not passively accept the idea that capitalism was good. Antonio Gramsci's concept of **hegemony** was used to understand how young people expressed their resistance to mainstream ideas in symbolic ways. In *Resistance through Rituals* (Hall and Jefferson, 1976) Stuart Hall brought together a collection of essays on youth subcultures including mods, rockers and punks. Punk, for example, can be seen as an expression of anger towards capitalism in several ways. The name and music of punk's most notorious band, the Sex Pistols, expressed hostility towards mainstream ideas, with titles such as 'Anarchy in the UK'. The clothing of punks, such as safety-pin earrings, can be seen as a rejection of commercial fashion.

In their analysis of the skinhead subculture, Clarke *et al.* (1976) claimed that the clothing style of skinheads – Doc Marten boots, drainpipe jeans, etc. – could be read as an attempt to recapture their working-class identity at a time of urban redevelopment and immigration. The smart suits of the Mods can be seen as expressing working-class aspirations to become middle class while the leathers of the Rockers can be seen as expressing traditional working-class masculinity.

Summary questions

13 Identify two ways in which youth cultures can challenge mainstream ideas.

14 Suggest two reasons why the concept of popular culture is less judgemental than the term 'mass culture'.

15 Using examples from a range of subcultures, explain how they show resistance to hegemony.

Global culture

Learning objectives:

■ Explain the process of globalisation.

■ Summarise emergence of global media corporations.

■ Understand the significance of global media on culture.

Hint

Think about the food you eat in a day. How much of your diet is influenced by the traditional foods of other cultures? Where does your food come from? Could you buy similar food in any country in the world? George Ritzer (1992) has written about McDonaldisation – we can buy an identical burger in identical surroundings in cities around the world.

Hint

The Walt Disney Company is one of the largest entertainment corporations in the world; it is an example of a **synergy**. It controls many types of media enterprises. Disney also controls the merchandising of its products in its stores. Count the Disney products you have read, seen or visited. Is the brand an example of **cultural imperialism**? Should we be concerned?

Key terms

Synergy: two or more agents working in harmony. For example, when a media organisation owns media operations in a variety of industry sectors and uses each operation to promote others.

Cultural imperialism: a process in which an economically powerful nation is able to impose its own culture on another smaller, less powerful nation.

Globalisation has caused much culture to be similar around the world. The influence on culture by local and even national boundaries becomes less important. The growth of global economic interdependence has influenced the growth of a global cultural system. It is argued that due to this process of globalisation there is a single culture where American commercialism dominates, with nation states losing their distinctive cultural identities.

As cultural commodities such as clothes, music and films become more and more globally produced, people in countries around the world increasingly share a set of symbols that are used to create their identity. In this global culture identity is increasingly based on consumption patterns as people all around the world express themselves and their identity in the fashion, music and other cultural commodities they buy. Distinctions between high and low culture become increasingly irrelevant as cultural forms from different countries interact with each other to produce new cultural forms at increasing speed. Bilton *et al.* (1996) suggest that the speed of change may result in us losing our sense of what is important to our identity in our own society; our identity is increasingly unstable as a consequence of globalisation. Politicians in many countries are concerned about the effects of globalisation on culture; in Britain, Gordon Brown has called for a debate about 'Britishness' and what this means.

There are growing ties of interdependence between countries and transnational corporations that conduct business across national boundaries. There is now a global economy and a global marketplace that affects many aspects of our lives including our personal identity.

The mass media is organised on a global scale and has become a very important leisure activity of most people in developed countries. The mass media communicates ideas, images and identities to people around the world. People in different countries are likely to be watching similar things on their TV and in the cinema as the same products are marketed around the world. Golding and Murdock (1991) point out that multimedia corporations, such as News International, not only own media concerns across the world but have created synergies that allow them to use each media concern to advertise another; this gives them a competitive advantage and may result in fewer local media concerns being able to establish themselves.

Advertising is an important part of the content of the mass media, commodities are often marketed around the world using the same campaign. Marxists would criticise advertising for creating false needs in the working class (think about how often fashion changes and ways in which, for example, young women are encouraged to wear the latest fashion) and in doing so providing more profit for the capitalist class.

Summary questions

16 Identify two reasons for the emergence of a global culture.

17 Explain how subcultures show resistance to hegemony.

Chapter summary

Further resources

T.W. Adorno, *The Culture Industry*, Routledge, 1991

S. Best, J. Griffiths and T. Hope, *Active Sociology*, Pearson Education, 2000

P. Bourdieu and J.-C. Passerson, *Reproduction in Education, Society and Culture*, Sage, 1977

M. Haralambos and M. Holborn, *Sociology, Themes and Perspectives*, HarperCollins, 2000

M. Jones and E. Jones, *Mass Media*, Macmillan, 1999

www.feralchildren.com

www.sociology.org.uk

- Society is not the same as culture – Society is made up of a system of social institutions. Culture is how people live within this system, the norms, values, mores and artefacts that are produced.

- Culture as a whole way of life – This is a sociological definition of culture. The concept of culture has been used in many different ways over time.

- The nature–nurture debate – Some of our behaviour is instinctual but much of it is learned. Geneticists claim that there are genes for a number of behaviours but evidence is not always conclusive.

- Primary and secondary socialisation – Socialisation is a lifelong process. Our family is the most important agency in the first few years but other agencies become important later.

- Subculture – In contemporary Britain many subcultures exist. A subculture is a culture within a culture. Subcultures can result from a shared cultural tradition within a group of people or can be a response to social inequality. There are several theories of subculture. Albert Cohen's theory is broadly functionalist. Marxist perspectives on subcultures are examined in the 'popular culture' section.

- High and low culture – Some writers suggest that some types of cultural product are intrinsically more valuable than others. Others argue that the ruling class have used their power to define their culture as superior and this gives their children an advantage in school as they have more cultural capital than working-class children.

- Mass culture – The Frankfurt School were concerned that the 'base' nature of mass-produced culture was robbing the working class of their revolutionary potential. Critics suggest that this is an elitist view of culture and there is no objective basis for claiming one type of culture is better than another.

- Popular culture – Neo-Marxist sociologists such as Stuart Hall rejected the view that cultural studies should focus on high culture. Using Gramsci's concept of hegemony, Hall and his colleagues suggested that cultural studies should seek to understand the meanings that ordinary people gave to the types of culture they enjoyed.

- Global culture – The idea that cultural diversity is being eroded by communications industries organised on a global scale. Note that new technology has allowed many local media producers to emerge (although successful ones are often bought by larger organisations). Religious fundamentalism and nationalism have been identified as responses to globalisation.

1.2 The role of society in culture

Different perspectives

- Explain the functions of cultural beliefs in contemporary society.

- Describe how cultural beliefs and behaviour might benefit powerful social groups.

- Understand how the structure of society shapes cultural beliefs and behaviour.

Key terms

Mechanical solidarity: found in pre-industrial societies. Most people carry out similar tasks and share the same values and symbols. Religion is an important unifying institution.

Organic solidarity: found in complex industrial societies. Institutions need to be in place to integrate individuals into the moral consensus of society. Schools and the mass media are important in transmitting this moral framework.

Infrastructure: services and facilities that support day-to-day economic activity such as roads, electricity, transportation.

Superstructure: the institutions of a society such as laws, politics, religion and education.

💡 Studies of cultures around the world show remarkable diversity in norms, values and mores – many cultural practices can be seen as a response to the needs of a society or particular groups within a society.

Macro-sociological perspectives explain culture as a result of the way social relationships are structured within a society. All societies are seen to operate as systems and the culture of the society will reflect the divisions present in the social system.

The functionalist view of how society shapes culture

Every social system needs a shared belief system if it is to function efficiently. In pre-industrial societies most of the population worked on the land in small rural communities. The structure of society was simple as everyone did more or less the same daily tasks. Durkheim (1947) claims that in this type of society there is **mechanical solidarity**. In this type of society religion is an important institution in binding communities together.

Fig. 1.1 *Mechanical solidarity – pre-industrial churchgoers*

In industrial societies there are many different types of work so it is more difficult to feel a strong connection to other people. This type of society is characterised by **organic solidarity**, where the tasks people do are different and therefore it is more difficult to maintain a collective conscience. Modern societies have developed new institutions to solve this problem. The education system and the mass media have largely replaced religion in socialising people into a shared culture.

The Marxist view of the role of society on culture

There are differences within Marxism, but it is agreed that the economic **infrastructure** of society will be the most important influence on culture. Marx claimed that the economic infrastructure determined the nature of all parts of the **superstructure**. Culture is part of the superstructure. Thus, as we have already seen, the ruling class will use their economic

■ Key term

Patriarchy: in general terms, this is a system of society or government ruled by men. In feminist theory, this becomes the notion that society is inherently and structurally biased in favour of men and against women.

■ Link

This material links to the Theory and Methods topic (A2).

AQA Examiner's tip

These sociological theories can be applied to a range of topic areas at AS and A2 level. At this stage it is worth compiling a list of five key points from each theory and comparing and contrasting them because this will help you to structure your exam responses.

power to ensure that the culture of society will benefit them. For example, the main aim of the ruling class is to keep making profit, the institutions in the superstructure such as schools and the mass media rarely challenge the idea.

■ The feminist view of the role of society on culture

Although there are differences within the feminist perspective, feminists would agree that our society is characterised by differences in power and status of two groups: men and women. Men have more power and status than women – feminists call this system **patriarchy**. Feminists claim that many cultural beliefs in contemporary society benefit men and disadvantage women.

■ Summary questions

1 Explain, using examples, the difference between mechanical and organic solidarity. Suggest two ways in which contemporary culture can be seen as patriarchal.

2 Explain why Marxists see the economic infrastructure as the most important part of the social system.

Agencies of socialisation: the family

Learning objectives:

- Explain the importance of the family in primary socialisation.

- Describe the ways that norms and values are learned in families.

- Understand the importance of the family in gender role socialisation.

Key terms

Agency of socialisation: a person or group of people who influence the socialisation of children, and later adults.

Nuclear family: a family consisting of two parents and their dependent children.

Primary relationship: this is a relationship in which a person has ongoing intimate, personal, face-to-face contact with those who are responsible for the primary socialisation process.

Role modelling: when an individual observes another person's behaviour and modifies their own behaviour to replicate theirs.

Symmetrical family: a family in which men and women are equal; they may do some tasks separately but there is a balance of responsibility between partners.

Link

This material links to the Families and Households topic (AS), the Sociological Methods topic (AS) and the Theory and Methods topic (A2).

When learning our culture perhaps the most important **agency of socialisation** is our family. We interact with members of our family from birth. We need to recognise that there are a variety of family types in British society today and should not assume that the **nuclear family** is the norm. All sociological theories see the family as essential in socialising new members into the norms and values of their culture. We have **primary relationships** with members of our family and we spend most of our time with them. As we get older our ties with our family become less important in the socialisation process but in the first few years most of our learning takes place in the family. There are many ways that we learn from our families and these include **role modelling**.

Fig. 1.2 *The family is where we begin to learn appropriate gender behaviour*

As infants we learn the basic norms that members of a society observe. We learn how to eat and we learn table manners. Later we learn how to use language – this allows us to communicate symbolically with other people. Basil Bernstein has suggested that there are differences in how we learn to use language that are based on the social class of our family. Working-class families tend to use grammatically simple sentences which take for granted many meanings, while middle-class families tend to use more complicated sentences with more explanation. This may have an impact on achievement at school.

Some sociologists suggest that child-rearing practices may be different for different social classes and that the norms and values learned during primary socialisation may have an impact on educational achievement and subsequent life chances. Haralambos and Holborn (2000) claim that research shows that compared to working-class families, middle-class parents emphasise high achievement at school and reward success. These differences in primary socialisation may help to explain why middle-class children tend to achieve better examination results than working-class children.

■ Learning our gender

We begin to learn appropriate behaviour for our gender in our family. Feminists claim that the traditional nuclear family is a patriarchal institution in which men dominate. There is a debate in sociology about whether nuclear families are **symmetrical**. The way roles are allocated in families is likely to influence the gender identity of boys and girls as they observe the tasks of their parents in their family and model their own behaviour on these.

Our culture teaches us what it means to be a boy or girl and how we should behave as men and women. From an early age boys and girls are dressed differently and tend to play with different toys.

■ Research study: Young and Willmott (1973) and Oakley (1974a)

Young and Willmott (1973) claim that families are becoming increasingly symmetrical, but Anne Oakley's (1974a) research disputes this claim.

■ Hint

The research methods of these two pieces of research were very different and provide a good example of positivist and interpretivist approaches in sociological research.

AQA Examiner's tip

The research conducted by Young and Willmott and Oakley can usefully be applied to a range of questions in a number of units. It would be helpful to make a list of the aims, methods, findings, conclusions and evaluation for each of these studies at this stage.

■ Summary questions

3 Identify two ways in which girls and boys may learn to behave differently in families.

4 Suggest two ways in which we learn from members of our family.

5 Explain why many sociologists see the family as the most important agency of socialisation.

Agencies of socialisation: education and religion

Learning objectives:

- Explain the importance of school in transmitting culture.

- Outline the positive and negative view of the role of schools in secondary socialisation.

- Understand why religion is a source of norms and values in contemporary society.

Key terms

Formal education: education delivered by specially created institutions such as schools, colleges and universities.

Formal curriculum: this is all the things we learn at school that appear on our timetable. It includes subjects like maths and English but may also include health education or study skills.

Hidden curriculum: everything learnt 'incidentally' at school, through the rules, regulations and roles adopted.

Link

This material links to the Education topic (AS) and the Theory and Methods and Stratification and Differentiation topics (A2).

Education

All societies must teach their new members the knowledge, skills and attitudes they require to interact with others in their culture. In traditional or tribal societies based on agriculture the family could teach children all the knowledge and skills they would need as adults. In modern industrial societies there is a complex division of labour. All industrial societies have a **formal education** system which transmits cultural norms and values to new generations. Education appears to be about teaching the knowledge and skills that are specified in the **formal curriculum**; however, some argue that the most important function of schooling is to pass on the **hidden curriculum** to young people. Sociologists have different views on whether this is good for everyone or good for powerful social groups.

Fig. 1.3 *The education system: an agency of socialisation*

The positive view of secondary socialisation at school

Talcott Parsons (1961), a functionalist sociologist, claims that in families children are taught particularistic values. Each family may have slightly different norms and values, meaning that some children may be allowed to do things that others are not. In schools children are taught universalistic norms and values – this means that all children must stick to the same rules. Parsons claims that children also learn that success at school is based on ability, so that those who get the best results in tests are suited for successful careers. The hidden curriculum is good as it teaches children what they will need to keep society functioning well.

The negative view of secondary socialisation at school

Bowles and Gintis, Marxist sociologists, claim that although schools teach children that the most intelligent get the best results in tests, this is not what actually happens. Bowles and Gintis (1976) claim that

Culture and identity

■ Hint

How has religion influenced your socialisation? Make a list of beliefs, norms and moral values that you think are based on your religion.

■ Link

This material links to the Beliefs in Society topic (A2).

AQA Examiner's tip

If you get a question that asks you to examine sociological explanations of the process of socialisation, you will be expected to consider a range of agencies of socialisation in your answer.

through the hidden curriculum children are taught to respect authority and accept boredom. Those who do best in tests are not the most intelligent but are those who behave in the way middle-class teachers expect. For Marxists, schools socialise children to accept that the way society is organised is fair. This is good for the ruling class in order to prevent working-class rebellion. Therefore, secondary socialisation at school is teaching working-class children to accept the culture of the ruling class and an unfair society.

■ Religion

In traditional societies families would learn norms and values from religion. Some sociologists claim that a process of **secularisation** has taken place and religion is now a less significant agency of socialisation. However, even those who do not attend religious ceremonies regularly may still see their religion as important. Also as religion, particularly Christianity, is part of the **National Curriculum**, it is taught to all children. Although church attendance may be declining, there are many faiths present in our culturally diverse society.

■ Summary questions

6   Identify two examples of behaviour learned through the hidden curriculum.

7   Suggest two ways that religion contributes to the socialisation of members of contemporary society.

8   Examine the view that the main function of schools is to teach acceptable behaviour to young people.

Agencies of socialisation: the mass media

Learning objectives:

- Explain the importance of the mass media in the socialisation process.

- Describe concerns about media content and social behaviour.

- Understand how media representations of gender, class and ethnicity might contribute to socialisation and identity.

AQA Examiner's tip

In studying media effects researchers have used a range of different research methods. The strengths and weaknesses of these methods could be discussed in questions on the Sociological Methods topic.

Hint

Make a list of all the products of the mass media you have accessed this week. When you have done this, calculate the total number of hours you have spent with the media and finally the total cost of the media that you have used. Do your calculations support the idea that we live in a media saturated society?

Key terms

Symbolic annihilation: a situation in which women are under-represented in the media and where their roles are seen as limited or negative in comparison with those of men.

Moral panic: sensationalised and exaggerated media reporting of a certain action or social group. This group come to be seen as a threat to the rest of society.

When learning the norms and values of our society we experience reality through interacting with people, but we also experience mediated reality through the mass media. Through the media we can experience the events that we are not involved in personally and we can learn norms and values from this mediated reality. The mass media are all forms of communication that are produced for consumption by a large audience. Examples of the print media are newspapers, books and magazines, but there is also electronically transmitted mass media such as TV, radio, music, films, computer games and the internet. It has been claimed that we live in a media saturated society and we are exposed to media products from a very young age. This is why we need to consider the importance of the mass media in the socialisation process.

We learn the norms and values of our culture in many ways, as we have already seen. One of the key ways we learn is through observing the consequences of our actions and the actions of others. We observe role models in our families, schools and religion, but we also see role models in the mass media.

For many years there has been a debate about the effects of the media on social behaviour, much of this research has focused on children as they are seen to be more vulnerable to the effects of the media. A major concern has been that children may imitate the violence they see in the media. Some researchers see the media having a direct effect on the behaviour of children while others see children as a media literate audience who can easily tell the difference between fantasy violence and real violence.

Feminists have long been concerned about how women are presented in the media. Gaye Tuchmann *et al.* (1978) suggests that women are '**symbolically annihilated**' in the media. This may result in girls and women learning that their roles are less important than those of men. A more recent controversy in terms of the role of the mass media in the socialisation process is that the media provide unrealistic images of the female body and this has been linked to the increase in eating disorders.

Media images of ethnicity have also been criticised for portraying minority ethnic groups in negative ways. Minority ethnic groups are often victims of **moral panics** in the media.

Link

This material links to the Mass Media and Theory and Methods topics (A2).

Summary questions

9 Identify two ways in which the mass media contribute to the process of socialisation.

10 Suggest two reasons why feminists are concerned about media representations of gender.

11 Explain how moral panics may lead to stereotyping of certain groups in contemporary society.

Agencies of social control: informal

Learning objectives:

- Identify the New Right concerns about informal social control in families in contemporary society.

- Describe a range of rewards and punishments used in the process of informal social control.

- Understand how a range of social institutions contribute to informal social control.

Link

This material links to the topics of Families and Households (AS), Crime and Deviance and Theory and Methods (A2).

Link

This material links to the topics of Beliefs in Society and Theory and Methods (A2).

Hint

The New Right has been influential in the development of social policies. The Conservative government of the 1980s and early 1990s adopted New Right ideas in a number of policy areas such as welfare reform, education and crime. New Labour have continued with many policies advocated by the New Right such as league tables in education and crime. A 1999 government document 'No More Excuses' is an expression of the government's intention to be tough on criminals; however, New Labour recognise the connection between poverty and crime.

Social control is how we are taught to stick to the rules that apply in our culture; it is part of the socialisation process. We learn to stick to rules by receiving positive and negative sanctions. Positive sanctions are rewards for behaving in socially acceptable ways; negative sanctions are punishments for behaving in unacceptable ways.

Informal agencies of social control are institutions that are not set up specifically to enforce rules. Informal agencies of social control include families, peer groups and the mass media.

Some sociologists have claimed that family structures are changing; this may have a negative impact on the ability of families to impose social control on children. Writers such as Charles Murray, from a **New Right** (see p107) perspective, claim that the number of female-headed single-parent families is increasing. In these families there is no male authority figure to impose discipline on children. If there is no male role model to impose social control on children then this may lead to a lack of respect for authority later in life and lead to social problems such as crime.

Feminists are very critical of the views expressed by the New Right. They claim that traditional nuclear families tend to be male dominated and make women and children vulnerable to domestic violence and even child abuse. These experiences are damaging to individuals and may lead to a range of social and emotional problems in later life.

Our peer group becomes more important to us as we get older. We look to people of our own age for guidance about appropriate ways to behave. In the transition between childhood and adulthood, interaction with our peer group allows us to experiment with the norms and values of mainstream culture. In our consumption of recreational goods the peer group are a source of positive and negative informal sanctions. We learn from them what tastes are acceptable and what are not.

The mass media are involved in the process of informal social control as they inform us about what happens to individuals and groups who break accepted norms and laws. In media reporting of crime we are informed about punishments given to criminals who break the law; this teaches us that if we break the law we are also likely to be punished.

Religion is also an agency of informal social control in many societies. Religious beliefs such as the Ten Commandments in Christianity encourage people to conform to socially acceptable ways of behaving. Many religions promise rewards in the afterlife for those who have lived according to the scriptures of their religion and punishments such as eternal damnation in hell for those who have not.

Summary questions

12 Outline New Right concerns about informal social control in the family in contemporary society.

13 Identify two ways that the media teach us to behave in socially acceptable ways.

14 Explain how religion acts as an agency of informal social control.

Agencies of social control: formal

The criminal justice system is the main agency of formal social control but some sociologists would argue that social control is a major function of schools.

Schools

Schools cannot operate in an orderly way unless pupils observe the rules of the institution; they are encouraged to stick to rules in informal ways, such as being told off or praised by teachers. Schools are also involved in formal social control as formal negative sanctions can be given to pupils who break school rules. Formal sanctions include detentions, suspensions and even permanent exclusion for pupils.

The police and the criminal justice system

The prime function of the police and the criminal justice system is social control. As agencies of social control the police enforce the law and make sure that everyone conforms to it. The courts then act as an agency of formal social control by dealing with those that are alleged to have broken the law. If someone is found guilty of breaking the law the courts can then punish them. The prison service acts as an agent of social control as part of the penal system to punish those guilty of a crime. It also acts as a crime deterrent.

Some say the police do not apply the same standards to all citizens. For example, the McPherson report following the murder of Stephen Lawrence concluded that parts of the police force were **institutionally racist**. Heindensohn (1985) identifies several aspects of police culture such as racial prejudice and misogyny, which may result in tighter social control for some groups than for others, but this study is dated, and police training has recognised some of the issues raised by Heindensohn. However, the police have the right to 'stop and search' anyone they see as acting suspiciously and statistics show that young black men are the social group who are most likely to be stopped and searched.

There has also been concern about the role of the police during industrial disputes. In the miners strike of 1984 the police were seen to be acting in the interests of the Conservative government rather than in the interests of the public. Although not an industrial dispute, the 2001 anti-capitalist protests in London where 6,000 police were deployed also illustrates this point.

The armed forces

The armed forces are retained and directed by the government and can be used as an agency of social control if necessary.

Learning objectives:

- Describe the role of schools in informal and formal social control.
- Understand the role of the police in the process of formal control.
- Evaluate the claim that the police apply increased formal social control to some social groups.

Link

This material links to the Education topic (AS) and the Crime and Deviance topic (A2).

Key term

Institutional racism: a term used to describe how organisations and structures and policies used by an institution deny equality to some ethnic groups.

Fig. 1.4 *The police enforce the law and make sure that everyone conforms to it*

AQA Examiner's tip

Try to apply Marxist, functionalist and feminist theories to the issue of social control. This will help you to improve your AO1 and AO2 marks in an examination question on social control.

Summary questions

15 Outline three formal and three informal sanctions that can be used in schools to teach pupils to stick to school rules.

16 Identify two pieces of evidence that suggest some social groups are subject to tighter formal social control than others by the police.

17 Explain the role of both the police and schools in the process of social control.

Chapter summary

Further resources

S. Best, J. Griffiths and T. Hope, *Active Sociology*, Pearson Education, 2000

M. Haralambos and M. Holborn, *Sociology, Themes and Perspectives*, HarperCollins, 2000

C. Murray, *Underclass: The Crisis Deepens*, Institute for Economic Affairs, 1994

T. Parsons, *The Social System*, Free Press, 1951

www.sociology.org.uk

www.ruthsociology.com

The role of society on culture
- Functionalist view – Society shapes cultural beliefs and behaviour and this is in the best interests of all social groups.
- Marxist view – The ruling class use their economic power to shape culture through all other social institutions. The ruling class benefit from cultural beliefs.
- Feminist view – Society shapes culture. Men have more power in society; this results in their interests being reinforced through patriarchy.

Socialisation in the family
- Functionalist view – The family teaches children the skills and behaviour they need to interact with others at school.
- Marxist view – The family teaches children the basic norms and values they need to become workers as adults.
- Feminist view – Gender role socialisation begins in the family. Girls and boys observe their parents and model their behaviour on these.

Socialisation at school
- Functionalist view – Education teaches children the norms and values they need to cooperate with others and transmits culture to the next generation.
- Marxist view – Education teaches working-class children to be passive. The culture transmitted by schools is elite culture.
- Feminist view – The formal and hidden curriculum reinforce gender role stereotypes.

Religion
- Functionalist view – Religion teaches children a moral code and binds a society together.
- Marxist view – Religion teaches the working class to accept their situation by promising rewards later.
- Feminist view – any religions teach women to conform to traditional gender role stereotypes.

Mass media
- Functionalist view – Through watching and reading the media we learn about acceptable standards of behaviour.
- Marxist view – The media reinforce ideas that benefit the ruling class. These are learned by all social classes.
- Feminist view – The media reinforce gender stereotypes by representing men and women in different ways.

Agencies of informal social control
- Functionalist view – Through informal social control in the family we learn to live in harmony with others.
- Marxist view – The informal sanctions we receive teach us not to challenge authority.
- Feminist view – Informal sanctions teach us to behave in ways that are acceptable for our gender.

Agencies of formal social control
- Functionalist view – Schools and the police apply the same sanctions to all.
- Marxist view – Schools and the police apply more formal social control to the working class.
- Feminist view – Schools and the police apply formal sanctions differently to different genders.

1.3 Concepts of self, identity and difference

Concepts of self; personal identity

Link

This material links to the Theory and Methods topic (A2).

AQA Examiner's tip

Make sure that you know why interactionism is different from the structural theories you have learned. You can pick up AO2 marks by comparing and contrasting theoretical approaches to a particular issue.

Hint

Think of your own example to illustrate Cooley's concept of the looking-glass self. Perhaps a person thinks they are very fashionable. How might the reactions of other people challenge or support their sense of self?

Marxist, functionalist and some feminist views of society see culture as a product of the needs of the social system. Marxists see culture as a result of an exploitative capitalist system, functionalists see culture as a result of the need for individuals to cooperate within existing social structures, while feminists see culture as a result of a system of male domination or patriarchy. All of these theories tend to see culture as imposed on the individual; society and the culture within society shapes the identity of people within their culture.

Symbolic interactionism or social action theory has a different view of the relationship between individuals and culture. These theories see individuals as actively creating culture through their interactions with other people. According to this perspective people are not passive; culture and identity is not imposed on them. Interactionists focus on small-scale social interactions, such as those in classrooms or workplaces, and try to understand how the way we interpret the actions of others influences our sense of who we are. Our culture is constantly changing as a result of an infinite number of these small-scale interactions.

The self

When sociologists refer to the self they mean how a person sees themselves as an individual. This is always influenced by our interactions with other people. Charles Cooley (1964) developed the idea of the looking-glass self to explain this process. The idea is that we cannot develop a sense of ourselves without interpreting the messages that we receive from others about our appearance and behaviour. This sense of self begins to develop from birth as we interact with our parents during primary socialisation and continues throughout secondary socialisation. The easy way to understand this process is by using an example. A teacher may think that they are very good at their job, that their lessons are always interesting, that students enjoy their lessons and will achieve high grades. However, in a sociology lesson they look around the class to see several students yawning and others gazing out of the window. As a result of this the teacher may reassess their view of their talent as a teacher, especially if their students achieve low grades in their A-level exams.

The issue of meaning

Humans are different from other living creatures because they have the ability to communicate with other people using symbols. Humans are also able to reflect on or think about their own actions and the actions of others and in doing this their perception of themselves may change. It is like having an internal conversation with ourselves. This issue of meaning is a very important one as different people may interpret the same action in different ways. Take the example of the teacher above; the teacher's concept of themselves may have changed as a result of the

Culture and identity

■ Hint

Think of the following social situations – how do you try to manage the impression you give to others in each one: a classroom, a job or university interview, a nightclub, an appointment with your doctor?

actions of the students, but it is possible that the teacher may still think they are a good teacher in spite of the reactions of their students. This is because the teacher may explain what has happened in a different way. The students were tired as they had just had a PE lesson, or it was the last lesson on a Friday afternoon and this explains why they were so tired. In this way the teacher's positive view of their own abilities remains.

Erving Goffman (1959), a symbolic interactionist, suggests that identities result from how we try to manage the impression we give to others in our everyday interactions. Most if not all social interaction is like a theatrical performance. Although Goffman recognises that the theatre is not the same as real life, he makes the analogy that 'all the world is a stage' and that people, as social beings, are continually engaged in managing the impression they give to others. We are not always aware that we are trying to manage our performance.

Goffman also looks at the way that actors work in 'teams', cooperating with each other and feeding each other lines in order to give a third party the desired impression. Think about teams such as polices officers, teachers and gangs. Settings and props are also used by individuals and groups to manage the impression they give to others; think about the doctor with her stethoscope, the smart suits of business executives and the Blackberry mobile phone – these all give messages about status to others. Goffman also describes how people move between the 'front region' and the 'back region' of social settings. 'Front region' is where the presentation takes place and where the desired impression is most carefully managed. 'Back region' or 'back stage' is private, where only insiders are allowed and where a very different version of reality is enacted. For example, staff in a restaurant are likely to behave differently depending on whether they are chatting in the kitchen or taking orders from customers.

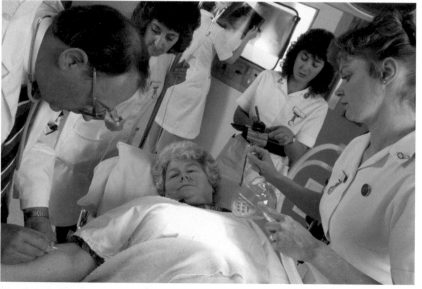

Fig. 1.5 *Goffman suggested we behave differently depending on the situation*

Our identity is formed through a combination of our understandings of how we see ourselves and how others react to us. These internal and external factors may contradict each other and this may make a stable identity difficult to achieve. This issue will be discussed further in relation to social stigma and labelling theory in the next sections.

■ Summary questions

1 Outline how one structural theory explains how personal identity is formed.

2 Identify and explain your own example of the concept of the looking-glass self.

3 Explain why the issue of meaning is so important in the development of personal identity.

Concepts of self; social identity

Learning objectives:

- Explain the concept of social stigma.

- Describe a range of strategies used to respond to social stigma.

- Understand that it is society that creates social stigma.

Key term

Stigma: a word that implies a negative association with something. A social group who has been labelled in a detrimental way could be described as being stigmatised.

Our social identity is our understanding of ourselves and who we are in relation to other people or groups. Social identity can be understood as a process of self-labelling or categorising ourselves by comparing ourselves to others. We notice that we are similar to some groups and different from other groups and this is how we come to develop our social identity. We should recognise that every person will have a unique social identity as everyone's experiences are different, but some aspects of our social identity may be more significant to us than others, for example our social class, gender or ethnicity.

Developing our social identity is a complex process – we are constantly negotiating who we are in relation to other people. As we age some aspects of our social identity change as our experiences lead us to think of ourselves differently in relation to other people and other people treat us differently. The social roles we occupy will also be a strong influence on our social identity.

There are various norms and values associated with different social roles and people occupying a social role are likely to try to meet the cultural standards associated with the role (for example, when becoming a parent).

The previous page discussed Erving Goffman's ideas about how our identity is constructed through impression management strategies and the reactions of others to these. In his later work on **stigma**, Goffman (1963) analysed the difficulties that some groups face in constructing a positive social identity.

Fig. 1.6 *What do you think when you look at this photo?*

23

■ Hint

Draw a table with three columns, one column should be headed 'physical', one should be headed 'personal weaknesses' and one should be headed 'social stigmas'. In each column write a list of five characteristics that fit into this category.

■ Link

This material links to the Crime and Deviance topic (A2).

AQA ✓ Examiner's tip

You can use historical as well as contemporary examples to illustrate the concept of stigma in your exam responses. For example, how were Jewish people stigmatised in Nazi Germany?

Goffman identified three main characteristics that form social stigmas: physical defects such as a missing limb; personal weaknesses such as a criminal record; and social stigmas such as membership of a religious or ethnic minority group. Some stigmas are therefore visible while some are not immediately apparent. All of these types of stigma tend to result in negative reactions from other people. Goffman suggests that to understand the process of achieving a social identity we need to analyse both the strategies people use to prevent the stigma from being applied and why people in society react to others in certain ways to create stigma. Goffman helps us to understand how stereotyping and prejudice in the wider society leads to stigmatised groups adopting a range of strategies to cope with their stigma and negotiate their social identity.

It is the interaction between so-called 'normal' people and those who are stigmatised that makes achieving a positive social identity difficult for some. Those who do not belong to stigmatised groups (or are able to hide their own stigma) label those with stigmas as different and communicate this through interaction. Through the reactions of others towards them, those with stigmas learn that they are not the same as everyone else, that they are looked down on. There are a number of strategies that can be adopted in order to create a positive social identity, these include:

■ Attempts to hide the stigma. This depends on the visibility of the stigma – cosmetic surgery might be a strategy here.

■ Admitting the stigma and accepting treatment from professionals. This may lead to withdrawal from society into a hospital or mental institution.

■ Protest against the stigma. This may take the form of organised protests. As we will see in a later section, this is a strategy that has been adopted by many disadvantaged groups in society such as those with disabilities.

In the following sections identity will be discussed in terms of how it is influenced by social class, gender, ethnicity, age and disability. The concept of stigma can be applied to any of these social bases of identity. Social inequalities are linked to prejudice and stereotyping in society and it is these social inequalities that lead people in disadvantaged groups to negotiate a range of strategies to gain a positive social identity.

■ Summary questions

4 Explain the concept of social identity.

5 Suggest three social groups who have a stigma in contemporary society.

6 Explain, using examples, a range of possible responses to social stigma.

Importance of self; individual and collective: identity, social and cultural life

Learning objectives:

- Describe the concept of labelling.

- Explain how labelling can lead to a deviant career.

- Understand how the media label groups through moral panics.

To understand how the actions of people working in social institutions can have an impact on both our sense of self and on future experiences it is useful to consider labelling theory. Labelling theorists question how and why some people committing an act are seen as deviant in the eyes of others while other people committing the same act are not defined as deviant. Howard Becker (1971) viewed criminals not as evil persons who engaged in wrong acts but as individuals who had a criminal status placed upon them by both the criminal justice system and the community at large. From this point of view, criminal acts themselves are not significant; it is the social reaction to them that are. The control of deviance is a social process which is key to an individual's social identity.

Labelling theory focuses on the reaction of other people, particularly the police, and subsequent effects of those reactions. When it becomes known that a person has engaged in deviant acts they are labelled 'thief', 'abuser', 'junkie', and so on. Becker noted that this process of segregation creates 'outsiders', who are outcast from society and who then begin to associate with others who are seen as 'different'. When more and more people begin to think of these individuals as deviants, they respond to them as such; thus the deviant reacts to such a response by continuing to engage in the behaviour society now expects from them. The following diagram simplifies Becker's labelling theory.

Link

This material links to the Education topic and the Mass Media topic (AS), and the Crime and Deviance topic (A2).

AQA Examiner's tip

Becker's labelling theory is similar to Goffman's theory of social stigma. If you make this connection in your exam responses you will show your understanding of a range of interactionist concepts and gain marks for both AO1 and AO2.

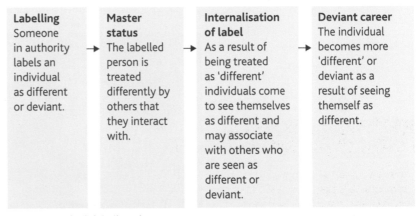

Labelling	Master status	Internalisation of label	Deviant career
Someone in authority labels an individual as different or deviant.	The labelled person is treated differently by others that they interact with.	As a result of being treated as 'different' individuals come to see themselves as different and may associate with others who are seen as different or deviant.	The individual becomes more 'different' or deviant as a result of seeing themself as different.

Fig. 1.7 *Becker's labelling theory*

Summary questions

7. Outline two possible responses to being labelled as deviant.

8. Explain, using examples, how groups are labelled in the mass media.

9. Explain how the labelling of individuals and groups might influence the self-concept.

Becker focuses on how individuals can be labelled in a negative way by the police, but other agents of social control such as teachers can label children in negative ways and this can have an impact on their self-concept. We should note that labels can be negotiated. It might be easier for some people to shake off a negative label. In his study of the activities of the police, Cicourel (1976) found that the parents of middle-class youths who were suspected of committing a crime were more successful in negotiating with police and their children were more likely to be released without charge than working-class youths.

It is not just individuals who are negatively labelled in society. Moral panics in the media label groups as deviant or dangerous, for example single parents or asylum seekers. This may lead to a negative reaction towards the group and eventually new measures being put into place to deal with the group that is seen to be a problem.

Role of agencies in defining identity and status

The agencies of socialisation influence our sense of identity in terms of social class, gender, ethnicity, age and disability. We will now consider a range of examples to illustrate this process.

Families

In our families we may learn that women and men do different tasks and that some of these tasks are more important than others. Parents may have different expectations of boys and girls and this has implications for the identity and status of children. Age may also be a factor, with older children having more responsibility in the home; again this is likely to have an impact on identity and status.

Peer groups

Our peer groups become a significant source of our identity and status during adolescence. Relationships with our peer group are quite different from the relationships we have with family members, they are likely to be more symmetrical, involving an exchange of problems and advice. It is through interaction with our peer group that we begin to develop a complex understanding of ourselves and our identity. In other sections of this chapter youth subcultures have been considered and these are a powerful source of identity for adolescents.

Fig. 1.8 *The Wall Game at Eton College. One of the traditions that form a child's sense of identity and status*

Education

The organisation of schools is likely to influence our identity and status. A child attending a public school such as Eton College is likely to gain a strong sense of identifying with the upper class and the traditions they observe. Within most secondary schools there is a system of streaming or banding. If a child is in the top band or stream, they are likely to have a more positive social identity than a child in the bottom band or stream.

Religion

Religion is an agency that still has a role in defining the identity and status of believers. Different religions have different views of women's roles and this is likely to influence the identity and status of members of the religion. For example, women cannot become priests in the Roman Catholic Church or become an Imam in the Islamic faith. Some sociologists suggest that religion is becoming increasingly significant in defining identity and status as people return to tradition as a reaction against globalisation.

Mass media

It is sometimes argued that we live in a media saturated society. The media provide us with a constant stream of information and images via television, film, newspapers and magazines that influence our understandings of ourselves and our status in society. The media labels groups as having low status in society through moral panics; this will influence the status and identity of these groups.

Workplace

The work we do is an important source of identity and status. In our society we have a complex division of labour with some occupations having a higher status in society than others. This, of course, is linked to social class with middle-class occupations having a higher status than working-class occupations. The lack of work is often seen to be something to be ashamed of. The term 'unemployed' is a source of social stigma for many people.

Summary questions

10 Identify two ways that education can shape our identity.

11 Explain how the mass media can shape the identity and status of social groups.

12 Assess the importance of religion in shaping identity and status in contemporary society.

Link

This material links to the Families and Households and Education topics (AS) and the Beliefs in Society and Mass Media topics (A2).

Hint

One of the first questions we ask when we meet someone new is 'What do you do?' This shows how important the job we do is in defining identity and status. Think about your reactions to people who give the following responses to this question: farm labourer, dentist, unemployed.

Chapter summary

Further resources

S. Chapman, *Revise AS Sociology*, Letts Educational, 2000

M. Haralambos and M. Holborn, *Sociology, Themes and Perspectives*, HarperCollins, 2000

G. Ritzer, *Sociological Theory* (3rd edn), McGraw Hill, 1992

www.sociology.org.uk

www.ruthsociology.com

Concepts of self: personal identity

- Key ideas – Structural theories see identity as imposed on the individual through the socialisation process. Social action theorists see the process of developing the self as dynamic and shaped by the meanings we take from our interactions with others.

- Commentary – Structural theories tend to see people as passive. Social action theories see people as active creators of meaning. This structure/action debate is central to many sociological debates in all areas of the syllabus.

Concepts of self: social identity

- Key ideas – Our social identity develops as we classify ourselves in relation to the many social groups we belong to. We try to manage the impression of ourselves that we give to others and this also contributes to our social identity.

- Commentary – Social action theories give useful insights into the significance of classification and impression management in the process of developing our social identity. However, Marxists would argue that the structures of capitalism are not recognised and feminists would make a similar point about patriarchy.

Importance of self; individual and collective: identity, social and cultural life

- Key ideas – The interactions between individuals and agencies of social control in forming individual and collective identity are recognised. Not all labels 'stick'; some people are able to shake off their labels.

- Commentary – Interactionists show how negative labels can influence both the identity and the future actions of individuals and groups. Marxists would link moral panics to capitalism as they are a way of dividing the working class and preventing class consciousness from developing.

Role of agencies in defining identity and status

- Key ideas – Although we all develop a unique identity, our experience of key social institutions will influence both our identity and our status. Our identity and status change throughout our lives as a result of new social experiences.

- Commentary – Interactionists recognise that our identity and status are fluid and are subject to change. Structural perspectives would argue that the social constraints on identity and status also need to be explained.

1.4 Postmodernism

Postmodernist theories

- Explain some key features of postmodern theory.

- Apply the postmodern idea of increased choice to the concept of identity.

- Understand the three levels of identity proposed by Harriet Bradley.

AQA Examiner's tip

Postmodernist theory is a challenge to structural theories. Make sure that you know why this is as it allows you to compare and contrast these theories in your responses to any 24-mark questions that ask you to 'examine sociological explanations' of a particular issue.

Link

This material links to the Mass Media and Theory and Methods topics (A2).

Some writers claim that contemporary society is different from society in the past and this has influenced both culture and identity. Theories of modernity include Marxism, functionalism and feminism. All these theories claimed that there were patterns to social behaviour and that these could be investigated and understood. Postmodernist theories challenge the assumption that there is an underlying order in society. If there were underlying patterns of behaviour in the past these have now broken down. In contemporary society there are so many choices available to us in relation to how we should live our lives that our identity is continually constructed and reconstructed through our consumption of cultural commodities and symbols. A key difference between modernist and postmodernist theories of identity is that for modernist theories it is possible to develop a coherent sense of who we are, whereas for postmodern theorists our identity is much more fluid and fragmented. We can play with our identity and change it if we want to.

Fig. 1.9 *We live in a postmodern media-saturated society*

Modernist theories of the role of the media claimed that the media either reflected reality (functionalist) or distorted reality (Marxist). In a postmodern society we have 'media saturation' and our constant interaction with media products has led to a situation in which the media actually creates our reality. As internet users we become part of virtual communities, we come to know people we have never had personal contact with better than we know our neighbours.

Image becomes more important than function. In postmodern society we care more about looks than substance. This is because signs are more important than underlying meaning. If we think of designer trainers, the logo becomes more important than the ability of the trainer to allow the wearer to play sport. Cosmetic surgery can be seen in the same way; looking young becomes more important than chronological age. We can play with our identity by buying into different lifestyles regardless of our class, gender, ethnicity, age or disability.

Harriet Bradley (1997) suggests that we need elements of both modernist and postmodernist theories to understand identity in contemporary society. For Bradley there are three different types of identity available to all of us and these can change as a result of personal, social and political circumstances. These three types of identity are illustrated below

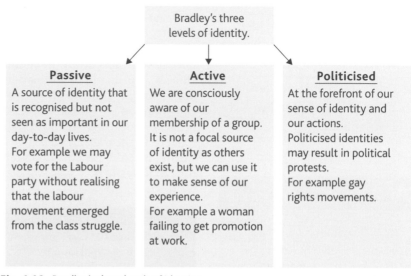

Fig. 1.10 *Bradley's three levels of identity*

These three levels of identity may become more or less important to us depending on our interactions with others. Bradley suggests that there are structural influences on identity but identity is fluid and subject to change in the light of experience.

Summary questions

1. Explain two ways in which postmodernists challenge the assumptions of modernist theories.

2. Identify two reasons why the mass media may be a more important source of identity in contemporary society than it was in the past.

3. Identify your own examples to illustrate Harriet Bradley's three levels of identity.

Identity and class

Learning objectives:

■ Recognise that a range of class inequalities still exist in contemporary Britain.

■ Describe how the class system in Britain has changed during the last 50 years.

■ Understand the impact of individualism and consumption on class as a source of identity.

Key terms

Life chances: the opportunities a person has to achieve good health, social prestige and economic prosperity.

Individualism: the notion that the individual is more important than the group as a whole.

Link

This material links to the Stratification and Differentiation and the Theory and Methods topics (A2).

When sociologists discuss social class they are referring to the way people can be grouped in terms of their occupation, income, lifestyle and attitudes, but there are also cultural differences between social classes. It is generally agreed that there are three main classes: the upper, middle and working class. Some sociologists also recognise a fourth social class – the underclass, who are the long-term unemployed. Others include this group in the working class.

Sociological research shows that children born into the working class have worse **life chances** than those born into middle-class or upper-class families. In 2002 a poll conducted by Mori found that 68 per cent of a sample of British adults agreed with the statement 'At the end of the day, I'm working class and proud of it'. This suggests that social class is still a significant source of identity for many people. In education, for example, working-class children still underachieve in comparison to middle-class children.

For Marxists our social identity is rooted in the work we do and different classes develop different social identities as a result of their different experiences in the workplace. Members of the proletariat (the working class) have strong class loyalty. Traditionally in industrial areas, particularly in mining and heavy industry, the trade union movement was strong and there was a keen awareness of class.

During the last 50 years middle-class occupations have declined and middle-class occupations have expanded. The workforce is becoming more diverse in other ways – we now have a core and peripheral workforce with core workers having permanent contracts with high wages and good working conditions and peripheral workers who have temporary contracts and poor working conditions. These changes, combined with the erosion of trade union power and the rise of **individualism** have undermined social class as a source of identity for many.

From a postmodernist perspective, class is no longer a significant source of identity in contemporary society. Rather than identity being derived from work or production it has come to be derived from leisure or consumption. The working class can now buy commodities traditionally associated with the middle or upper class.

In terms of Harriet Bradley's levels of identity, social class can be seen as a passive identity. We all recognise that inequalities exist in society, but our class is not recognised as a central part of who we are in our everyday lives; our individual talent and attributes have come to be seen as more important in a society characterised by individualism. However, in some circumstances such as industrial unrest or economic slump our class may become a more important source of identity to us.

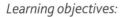 **Examiner's tip**

Try to give examples of how working-class identity may be different from upper-class identity in your exam responses to questions on class and identity.

Summary questions

4 Identify two examples of life chances that differ according to social class.

5 Explain two changes in the class system during the last 50 years.

6 Suggest two reasons why postmodernists claim that class is a less significant source of identity today than it was in the past.

Identity and gender

The relationship between sex and gender seems to be a straightforward one. Males and females are biologically different and through the socialisation process they learn the appropriate ways of behaving as a man or a woman in their culture. However, in some cultures there are more than two genders. For example, in some Polynesian cultures a third gender of people who are biologically male but behave in ways that are seen as typically female is recognised.

In their analysis of identity and gender, feminists distinguish between sex and gender. Our sex is derived from our biological make up while our gender results from cultural expectations. Both our status in society and our gender identity depend on the culture of our society. Feminists argue that our culture is characterised by patriarchy and girls and boys internalise this culture through the socialisation process. Anne Oakley (1972) analysed how girls were socialised into their gender role and found by the age of five most girls had a strong sense of their gender identity.

Hint

Identify the 'rules' for gender roles in our society. Draw a table of two columns, one headed 'men' and one headed 'women'. Identify 10 behaviours or characteristics in each column. Was this an easy task? Do you think the task would have been easier or more difficult at different historical periods?

Masculinity

Some sociologists have claimed that there is currently a 'crisis in masculinity' as men seek to come to terms with changing gender roles. Mac an Ghaill (1994) suggests that the changes in the labour market mean that the traditional male role of breadwinner and protector has been undermined, resulting in confusion about how to respond to these changes. The 'new man' has been posited as one response. However, another response to the crisis in masculinity is to revert to the macho stereotype, an expression of which can be seen in magazines such as *Loaded* and *Nuts*.

A postmodernist analysis of gender identity suggests that the distinctions between masculinity and femininity are becoming blurred; gender identity is more fluid than it was in the past. Traditional gender roles are no longer as significant in social life as more women are focused on their careers and house-husbands are not uncommon. In the media there is a diversity of role models who transgress traditional gender stereotypes; examples include Eddie Izzard, Pete Burns and K.D. Lang. We have more choices in our gender identity, which no longer depends only on our biology – sex reassignment is possible. We can express our gender identity in a range of different ways at different times.

AQA Examiner's tip

In exam questions on gender and identity you should make sure that you address the issue of masculinity as well as femininity. This will show the examiner that you are aware of social changes in gender roles and gender identity.

In terms of Harriet Bradley's typology of identity, gender may have been transformed from a passive to an active identity. Gender may be higher in the consciousness of women and men in understanding their everyday experiences. Feminism is also a political movement and gender may be a politicised identity for some. However, we must note that there are many differences in the experience of gender as a source of identity. For example, black feminists would combine ethnicity and gender as a source of identity.

Fig. 1.11 *Gay rights protesters*

Identity and sexuality

Attitudes to sexuality and expressions of sexual identity have changed in recent decades. Gender and sexual identity will be experienced differently by different social groups; for example, lesbians and gay men will experience masculinity and femininity in different ways. For some, sexuality has become a politicised identity – protest movements such as radical feminism and 'Outrage' illustrate this. Michel Foucault (1976) suggests that the way sexuality is expressed is dependent on the **discourses** present in a society at a particular time. Fifty years ago homosexuality was thought of as deviant or as an illness whereas today it is discussed as just one of many sexual orientations. In terms of Goffman's concept of stigma (1968a), homosexuality carries less social stigma than it did in the past; therefore, establishing a sexual identity is likely to be less psychologically painful for those who are not heterosexual than it was 50 years ago. We should note, however, that in different cultures homosexuality is still seen as deviant or evil and in these cultures identity based on sexuality may remain hidden.

Key term

Discourse: a way of writing, speaking, seeing and understanding a particular social group or activity.

Summary questions

7 Explain, using examples, the difference between sex and gender.

8 Identify two differences between modernist and postmodernist views of gender and identity.

9 Suggest two examples to illustrate the claim that sexuality has become a politicised identity for some groups in contemporary Britain.

Identity, ethnicity and nationalism

Learning objectives:

- Describe a range of reasons why ethnicity might be a key source of identity for some groups in contemporary Britain.

- Understand how contemporary debates about 'Britishness' may impact on the identity of different social groups.

- Recognise that ethnicity is still a source of disadvantage in contemporary Britain.

Link

This material links to the Mass Media topic (A2).

Key terms

Ethnicity: the characteristics of religion, language and cultural tradition that are shared by a group of people with common ancestry.

Race: the belief that distinct biological categories of humans exist and these are 'races'. In the nineteenth century scientists classified and ranked 'races' in terms of superiority.

Hint

Conduct some research on ethnic groups and life chances using secondary data. Include wealth, housing, crime and educational achievement. Look for patterns – do these suggest that some minority ethnic groups might experience life in contemporary Britain as hostile?

There is much evidence to suggest that **ethnicity** is still a source of social inequality despite laws designed to prevent discrimination on the basis of ethnicity. Ethnic group membership appears to have an impact on life chances such as wealth, status and power, but it may also give a sense of identity and community to individuals in a society they experience as hostile.

Almost 5 million people in the UK population are from non-white backgrounds, but as well as this we should remember that ethnicity is not necessarily about skin pigmentation alone; there are many 'white' communities who share a very strong sense of shared identity and feel themselves to be victims of discrimination.

Although the concept of '**race**' has been discredited, beliefs based on the notion that those with different cultural traditions are 'not like us' can have a real impact on the social identity of ethnic minority groups. Earlier in this chapter the skinhead youth subculture was considered (see page 10); this subculture scapegoated ethnic minority groups for economic problems that were not of their making, such as high unemployment. The mass media have also scapegoated ethnic minority groups in moral panics as Stuart Hall's analysis of mugging shows (Hall *et al.*, 1978, 1979). Young black men became identified as a threat in media reporting of mugging in the 1970s.

In terms of Bradley's levels of identity, ethnicity may be an active or politicised identity for ethnic groups in making sense of their experiences of racism in contemporary Britain.

In constructing a social identity in Britain today there is often a conflict for young people between holding on to the traditional cultures and those of their parents and the mainstream culture they are taught at school. Subcultures can also develop as an expression of resistance to oppression. One example of this is Rastafarianism which stresses white oppression and the fall of Babylon (the West). This may give support and a positive sense of identity and belonging in a society that appears hostile.

Ethnicity is likely to be a key source of identity, our self-concept is constructed through our interactions with others and with what we see as reference points in society, particularly in terms of cultural and media representations. Just as we are likely to construct aspects of our self-concept in terms of gender, in a socially diverse society where ethnicity is a source of social difference and inequality we are likely to refer to external representations of ethicity in our construction of self identity.

Nationality

Benedict Anderson (1983) claims that a nation is an imagined community in which millions of people who will never actually meet each other in person see themselves as belonging to a country.

Agencies of socialisation tend to promote a sense of shared national culture. We can see this in the mass media with its reporting of sporting events, such as football, and the royal family.

Politicians have become involved in the debate about British culture. Prime Minister Gordon Brown called for a day for Britain to celebrate its national identity. However, we must recognise that within Britain there are also many different regional identities such as Scottish, Welsh and Irish. Ethnic minority groups may feel increasingly excluded in a society that promotes 'Britishness' if their own cultural traditions feel challenged.

In 'Our Mongrel Selves' (1992) Stuart Hall points out that most modern nation states are culturally diverse and this may result in a confused sense of national identity. Tariq Modood (1997) also recognises the development of hybrid identities in contemporary Britain such as Black British and Asian British.

As well as being a source of disadvantage in contemporary Britain, ethnicity of course has a positive influence as well. For example, high academic achievements in Chinese and Asian minority ethnic groups and highly popular celebrations such as the Notting Hill Carnival.

Summary questions

10 Explain, using examples, the difference between the concepts of 'race' and ethnicity.

11 Suggest two ways in which moral panics might reinforce ethnicity as an active or politicised identity.

12 Suggest one positive and one negative consequence of an agreed definition of 'Britishness' on the identity of groups in society.

Hint

Think about recent examples of media reporting of ethnic groups – have any groups been presented as a 'problem'?

Hint

The debate about Britain's involvement in Europe, particularly in adopting the euro, is often reported in terms of the loss of British identity and sovereignty.

AQA Examiner's tip

You should look for developments on the issue of British identity in the mass media as this can be used in your responses to an exam question on sources of identity. You will impress the examiner with your awareness of current political issues.

Identity, age and disability

Learning objectives:

- Identify reasons why age might be a key source of identity in Britain today.

- Understand why the identities of older people might be more politicised today than in the past.

- Recognise how social stigma and discourses might impact on the identities of people with disabilities.

Link

This material links to the Mass Media and Stratification and Differentiation topics (A2).

Hint

The interactionist concept of social stigma is relevant to age, particularly old age. Consider a range of stereotypes of older people. Could these stereotypes be a source of social shame and therefore create a sense of social stigma for older people?

Hint

Think about villains in James Bond films. How many of these are disabled? Think about the villain in *Casino Royale*. What message does this give us about disabled people?

Contrast this with positive examples of disability such as athlete Tanni Grey-Thompson.

Identity and age

There are many stereotypes based on age in our society and these may be internalised and contribute to our sense of identity. The most economically advantaged age group is the middle aged, however, although younger people and older people are both stereotyped and suffer economic disadvantage.

Youth cultures have been considered and are clearly important sources of identity for their members but this is, for most, an active source of identity for a limited period of time. As we grow older we gain our identity from a wider range of sources. However, there are examples of young people developing a politicised identity, from the civil rights protests of the 1960s to the recent campaigns against university tuition fees.

Older people who have retired from full-time work are likely to experience a range of social and cultural disadvantages, such as limited income and negative stereotyping. We should note that older people are becoming more powerful consumer groups as they have more disposable income and can, therefore, according to the postmodern perspective, construct a range of identities through consumption.

Old age may be becoming a more politicised identity for some. In Britain there have been many protests organised by older people about pension levels and the community charge. In May 2007, The Zimmers had a hit song with 'My Generation' which was released as part of a protest about age inequality in contemporary Britain.

Identity and disability

Like class, gender, ethnicity and age group, there is a huge diversity in experience of people in the category and this will result in different social identities. We should also note that the experience of disability is socially constructed. Physical or psychological characteristics may lead to differential abilities, but it is culture of society that makes disability significant. In terms of interactionist theory disabled people may come to see themselves as others see them. Erving Goffman (1963) writes of a stigmatised identity; this is when an individual comes to be seen as different to others. It is the internalisation of this stigma that is likely to make disability an active level of identity for many disabled people.

Like the feminist movement and the anti-racist movement, the disability movement has become increasingly political, arguing that public attention needs to shift from individual impairments to social oppression. This may mean that disability is more central to identity for many, as people challenge the dominant discourses surrounding disability.

Summary questions

13 Identify two reasons why retirement might be experienced differently by people in different social classes.

14 Explain why disability is socially constructed.

15 Suggest two reasons why disability is a more politicised identity today than it was in the past.

Chapter summary

Further resources

S. Best, J. Griffiths and T. Hope, *Active Sociology*, Pearson Education, 2000

T. Bilton, K. Barnett, P. Jones, D. Skinner, M. Stanworth and A. Webster, *Introductory Sociology*, Macmillan, 1996

M. Haralambos and M. Holborn, *Sociology, Themes and Perspectives*, HarperCollins, 2000

M. Jones and E. Jones, *Mass Media*, Macmillan, 1999

www.ruthsociology.com

www.sociology.org.uk

In the first part of this chapter postmodernism was discussed and compared to modernist theories such as Marxism, functionalism and feminism.

- Modernist theories – Emphasise structures in society that shape identity. Social life is patterned and predictable, therefore identity is stable. Class, gender and ethnicity are important sources of identity. Economic power is a key factor in shaping identity.

- Postmodernist theories – Emphasise choice in shaping identity. Traditional sources of identity such as class, gender and ethnicity are fragmenting and unstable. Identity is fluid. Cultural and symbolic power are important in shaping identity.

In the remaining sections of this chapter a range of sources of identity were discussed in relation to modernist and postmodernist theories.

Class

- Modernist view – Social class is a key source of social inequality and identity.

- Postmodernist view – The class system has become open and movement between classes means that class has become less significant in shaping identity.

Gender

- Modernist view – There are still social inequalities based on gender. This means that gender is still important in our sense of who we are.

- Postmodernist view – Gender roles are disappearing. Men and women express their gender identities and sexuality in many different ways depending on the choices they make.

Ethnicity

- Modernist view – Ethnicity is still a key source of social inequality. Racism still exists in contemporary Britain and this will have an impact on the identity of ethnic minority groups.

- Postmodernist view – Ethnicity is becoming less significant as a source of identity. Any person, regardless of ethnic origin, can choose from a vast array of possible identities. Hybrid identities can emerge through consumer activity.

Age

- Modernist view – Age is a key source of social inequality. As a result of ageism people identify with people of the same age group.

- Postmodernist view – In the past some behaviours were unacceptable for people of different ages. Today people of all ages can enjoy similar consumption and leisure activities.

Disability

- Modernist view – Disability is a key source of social inequality, this is likely to have an impact on identity.

- Postmodernist view – Disabled people are free to express themselves in many more ways than in the past due to technological advances.

1.5 Leisure, consumption and identity

Introduction to leisure and how it shapes identity

In the process of industrialisation, work became separated from the home, work took place in special places such as factories and people were paid for their time spent at work. Before this, work took place in and around the home and work and non-work were not separated. It is the way work is organised that creates leisure time. Perhaps the best way to think of leisure is the time we have that is free from other demands on our time.

Modernist theories focus on work as the major influence on our identity. Throughout the 20th century there have been huge changes in both work and leisure; average working hours have decreased and people have more disposable income. This means that there is more time and money to be spent on leisure activities. There is huge variety in the leisure activities available to us, and our class, gender, age and ethnicity will influence the goods we consume. An example of this might be clothing where there are different conventions surrounding class, age, gender and ethnicity.

Since the Second World War there has been rapid growth in the production of consumer goods leading to mass consumption. People in countries around the world share the same images, sounds and brands. Consumption of leisure goods, especially the mass media, has increased. Postmodern approaches suggest that the leisure industries, especially the mass media, have become more important sources of personal identity than the work we do. What we do in our leisure time becomes an important part of the image of ourselves that we present to others. Leisure becomes a series of **lifestyle** choices.

From a Marxist perspective the increase in consumerism benefits the ruling class in several ways. First, it provides massive profits for big business – it does this by creating false needs in the working class through advertising. Secondly, it prevents class consciousness developing by manipulating the working class through the ideological content of the mass media. Marxists suggest that the misery of working in a capitalist society is made bearable in the sphere of leisure. Marxists would see leisure as a form of social control because the state is involved in the regulation of leisure through the licensing and censorship laws and through the control of public spaces by the police.

From a postmodern perspective work is not the most significant source of identity in contemporary society; our identities are constructed by what we consume. We now have much more choice in what to do with our leisure time: we are what we buy. Leisure has become consumption.

Summary questions

1 Describe how the changing organisation of work influenced leisure.

2 Identify two reasons why leisure is a more important source of identity in contemporary society than it was in the past.

3 Outline the differences between Marxist and postmodernist perspectives on leisure.

Leisure, class and identity

Learning objectives:

- Identify variations in leisure activities by social class.

- Explain why postmodernists see class as a less significant factor in leisure choices than it was in the past.

- Understand changes in youth culture and leisure activities.

Key terms

Extrinsic rewards: this is when jobs are not enjoyed, we only do them for the wages we receive.

Intrinsic satisfaction: this is when the job done gives a sense of personal fulfilment. Money is not our prime motivation for work.

Links

This material links to the Theory and Methods topic (A2).

This material links to the Mass Media topic (A2).

Hint

Make a list of different ways of spending leisure time. Are different types of leisure associated with different social classes? You could focus on sport.

AQA Examiner's tip

Postmodernists claim that class is less important in terms of tastes in leisure as the distinctions between high and popular culture have broken down. Try to apply examples of this in your exam responses, for example the popularity of classical film music in Hollywood films.

Parker (1976) suggested that social class influences the type of leisure activities we choose. Those in traditional working-class occupations such as manual work, which is done for **extrinsic rewards**, choose leisure activities that provide an escape from work such as drinking in the pub. Middle-class professionals, who work in jobs with high levels of **intrinsic satisfaction** are willing to allow activities associated with work to be part of their leisure time, for example having dinner or playing golf with business associates.

From a postmodern perspective the boundaries between social class and leisure have become blurred. This is a result of the fragmentation of experience that characterises the postmodern condition. Regardless of our social class we can all pick and choose how we spend our leisure time.

Postmodernists have an optimistic view about everyone having the ability to express their identity through their activity as consumers. However, it is important to recognise that while most people can afford a range of leisure activities such as a holiday, income does limit our choices in leisure and consumption. We can all visit the same shops but some can afford more choices than others; some leisure activities are not accessible to all.

Youth culture, participation and identity

It has been argued that in the last 50 years the fashion and entertainment industries have been dominated by a 'cult of youth' in which youth and the lifestyle and tastes of young people are celebrated. This is linked to the increasing amount of disposable income held by young people.

The mass media are important in the development of youth subcultures as new trends are rapidly communicated to young people. There have been many different youth subcultures since the 1950s; many of these reflect the social class, gender and ethnicity of their members. Some sociologists suggest that the age of spectacular youth subcultures is now over. Today, young people can pick and mix the fashion and music from all the youth subcultures that have existed in the past and create new combinations of fashion and music. It is interesting to note that these styles sometimes emerged as an expression of protest in the past but are now sold as commodities by global manufacturers.

Electronic games consoles and the internet are popular leisure pursuits of young people and can be interpreted as a new type of 'virtual youth' subculture. New technology allows young people to play games on the internet with others from around the world, and they can talk to them as they are playing. Using chat-rooms accounts for an increasing amount of their leisure time.

Summary questions

4 Suggest two differences in leisure patterns of different social classes.

5 Identify two claims made by postmodernists about the relationship between class and leisure.

6 Explain how new technology might influence how young people spend their leisure time.

Leisure, gender and identity

Link

This material links to the Families and Households topic (AS) and the Theory and Methods topic (A2).

Hint

Feminists have raised awareness of gender stereotypes, and as a result of this gender stereotypes are being challenged. Put the following activities into two groups – which ones are associated with men and women? Has this changed in recent years? Rugby, aerobics, shopping, ballet dancing, football, snooker, golf, gambling, guitar playing, soap opera viewing.

Key term

Hybridity: a combination of different styles and cultural forms.

AQA Examiner's tip

Although class, gender and ethnicity are often analysed separately in terms of leisure, you need to show the examiner that you are aware that these factors overlap and will be experienced in different ways according to the social characteristics of each individual.

There are gender differences in leisure activities. Men are more likely to go to the pub than women and are more likely to watch sporting events. Also, the ongoing responsibilities of women mean that they are less able to put time aside for leisure. Feminists suggest that gender role socialisation has an impact on women's expectations of leisure and that the lack of affordable childcare stops women from accessing the leisure activities of their choice. Feminists argue that the leisure opportunities that women have are restricted by men who expect women to choose home-based activities in their leisure time rather than going out. Research also suggests that women have less disposable income than men. Women tend to combine their leisure with other obligations, for example looking after children, and are also likely to become involved in leisure activities for the sake of their husbands.

Women are further restricted from pursuing certain leisure activities because men still dominate many sporting and social venues and women may feel uncomfortable on their own in these settings. A fear of being a victim of crime in the evening may result in a reluctance to pursue leisure interests outside the home in the evening.

There are differences between the leisure activities depending on the age, social class and marital status of women. Middle-class women are more likely to belong to gyms and go to keep fit classes. Single women are more likely to go out to pubs and nightclubs.

Leisure, ethnicity and gender

The influence of the blues, reggae, hip hop and bangra show how significant the music of different ethnic groups has been on contemporary popular music. These expressive forms emerged from the experience of minority ethnic groups.

There are many examples of successful black sports stars, musicians and actors in the media and these may influence the identity and leisure of minority ethnic groups. However, in some sports such as swimming, golf and tennis, ethnic minorities are still under-represented.

Postmodernists claim that in contemporary culture a **hybridity** of cultural forms has emerged that celebrates diversity and is used by people of all social backgrounds as a shared symbol and source of identity. Ethnicity, according to postmodernists, will become less and less significant in terms of inequality as everyone gains access to the same symbolic universe.

We should remember that unemployment is still higher for ethnic minority groups and this may limit their leisure choices. Ethnic minorities may well use the products of the culture industries as a source of social identity but this may reflect their resistance to racism rather than being freely chosen.

Summary questions

7 Identify two reasons why the leisure choices of women may be restricted in contemporary society.

8 Explain the feminist perspective on gender and leisure.

9 Explain how ethnicity might impact on leisure choices.

The leisure industry: globalisation, leisure and identity

Although nation states in different parts of the world are at different stages of development, most countries are now industrialised to some extent and global processes associated with capitalism such as mass production and mass consumption are organised across national boundaries. Mass communications technology has been central to the process of globalisation. Electronic banking and instant communication has made it easier for transnational corporations to conduct their business.

The leisure industry is made up of organisations that provide entertainment, tourism and leisure products. Through our lifestyle choices we use the products and services of the leisure industry to express our identity. New technology has led to many changes in the leisure industry – for example, travel has become much easier and cheaper as new transport technology has developed. It is now possible for many of us to travel around the world due to the low cost of transport. This means we can see for ourselves how people live in different countries. However, we can also see how people live around the world through the mass media and these images can motivate us to use the services of the travel industries.

The tourism industry is a large sector of the leisure industry. John Urry (1990) has analysed the way that tourism has changed in recent years. A key motivation for tourists is to look at things they would not normally see. Urry calls this the tourist 'gaze'. We often visit countries and cities that we have seen images of in the media and take our own images home with us in the form of photographs or videos. Urry identifies two types of gaze: the **collective gaze** and the **romantic gaze**.

Key terms

Collective gaze: this is when other people are needed to give the 'atmosphere' to a place that we visit; for example, a club in Ibiza needs to be busy so that we can enjoy the experience more.

Romantic gaze: this is when we want to be alone to see the place we are visiting; for example, to contemplate the beauty of a mountain.

Hint

Tourism is a case study of one aspect of leisure. There are many more sectors in the leisure industries that could also be used to illustrate postmodernist ideas. For example, fashion and music could be used.

Link

This material links to the Theory and Methods topic (A2).

Fig. 1.12 *An example of Urry's collective gaze*

Fig. 1.13 *An example of Urry's romantic gaze*

Urry claims that tourism can be seen to illustrate some of the themes of modern and postmodern culture. In modern tourism built-up tourist resorts would appeal. The emphasis is on the collective gaze – many other tourists would help to create a holiday atmosphere. Thus built-up resorts like Benidorm would appeal with mass-produced entertainment consumed by all. The postmodern tourist would shun this type of tourism – they would base their choice of holiday on trying to achieve the romantic gaze.

This research illustrates some key postmodern ideas in terms of the leisure industry and how it might shape identity. Most people can afford an annual holiday and the reasons for choosing different holiday experiences is not determined by social class, gender or ethnicity. We can all choose from the vast array of holiday options available to us and through this choice we can make symbolic statements about who we are and what is important to us.

Summary questions

10 Suggest two reasons for the development of global tourism.

11 Identify two characteristics of the tourist gaze.

12 Explain, using examples, the differences between modern and postmodern tourism.

Inequalities in leisure: aspects of negative identity

Learning objectives:

- Recognise how the boundaries between work and leisure are changing.

- Explain the optimistic and pessimistic view of a key leisure activity: watching television.

- Understand how income constrains leisure choices.

Link

This material links to the Mass Media topic (A2).

Key term

Polysemic: literally 'many signs'. Having several possible meanings.

Link

This material links to the Theory and Methods topic (A2).

Hint

In Britain many of us pay a monthly subscription to receive satellite television. Satellite television is therefore a commodity we pay for and thus it makes profits for the companies delivering the product. However, as an audience we ourselves become a commodity that is sold to advertisers for more profit for the companies.

There have been many developments in leisure and the leisure industries during the last 50 years. Boundaries between work and leisure have become blurred as new technology has allowed us to read our business emails in our leisure time, many of us work in the leisure industries and some of us set up businesses as a result of our leisure interests. Consumption is central to our experience of leisure and much of our leisure time is spent interacting with the mass media, particularly television.

In recent years we have witnessed a multi-channel revolution in television. This has implications for the way television programmes are produced and the way we watch television. The production of programmes has become fragmented with many independent production companies; the audience has become more fragmented as many are able to choose from hundreds of channels.

The aim of producers is to attract the largest audience for the cheapest cost; companies are often unwilling to take risks with new programmes. As a result they tend to 'clone' hit series. The reliance on advertising and sponsorship may also limit the types of programme that are made as advertisers want their products to be associated with desirable lifestyles that encourage consumption. This may explain why so many television programmes are about DIY, cooking and gardening.

From a postmodern perspective we can interpret the fragmentation of television channels and texts in an optimistic way. All texts are **polysemic** and can be interpreted in a range of ways that allow individuals to make sense of their experiences and continually create their own sense of identity. New commodities are continually produced and as consumers we can use these to continually change our identity should we choose to do so.

A more pessimistic view on mass consumption came from the Frankfurt School. In earlier sections writers such as Adorno were concerned that mass consumption would lead to a passive working class who could not distinguish between what is worthy and what is not (see page 7).

The postmodern idea that we all have incessant choices in terms of constructing our identity seems to have some support in some aspects of our culture. However, we need to consider what happens to those who cannot afford the choices we are all assumed to have. Those who cannot 'buy in' to the lifestyles they desire may experience negative feelings about themselves and their society. Critical sociologists suggest that we still need to recognise and understand the social inequalities such as class, gender, ethnicity and disability that have profound effects on our daily lives and the choices that we have.

Summary questions

13 Identify two examples to illustrate the claim that the boundaries between work and leisure are becoming less distinct.

14 Suggest two consequences of multi-channel television.

15 Evaluate the postmodernist claim that we all have similar choices in what to do in our leisure time.

Chapter summary

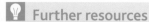
Further resources

R. Barker, *Leisure Studies*, Collins, 2006

S. Best, J. Griffiths and T. Hope, *Active Sociology*, Pearson Education, 2000

T. Bilton, K. Bennett, P. Jones, D. Skinner, M. Stanworth and A. Webster, *Introductory Sociology*, Macmillan, 1996

M. Haralambos and M. Holborn, *Sociology, Themes and Perspectives*, HarperCollins, 2000

M. Jones and E. Jones, *Mass Media*, Macmillan, 1999

✔ In this chapter the influence of leisure on culture and identity has been considered.

Introduction to leisure and how it shapes identity

- Modernist view – Leisure is separate from work. Work is more important in creating our identity than leisure: we are what we do.

- Postmodernist view – Work and leisure are becoming less interrelated. Consumption activities in our leisure time are more important sources of identity than work: we are what we buy.

Leisure, class and identity

- Modernist view – There are differences in leisure activities for different social classes. The choices we make in our leisure activities reflect the characteristics of the work we do.

- Postmodernist view – Different social classes can choose the same leisure activities. Distinctions between high and popular culture have blurred.

Youth culture participation and identity

- Modernist view – Distinctive youth cultures are based on class experiences.

- Postmodernist view – Pick-and-mix fashion and music, class is insignificant in youth culture. Virtual communities have resulted from the availability of the internet.

Leisure, gender and identity

- Modernist view – There are different patterns of leisure for men and women, these result from learned social roles.

- Postmodernist view – Both men and women can choose from a range of different leisure activities that are open to all.

Leisure, ethnicity and gender

- Modernist view – Distinctive cultural forms of ethnic minority groups reflect experiences of stereotyping and discrimination.

- Postmodern view – Ethnicity is becoming irrelevant in understanding leisure as hybrid cultural forms combine traditions from many cultures.

Globalisation, leisure and identity

- Modernist view – Modern tourism involves travelling to a different place to take part in a collective experience with other tourists. Tourist experiences are mass produced.

- Postmodernist view – Postmodern tourism involves the search for the natural and authentic experiences of different places and cultures.

Inequalities in leisure, aspects of negative identity

- Modernist view – Leisure activities reflect socio-economic status. Mass production and consumption may lead to a passive working class.

- Postmodernist view – Production of leisure goods has become fragmented and available to all. Consumers use leisure products in different ways to express our identity at any particular time.

AQA Examination-style questions

☑ Read Items 1(a) and 1(b) below and answer parts (i) to (v) that follow.

1   (a)   When describing pre-industrial societies in Europe, a distinction is made between the high culture of the aristocratic elite and the folk culture of the ordinary people. Folk culture consists of local customs and beliefs that directly reflect the lives and experiences of the people, such as folk songs and stories that are handed down from one generation to the next. With industrialisation and urbanisation a new, increasingly commercialised, culture has emerged, shaped by media influences and technology. Some sociologists refer to this as mass culture.

(b)   Traditional sociological approaches emphasise the way in which our identities and leisure patterns are strongly influenced by our social position. For instance, Parker (1976) argues that occupation is a crucial factor in shaping our leisure patterns: those engaged in heavy unskilled manual labour tend to adopt an opposition pattern, where leisure is sharply distinct from work.

More recently, however, postmodernists have argued that our identities are no longer shaped by occupation, class, gender, age and so on. They argue instead that today's society offers us a great variety of identities from which we can freely choose, particularly in the sphere of leisure and consumption. Through these, we can construct our own lifestyles and express our individual identities.

(i)   Identify two ways in which mass culture differs from folk culture apart from those referred to in Item 1(a).   *(4 marks)*

(ii)   Suggest two ways in which technology and/or industrialisation have influenced culture (Item 1(a)).   *(4 marks)*

(iii) Suggest two ways in which old age may be a stigmatised social identity.   *(4 marks)*

(iv)   Examine sociological explanations of the process of socialisation.   *(24 marks)*

(v)   Using material from Item 1(b) and elsewhere, assess the view that people's leisure patterns and identities are no longer shaped by their social position.   *(24 marks)*

AQA specimen question

Read Items 2(a) and 2(b) below and answer parts (i) to (v) that follow.

2   (a)   Our peer group becomes a significant source of our identity and status during adolescence. Relationships with our peer group are different from the relationships we have with family members; they are likely to be more symmetrical, involving an exchange of problems and advice. It is through interaction with our peer group that we begin to develop a complex understanding of ourselves and our identity. In other sections of this chapter youth subcultures have been considered and these are a powerful source of identity for adolescents.

(b)   Labelling theory focuses on the reaction of other people, particularly the police and subsequent effects of those reactions. When it becomes known that a person has engaged in deviant acts they are labelled 'thief', 'abuser', 'junkie', and so on. Becker noted that this process of segregation creates 'outsiders', who are outcast from society, and who then begin to associate with others who are seen as 'different'. When more and more people begin to think of these individuals as deviants, they respond to them as such; thus the deviant reacts to such a response by continuing to engage in the behaviour society now expects from them.

Both extracts taken from Culture and identity Chapter 3 of this textbook

(i)   Identify two agencies of socialisation, apart from those referred to in Item 2(a).   *(4 marks)*

(ii)   Suggest two ways in which our peer group influences our sense of self.   *(4 marks)*

(iii) Suggest two ways in which social roles influence our identity.   *(4 marks)*

(iv)   Examine sociological explanations of the process of identity formation.   *(24 marks)*

(v)   Using material from Item 2(b) and elsewhere examine the influence of labelling on social status.   *(24 marks)*

Families and households

Introduction

Family is often the first topic studied by sociology students, and this makes sense. After all, we have all experienced family life and have experiences to draw upon. It introduces some of the key sociological theories, and shows that there are many competing views on every aspect of the family. Some sociologists look at the family in a positive way and others take a more critical view. The topic illustrates the complexity of social life – what appears simple on the surface often needs to be examined in more detail to get a more truthful picture. Family is often in the news, and some types are often presented more favourably than others. The subject of family arouses strong views, and it is important to try to look at the subject without prejudice. The way we have experienced family life may be very different to how others have experienced it.

A number of important areas have emerged in the sociology of the family, and this chapter will explore each in turn:

- Sociologists examine the wide range of families that exist today – family diversity. They are also interested in the decline in the number of children being born, longer lifespans and how immigration has affected the family.
- Some look at these changes in a positive way, and others are more critical. These views are discussed in the section on theoretical views on the family. The section on social policy examines laws that influence the family.
- Patterns of marriage, divorce and cohabitation are discussed, as are reasons for changes in these areas and sociological views on them.
- The section on childhood looks at the reasons for the changes that have taken place in this area, and at the different ways sociologists view childhood.
- The last section examines relationships between men and women in the family, with a particular focus on housework, childcare and power relationships.

What is a family?

Defining the family is not easy, and all definitions can be challenged. The conventional definition is that it involves a married couple with one or more children. Hopefully you will be able to challenge this definition, see how it is flawed and come up with your own improved definition. You might like to consider whether you need children to make a family, or if you need two adults of the opposite sex.

What is a household?

Defining a household is easier. It is generally seen as a person living alone or a group of people living together who may or may not be related to each other. A group of students are a household but not a family. All families are households but not all households are families.

Specification	Topic content	Page
The relationship of the family to the social structure and social change, with particular reference to the economy and state policies.	Functionalist and New Right views on the family	59
	Critical views of the family – feminism	61
	Radical psychiatry and Marxism	63
	Social policies in the UK and around the world	64
	Social policy and the family	65
Changing patterns of marriage, cohabitation, separation, divorce, child-bearing and the life course, and the diversity of contemporary family and household structures.	Marriage, divorce and cohabitation	68
	The increase in divorce	69
	Declining marriage/increasing cohabitation	70
	Theoretical views	71
	Family types in the UK	48
	Nuclear and extended families	50
	Single-parent families	51
	Singletons, same-sex and reconstituted families	53
	Migration to Britain	56
The nature and extent of changes within the family, with reference to gender roles, domestic labour and power relationships.	Domestic labour and gender roles	81
	Domestic labour and gender roles – research	82
	The impact of paid work	83
	Power relationships/domestic violence	84
The nature of childhood, and changes in the status of children in the family and society.	Children as a social construct	73
	Childhood in the UK	74
	Changes in the position of children	76
	Children in different cultures	77
	The future of childhood	79
Demographic trends in the UK since 1900: reasons for changes in birth rates, death rates and family size.	Childbirth, family size and mortality rates	54

2.1 Family diversity in the UK and demographic trends

Family types in the UK

Learning objectives:

- Understand sociological views on family diversity.
- Consider social class and family diversity.
- Explore the family life cycle.

When you are asked to define the family, most people will probably say a mum, dad and children. This is often seen as the typical, 'normal' or conventional family. It has also been called the 'cereal packet family' because of family TV adverts for breakfast cereal. The correct name for this type of family is the nuclear family, and although the nuclear family is an important and common family form throughout the world, in the UK only about 25 per cent of all households are made up of this type of family. In fact the nuclear family has been declining in the UK for at least the last 30 years, and other types of family and household are becoming more important. These growing types include the single-parent family, reconstituted or stepfamilies, cohabiting couples and their children, singletons (people living by themselves) and same-sex families. All of these types are discussed in more detail in subsequent sections.

Sociological research and views on family diversity

Robert and Rhona Rapoport (1982) were among the first sociologists to identify the changes that were taking place in UK families. They argued that the nuclear family was no longer the main family type, and that a range of alternative family types and households existed and were growing in size, especially single-parent and reconstituted families. Unlike some sociologists and politicians, the Rapoports were hopeful and optimistic about these changes. They celebrate the fact that people now have freedom and choice, and no longer have to live in a certain type of family. They argue that there is not a 'right' type of family – all families should be accepted and not criticised. More recent research by Rhona Rapoport (1989) confirms the earlier research. She argues that the decline of the conventional nuclear family is part of a European trend, and not just confined to the UK.

Feminists also tend to be supportive of family diversity. They generally see the nuclear family as benefiting men more than women, and other types of family and household as giving women more freedom. On the other hand, functionalist and New Right sociologists are critical of family diversity and support the conventional nuclear family. They particularly dislike the single-parent and same-sex family. These views are discussed in more detail in the next section.

Social class and family diversity

One area of diversity that the Rapoports point out, and one which is often overlooked, relates to differences between families with regard to social class. These differences could include such things as:

1 Middle-class parents may use nannies or au pairs to look after children whilst they go to work. Working-class parents may be more likely to use families or friends.

2 Differences in disciplining children. Working-class parents may be more likely to use physical punishments like smacking, and middle-class parents may be more likely to use verbal punishments.

3 Children from the upper middle class and upper class are more likely to attend fee-paying independent schools. They are also more likely to board, i.e. live away from home whilst at school.

■ The family life cycle

When discussing family diversity it is important to consider the family life cycle. This means the types of families and households an individual is likely to experience in their life. Each of us will have a different life cycle, linked to when and where we are born, our class, gender, ethnicity, and the choices we make throughout our lives. One possible family life cycle for someone born in the 1990s might be as follows.

The (made-up) life cycle of 'Nikki' (born in 1990; died in 2090)

1 Nikki is born into a nuclear family (age 0–13).

2 Nikki's parents divorce. Nikki stays with her mother, and experiences life in a single-parent family (age 13–18).

3 Nikki goes to university and shares a flat. This is a communal household (age 18–21).

4 Nikki lives alone as a singleton (age 21–25).

5 Nikki falls in love with Pete and they live as a cohabiting couple (age 25–28).

6 Nikki and Pete marry and have two children. Nikki is in a nuclear family again (age 28–48).

7 The children leave home and Pete and Nikki are an 'empty nest family' (age 48–78).

8 Pete dies and Nikki lives alone again as a singleton (age 78–100).

Robert Chester and the rise of the neo-conventional family

Robert Chester (1985) has looked at diversity and the family life cycle, and argues that for most people the nuclear family remains the most typical family type. He argues that single-parent families, for example, normally come from nuclear families, and many single parents will remarry and become nuclear families again. Although many people are singletons, most of these will marry eventually or, if they are elderly, will be widows who have already been married. Chester argues that even though most couples cohabit, most will marry the person they cohabit with, and most marriages continue until death. In Chester's opinion, the extent of family diversity has been exaggerated. For Chester, the only significant change in the past 30 years has been women working, hence the term 'neo-conventional' family. ('Neo' means new.)

Fig. 2.1 *The Rapoports pointed out that people from different social classes discipline children differently*

Families and households

AQA Examiner's tip

Be careful to use 'cautious' phrases in your essays. Do not say things like 'all middle-class families use nannies', but rather 'middle-class families may be more likely to use nannies'. Other useful cautious phrases are 'there is a trend towards ...' and 'this seems to indicate ...'.

■ Summary questions

1 What do sociologists mean by the term 'family diversity'?

2 What is meant by the term 'family life cycle'?

3 Name two social class differences that could exist between families.

Nuclear and extended families

Learning objectives:

- Understand what is meant by nuclear, extended and beanpole families.
- Understand ethnic differences in family patterns.

Key term

Geographical mobility: the ability to move around the country, normally in pursuit of employment.

AQA Examiner's tip

Be careful to avoid making stereotypical comments. Although extended families are more common amongst Asians, they are by no means the most typical family type.

Links

This area links to Education. African-Caribbean boys underachieve at school compared to other groups, and one reason sometimes put forward for this underachievement is lack of a male role model due to the extent of the single-parent family.

Summary questions

4 What is meant by an extended family?

5 What is a beanpole family?

6 Name two ethnic differences in family patterns.

7 What did Finch and Mason discover?

Nuclear families

The nuclear family consists of a mother, father and dependent children. As pointed out by Robert Chester, it is still the family most people experience at some point in their lives. One reason for the strength and appeal of the nuclear family is its **geographical mobility**.

Extended families

An extended family is a family of three generations living together. The extended family was strongest in working-class families. It is less important today because of geographical mobility, but research by Finch and Mason (1993) shows that kinship ties are still important for most. They discovered that 90 per cent of those researched had given or received financial help from their extended family. They also found that women were more actively involved with the extended family.

Beanpole families

A beanpole family is a nuclear family with one or two children who maintain regular contact with grandparents. As the family size shrinks, the relationship between grandparents and grandchildren becomes more intense. This is due to fewer children being born and longer life expectancy. Grandparents are increasingly being used to look after grandchildren.

Ethnic differences in family patterns

Asian families

The stereotypical image here is that of the extended family. In reality, only about a quarter of Asian households in the UK are extended. Although the nuclear family is the most typical family form, most studies show that extended family ties remain strong in most Asian families, and many Asian families live close to each other.

Marriage tends to be arranged. Divorce is uncommon. Relationships between Asian parents and children tend to be different to white families. Asian families tend to be larger than those of other ethnic groups. About three-quarters of Asian families include children, compared to about a third of white families.

African-Caribbean families

African-Caribbean families are more likely to be single-parent – 50 per cent compared to 25 per cent in the population as a whole. Reasons that have been suggested for the higher rate of black lone parents are as follows:

1 A legacy of the slave trade when families were often split, and children stayed with the mother.
2 Black unemployment, which is linked to male underachievement at school.
3 Tradition, the woman is in charge of the household.

Single-parent families

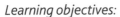

Learning objectives:

- Understand the growth of single-parent families.
- Explain why single-parent families are normally headed by women.
- Evaluate critical and positive views on single-parent families.

The percentage of single-parent families in the UK has more than tripled since the 1970s. About 25 per cent of all families with dependent children are single-parent families, and about 90 per cent of them are headed by women. One child in five now lives with a lone parent. Britain has one of the highest rates of lone parenthood in Europe. In the past, single-parent families obviously existed, but they were fewer in number and normally caused by the death of the male partner. Now most single-parent families are the result of divorce and women not marrying.

Reasons for the growth of single-parent families

1   Divorce. Divorce was made much cheaper and easier in the UK in the early 1970s, and this is one explanation for the growth in lone parents since then.

2   Greater social acceptance. There is a lot less stigma to being a single parent today compared to the past. This is linked to secularisation, which means the decline in religious practice and thinking. For many people today, religion has very little influence or control over their lives, which leads to a wider range of options with regard to the type of family or household they choose to live in. The media also portrays single parents in a more positive light today than in the past, and it is no longer seen as 'deviant' or 'sinful' to be a single parent.

3   The welfare state. The New Right (discussed in more detail in the next section) in particular argue that it is 'too easy' to be a single parent today as the state will support the mother with a range of benefits. Women no longer have to rely on a man or marriage to support them.

4   An increase in the never-married single mother, which now accounts for about 40 per cent of all lone parents. Despite the moral panics in the newspapers, though, at any one time less than 5 per cent of all lone parents are teenagers, and the average age of a lone parent is about 34.

5   Changing attitudes to marriage.

Why are single-parent families normally headed by women?

1   When couples divorce women are far more likely to be given custody of the child.

2   Men tend to have better-paid jobs so may be reluctant to give these up and become single parents.

3   Many men may be reluctant to give up work and care for a child as it could threaten their masculinity.

4   Women are socialised to be nurturing and to expect to be mothers, so being a single parent is more socially acceptable to them than it would be to a man.

Families and households

Fig. 2.2 *90 per cent of single-parent families are headed by women*

■ Critical views on single-parent families

1 Functionalists and the New Right (see next section) argue that a single parent cannot provide adequate socialisation, and that two parents are needed. In particular, children need a male and a female role model, and in a single-parent family they will normally only experience the female role and not the male role.

2 Single parents are more likely than other households to be dependent on the welfare state and not in work. Some commentators argue that this is not fair to those that do work and pay their taxes. The never-married young mum is often targeted here.

3 Research summarised by McLanahan and Booth (1991) indicates that children from single-parent families do less well at school compared to children from nuclear families, and are more likely to become delinquents. Children from single-parent families are also more likely to become single parents themselves and experience lower earnings as adults. However, do these differences stem from the absence of the second parent, or from the lower average incomes of single-parent families?

■ Positive views on single-parent families

1 Many children from single-parent families do well educationally and take up professional jobs. Many single parents raise their children well and the children do not become delinquents.

2 Cashmore (1985) has pointed out that one good parent is better than two bad parents. If the two parents are always arguing and fighting, the single-parent family may in fact be better for the child.

3 Feminists are often supportive of the single-parent family for the independence it provides women. Also the woman may have left her partner because of domestic violence, so the single-parent family is better for the woman and children.

4 Most women do not choose to be single parents, and being a single parent is often just one stage in a person's family life cycle. As Chester (1985) pointed out, most single-parent families come from nuclear families and most will become nuclear again when the single parent forms a new relationship.

5 Other family types are not perfect either. It is easy to attack lone parent families, but what about the many nuclear families that are not working?

■ Summary questions

8 How many single-parent families in the UK are headed by women?

9 Name two reasons why single-parent families are normally headed by women.

10 Name three reasons for the growth of single-parent families.

Singletons, same-sex and reconstituted families

Hint

Do not confuse 'singletons' with 'single-parent families'.

Key term

Surrogacy: an arrangement where a mother has a child for another couple.

Summary questions

11 What is meant by the term 'singleton'?

12 What is a 'reconstituted family'?

13 Give two reasons for the growth of singletons.

14 Give two reasons for the growth of same-sex families.

Singletons

A singleton is someone who lives by themselves. About three in 10 households contain one person. Singletons are growing for a number of reasons:

1 More people in their twenties and thirties live by themselves because they can afford to, and there is less stigma about it. Women especially are able to pursue careers and do not face as much pressure to marry. People tend to marry later.

2 More men in their forties and fifties live by themselves because of divorce. Divorced women normally gain custody of children, so men are left by themselves unless they remarry.

3 There are an increasing number of women who live by themselves because of the death of their husbands, as women live longer than men.

Same-sex families

This family type has increased in recent years. It is difficult to estimate the numbers of same-sex families as until recently same-sex partnerships were not legally recognised, so records were not kept. Following the Civil Partnership Act 2004, though, which came into force on 5 December 2005, gay couples now have legal recognition of their relationships. This gives them equal treatment to married couples.

Why have same-sex families increased?

1 Increased social acceptance. Homosexuality was legalised in the UK in 1967, and the age of consent has gone down from 21 to 18 and is now 16, the same as for heterosexuals. Homosexuality is far more socially acceptable now.

2 Secularisation. Most religions condemn homosexuality, but as less people in the UK are religious they can be more accepting of homosexuality.

3 Reproductive technologies like IVF ('test-tube babies') and **surrogacy** allow gay couples to have children. Adoption is another possibility.

Reconstituted families

A reconstituted family is made up of an adult couple, married or unmarried, living with at least one child from a previous relationship of one of the partners. It is also known as a step- or blended family. This is a growing family form because of the increase in divorce since the 1970s. About 10 per cent of all children live in a stepfamily. Issues with reconstituted families are that children may find themselves pulled in two directions emotionally, and be subject to sibling rivalry.

Childbirth, family size and mortality rates

Families and households

- Understand why women are having fewer children.
- Understand why more children are born outside of marriage.
- Understand mortality rates and why people are living longer.

Key terms

Infant mortality rate: the number of deaths in a population of infants under one year of age per thousand births.

Child-centred: the idea that children are now the most important aspect of society.

Hint

Any 'rate' is always per 1,000 per year, whether it is referring to marriage, divorce or deaths.

Childbearing and family size

In the 1870s women would have on average six children. In the 1960s the average was 2.7, and today the average is 1.6. In the 1970s most women had their first child in their mid twenties; today it is nearer 30. Also an increasing number of children are now born to unmarried couples.

Why are women having fewer children?

1 The decline in the **infant morality rate**. More children survive into adulthood.
2 The introduction of reliable contraception in the 1960s, particularly the pill.
3 The increased expense of children. This links to society becoming more **child-centred**.
4 Women are having children later, leaving less time to have more children.
5 The impact of feminism and prioritising careers.

Why are more children born outside of marriage?

1 The increase in the number of people cohabiting.
2 Couples are less stigmatised for having children outside of marriage.
3 Secularisation. People are less influenced by religion and are more likely to have sex outside of marriage.

Mortality rates

People are living longer. The average life expectancy for a woman today is 80, for a man it is 75. This has consequences for the elderly and society in general. One issue is financial; more money is needed for pensions and health care. Another issue is elderly care – should the state or families themselves be responsible? An ageing population can be seen as an asset rather than a problem, and employers are encouraged to employ people beyond retirement age.

Why are people living longer?

1 Better medical care and improved medical knowledge, especially over disease.
2 The welfare state, support for the elderly in the form of pensions and help with fuel and transport.
3 Improved knowledge about the importance of diet and exercise.
4 Improved hygiene, cleaner water, refrigerated food and effective sewage disposal.
5 Women are having fewer children, more births take place in hospitals.
6 Jobs are less physical. Most people work in comfortable offices and businesses.

Fig. 2.3 *Why are people living longer?*

7 The last world war ended in 1945, you are unlikely to die in a war.

8 We are protected from many of the hazards of the past. We have a '**nanny state**' to protect us. A recent example is the smoking ban.

> **Key term**
>
> **Nanny state:** the idea that the government regulates and controls all aspects of our life and attempts to protect us from dangers.

Summary questions

15 What percentage of all children are born outside of marriage?

16 Give two reasons why women are having fewer children.

17 Give two reasons why more children are born outside of marriage.

18 Give two reasons why people are living longer.

Migration to Britain

Learning objectives:

- ■ Describe the history of migration to the UK.
- ■ Understand issues surrounding migration.
- ■ Examine emigration out of the UK.

Britain is a multicultural society. According to the 2001 census, where people were given the chance to describe their ethnic origin, 8 per cent of the British population described themselves as belonging to a non-white ethnic minority group. This amounts to about 4.6 million people out of a total population of about 60 million. Indians are the largest of these groups (1.8 per cent of the population), followed by Pakistanis (1.3 per cent), those of mixed ethnic background (1.2 per cent), black Caribbeans (1.0 per cent), black Africans (0.8 per cent), Bangladeshis (0.5 per cent) and Chinese (0.4 per cent).

The census also showed that Britain's ethnic minority population is not evenly distributed throughout the country, with London being the most multicultural. Other multicultural areas include Yorkshire, especially cities like Bradford, and the West Midlands, particularly Birmingham.

The history of migration to the UK

Britain has a long history of immigration. Throughout the years there have been Romans from Italy, Saxons from Germany, Vikings from Denmark and Normans from France. In the 16th and 17th centuries England accepted many people from France and Holland who were escaping religious persecution, and in the 19th century many left Ireland to escape starvation and poverty. After the Second World War many refugees came to Britain from Europe, especially Poland. The biggest groups of immigrants to Britain since then have been from Asia and the Caribbean. Many of the early immigrants were recruited to do low-paid and relatively low-status work which employers could not fill with white British workers. London Transport, for example, recruited thousands of workers from Barbados, and many more ethnic minorities got jobs in the NHS and service sector. More recently changes in the European Union have allowed many eastern Europeans to work in the UK, and many have come from Poland. Estimates vary on the actual number of eastern Europeans in the UK, with figures ranging from half to two million.

Issues surrounding migration

Migration is a complex and sometimes controversial area, and this section will simply highlight some of the issues that have arisen in recent years:

1 One area that has already been discussed is how ethnicity can influence family structure. Asian families are more likely than other groups to be extended, and one reason for this is that it reflects family patterns in countries such as India, Pakistan and Bangladesh where the extended family is more common.

2 Migration is often a 'hot' political issue. Many Conservative politicians, especially in the past, have spoken out against immigration. One famous (or infamous) politician was Enoch Powell who in 1968 gave his 'rivers of blood speech' in which he spoke out against unchecked immigration and implied that the British way of life was under threat. Other far-right political parties

like the British National Party (BNP) have also argued against immigration, and have even won a limited number of seats on some local councils.

3 **Integration** and issues of **cultural identity** are of interest to sociologists. To what extent should minority groups that have migrated to another country integrate or 'fit in'? To what extent should your ethnic identity, be it Indian, Irish or Polish, or your religion, take priority over your identity as 'British'. This raises further questions as to what being 'British' actually means!

■ Emigration

Emigration refers to people leaving their county of birth and moving to another country to live there. People have obviously been emigrating since transport made it possible, but in recent years emigration from the UK has become more popular than ever before. It has been estimated that since the millennium (AD 2000) about 1.1 million British citizens have left the UK and moved abroad, and about 600,000 others have returned from abroad. This is a loss of about half a million British citizens. The number of British citizens who emigrate each year has gone up by more than a third since the mid-1990s. The most popular destinations in Europe are France and Spain. Half a million Britons live in the US and more than 600,000 people in Australia hold UK passports. Reasons given for leaving normally include to have a better 'quality of life', a higher standard of living, less crime and better weather! The high numbers of people returning, though, shows that sometimes the new life does not work out as planned.

■ Key terms

Integration: the subjective feeling of 'belonging' to society and its structures.

Cultural identity: the culture that you most closely identify with.

■ Summary questions

19 What percentage of the UK population is non-white?

20 What is the largest ethnic minority group in the UK?

21 What is meant by the term 'integration'?

Families and households

Chapter summary

Further resources

www.gingerbread.org.uk –
Information and support for
single-parent families.

The Simpsons are a good example of
a nuclear family – Homer and Marge
as the married couple with their
three dependent children. Homer
is the breadwinner and Marge the
housewife, except when she became
a police officer!

Soap operas today tend to show
a range of family and household
types including singletons, gay
couples, ethnic minority families and
cohabiting couples. In the past they
would have mainly featured nuclear
families.

Bridget Jones's Diary (2001) and
About a Boy (2002) are good
examples of the singleton lifestyle.

- There are many different types of family in the UK.

- Although the nuclear family is often presented as the main family type, most people do not live in nuclear families.

- Some sociologists take a positive approach to family and household diversity and others take a more critical approach.

- The family life cycle refers to the types of family and household a person will experience in their lifetime.

- Growing family and household types include single-parent families, singletons and reconstituted families.

- Women are having fewer children than in the past and people are living longer.

- The UK is becomingly increasingly multi cultural, and this is adding to the types of families and households that exist.

Theoretical views and social policie the family

Functionalist and New Right views on the family

Learning objectives:

- Understand functionalist and New Right views on the family.

- Evaluate criticisms of functionalist and New Right views on the family.

Key terms

Consensus: agreement or harmony.

Socialisation: the process of learning the norms and values of society.

Fig. 2.4 *Functionalists favour the male and female parental role models in the nuclear family*

A theory is simply an idea about how something works. The two theories on the family examined in this chapter, functionalism and New Right, look at the nuclear family in a positive way but are more critical of other family types. Although these two perspectives do overlap in places, functionalism is an academically well-established and very detailed sociological theory, whereas the New Right is more of a political and journalistic viewpoint, and academically less well regarded.

Functionalist views on the family

Functionalists always ask about the purpose or function of an institution. What good does it do for society? How does it help to maintain order and **consensus**? They are interested in the positive functions of the family. How does it contribute to a healthy society? Two key functionalist writers on the family are the American sociologists George Peter Murdock and Talcott Parsons.

George Peter Murdock (1949) looked at a sample of 250 societies, from small hunting and gathering societies to modern industrial countries like the US. In all of these societies families were the most important institution. By looking at these societies he was able to define the family:

> The family is a social group characterised by common residence, economic cooperation and reproduction. It includes adults of both sexes, at least two of whom maintain a socially approved sexual relationship, and one or more children, own or adopted, of the sexually cohabiting adults.

Murdock argued that all families fulfil four vital functions. These are:

1 Sexual – married adults enjoy a healthy sex life which prevents them having affairs and ensures children are raised by their natural parents.

2 Reproductive – making the next generation.

3 Economic – by this Murdock means providing food and shelter. Ideally the man will go out to work and the woman will look after the house and children.

4 Educational – by this Murdock means **socialisation**.

Talcott Parsons (1959) focuses on the American family. He argues that the family has two key functions:

1 Primary socialisation.

2 Stabilisation of the adult personality. The family is a warm, friendly place where the adults can relax. This is sometimes called the 'warm bath' theory of the family, as the family is seen like a warm bath where all the cares and stresses of everyday life are soaked away.

Functionalists favour the nuclear family. Children are provided with a male and female role model and socialisation from two parents. Functionalists do not like single-parent families or gay families.

Families and households

■ Key terms

Instrumental role: the economic or breadwinner role.

Expressive role: the nurturing or caring role.

Underclass: a group of people who exist outside the main culture and at the bottom of the class system, often associated with welfare dependency, criminal activities and lone parents.

Functionalists argue that ideally the man will take the **instrumental role** and the woman the **expressive role**. Functionalists prefer marriage to cohabitation as it is seen as more stable; they do not like divorce.

■ Criticisms of the functionalist view of the family

- ■ Murdock's definition of the family is criticised for being too narrow, it excludes single-parent and gay families.
- ■ The idea of different gender roles in the family has been criticised by feminists. Feminists point out that the family benefits men more than women.
- ■ The theory is seen as too positive and optimistic. It ignores negative aspects of some families such as domestic violence.
- ■ Functionalists focus too much on the positive aspects of the nuclear family and criticise other family types like the single-parent family. There are many very successful single-parent families.

■ New Right views on the family

These are usually conservative commentators. They were perhaps most influential in the UK in the 1980s when Margaret Thatcher was prime minister. They have very similar views on family as the functionalists. They are critical of the single-parent family for two reasons. First, they believe that children need a male and female role model for adequate socialisation. Secondly, they argue that single-parent families cost too much in welfare benefits. They argue that men should be the bread winners and women the home makers. They are against cohabitation and divorce, and in favour of marriage.

One key New Right sociologist is the American sociologist Charles Murray (1989). He wrote about the emergence of the **underclass** in America and said that it is increasing in the UK. He identified two groups: the New Rabble, which includes the long-term unemployed, welfare dependents and single mothers relying on benefits – this group is dangerous for society because children are not socialised properly; and the New Victorians, who are the respectable middle class who marry, socialise their children properly, work and pay taxes.

■ Summary questions

1 What is meant by the term 'consensus'?

2 What is meant by the 'expressive role'?

3 What are Parsons' two functions of the family?

4 Give two New Right views on the family.

■ Criticisms of New Right views on the family

- ■ The New Right tend to group all single-parent families together and criticise them, without acknowledging many nuclear families that fail to socialise their children properly.
- ■ Feminists argue that the New Right hold sexist views on women, and that women increasingly go out to work as the family can no longer survive on a single male wage.
- ■ If welfare benefits were cut for single parents, it is the children who would unfairly suffer.

Critical views of the family – feminism

Learning objectives :

- Understand the different feminist views on the family.

- Evaluate criticisms of feminist views on the family.

Feminism is a movement that argues that women suffer injustices in society because of their gender. Feminists believe that women need to fight for their rights and free themselves from patriarchy. When looking at the family most feminists take a critical view, and see the family as an institution that benefits men more than women and children. There are many different types of feminism, and this chapter will examine four of the most important ones.

Liberal feminism

Liberal feminists tend to have an optimistic view on the family. They focus on the increased equality that exists between men and women, and the fact that many couples see their relationship as an equal partnership. They look at the emergence of the 'new man', a man who will take an active role in housework and childcare and is in touch with his 'feminine side'.

Radical feminism

Radical feminists tend to look at the family in a more critical and negative way than liberal feminists. They argue that men benefit more from family life than women. They have conducted much research into housework and childcare, and argue that men do very little compared to women. They often see marriage as a type of prison for women, and argue that men may use violence against women if they do not get their own way. Radical feminists support family diversity, especially single-parent and gay families, and disagree with functionalists and the New Right that the nuclear family is always the best family type. They are also supportive of divorce because they argue that it allows women to escape marriage. A more extreme version of radical feminism is called 'radical separatism', and these feminists tend to see men as 'the enemy' and argue that men and women should live apart.

Marxist feminism

Marxist feminists also look at the family in a negative and critical way. They argue though that the main cause of women's oppression is not patriarchy but capitalism – the economic system that exists in most countries in the world. Under capitalism those who own the factories, businesses and offices – the capitalists or upper class – exploit those who have to work for them – the proletariat or working class. Women serve capitalism in the following ways:

- Women look after the men who work for the bosses. They satisfy their physical, emotional and sexual needs, and 'service' the men like a car going to a garage. Margaret Benston (1972) argued that women are 'the slaves of wage slaves' (men are the wage slaves).

Fig. 2.5 *Feminists believe women need to fight for equal rights and that the family benefits men more than women*

■ When men have a bad day at work they take out their anger, frustration and aggression on their wives and children. Fran Ansley (1972) argued that in this way women are 'takers of shit'.

■ Women give birth to the next generation of workers.

■ Women are used in the job market as a 'reserve army of labour' – useful when there are plenty of jobs to fill, but when there is not they are 'sent back' to be housewives.

■ Black feminism

Black feminists are often critical of other feminists. They argue that most white feminists tend to group all women together and ignore the ethnic differences that exist between women. African-Caribbean women, for example, are more likely to be single parents than white or Asian women. Asian women may experience more patriarchy in their families than white women, and may have to do more housework and childcare. They may have more religious and cultural responsibilities than other groups too, and arranged marriage could be an issue. Black feminists argue that for many women their ethnicity is at least as important as their gender.

■ Criticisms of feminism

■ There is not just one variety of feminism, and they tend to criticise and challenge each other, which may weaken their overall message.

■ Feminist views can be seen as dated, as women now have equality in terms of job opportunities and equal pay. Some commentators argue that the battles have been fought and the gender war is over. Marxist feminism in particular can be seen as dated as most women now work, and the idea that they spend their time 'servicing' their husbands would be treated with scorn by most modern women.

■ For most women men are not the enemy to be avoided. Most women want to spend time with men and even marry them and have children together!

■ The New Right would argue that equality is not always a good thing, as most women are now working full-time and children are suffering as they are being neglected. Women themselves are suffering as they are doing too much, and would actually have an easier life as 'just a housewife'!

Summary questions

5 What is meant by the term 'patriarchy'?

6 What do radical separatists believe?

7 What do black feminists argue?

8 Give two criticisms of feminism.

Radical psychiatry and Marxism

Families and households

Learning objectives:

■ Understand and evaluate radical psychiatry and the family.

■ Understand Marxist views on the family.

Most feminists take a critical view of the family. Other critical views are taken by radical psychiatry and Marxism.

Radical psychiatry and the family

Radical psychiatry emerged in the 1960s and 1970s and takes a critical view of family life, particularly the nuclear family. Three important radical psychiatrists are Leach, Laing and Cooper.

Leach (1967) argues that the nuclear family is too isolated and lacks the support of the extended family. This puts too much pressure on the parents who lack emotional support and often take out their anger and frustration on each other and their children.

Laing (Laing and Esterson, 1964) argues that the family can cause mental illness such as stress, depression and anxiety because parents and children spend too much time with each other. Parents expect too much of their children and the children feel suffocated. Laing wrote about a girl called Jane who became schizophrenic and thought she was a tennis ball because she was bounced between her parents emotionally.

Cooper (1972) takes a more Marxist approach to the family and focuses particularly on how children are treated. He argues parents teach children to be obedient, so when they go to work they are easily controlled. Parents make children aim at getting 'respectable' jobs, and any dreams are stamped upon. Parents are like the capitalists or bosses, and the children become the proletariat or workers.

Fig. 2.6 *Friedrich Engels argued that the nuclear family was an attempt to control the sexual behaviour of women*

Criticisms of radical psychiatry

Radical psychiatry is often accused of taking too negative a view on the family. Leach ignores the contacts that are maintained between the nuclear and extended family, Laing over-states the link between mental illness and the family, and Cooper is too critical of the relationship between most parents and their children. Functionalists would accuse the radical psychiatrist of ignoring the positive aspects of family life.

Marxism and the family

Marx's friend Engels (1820–95) wrote a lot about the family. He argued that as capitalists became rich, they needed to ensure they passed their property on to their rightful heir, especially their first-born son. The nuclear family and monogamous (faithful) relationships were an attempt to control women's sexual behaviour. This was before DNA testing for paternity was available, which enabled men to be as certain as possible that their son was their own.

Other Marxist views on the family already discussed include the arguments put forward by the Marxist feminists such as Ansley and Benston, and also the Marxist radical psychiatrist, David Cooper.

Summary questions

9 What does Leach argue?

10 How does Cooper see the family?

11 Give two criticisms of radical psychiatrists' views on the family.

12 Name three Marxists who have looked at the family.

Social policies in the UK and around the world

Families and households

Learning objectives:

■ Outline social policies in the UK.

■ Outline social policies in other countries.

Social policy refers to laws made by the government. Social policies that affect the family include laws made about marriage, divorce, children, welfare, domestic violence and child abuse. Social policies are very important because they regulate family life and decide what is and is not possible, and they may influence the structure and roles within the family. This chapter will examine some social policies that are specific to the UK, and then social policies in other countries.

Social policies in the UK

Social policies that affect marriage in the UK include being able to marry only one person at a time and only someone of the opposite sex, although civil partnerships now exist.

Social policies that affect divorce include whether or not divorce is legal, the amount of time you have to stay married before a divorce is possible and who gains custody of any children.

Social policies that affect children include children having to go to school between the ages of 5 and 16, not being able to work part time until they are 13 and full time until they are 16. There are also a whole range of laws to do with smoking, drinking, sexual behaviour and even going to the cinema.

Social policies that affect welfare include the child benefit that all primary carers of children receive, benefits available to single parents, and unemployment, housing benefits and pensions.

Social policies that affect domestic violence and child abuse include the laws that protect all members of the family against violence, and give the police and courts the power to intervene within the family, remove violent members and place children in care.

Social policies in other countries

Clearly all countries have very different laws that affect the family, and these laws are constantly changing to fit in with different circumstances and the political ambitions of the countries' leaders. Some of these may be seen as sensible and necessary, and others as indefensible.

In Nazi Germany in the 1930s, for example, the government decided that only the 'racially pure' should be able to have children. Many of those who were not seen as fit to breed, such as the mentally and physically handicapped, were compulsorily sterilised.

In Romania in the 1980s the government tried to increase the birth rate by restricting contraception and abortion. They made marriage more financially attractive and restricted divorce.

At the other extreme, in China they have a one child policy, and couples that comply get higher tax allowances and other benefits.

AQA Examiner's tip

Social policies are changing all the time, so it is important to try and keep up to date by reading a good-quality newspaper and watching the news on a regular basis.

Summary questions

13 What is meant by the term 'social policies'?

14 Name two social policies that affect marriage.

15 Name two social policies that affect children.

16 Name two social policies that have existed in other countries.

Social policy and the family

Learning objectives:

- Understand functionalist views on social policy.
- Understand New Right views on social policy.
- Understand feminist views on social policy.
- Understand marxist views on social policy.

Theoretical views

Theoretical views on social policies are held by functionalists, the New Right and feminists.

Functionalist views on social policy

Functionalists have generally taken a positive view on social policy. The welfare state takes a lot of pressure off the family with regard to education and health care, and allows the family to concentrate on socialisation and nurturing. As previously mentioned, Murdock argues that the modern family has four key functions, and Parsons argues it has two key functions. The existence of the welfare state allows the family to concentrate on these key functions. The welfare state should work alongside the family and they can support each other. When a family member becomes ill, for example, they can be cured in hospital and then cared for in the family.

New Right views on social policy

The New Right takes a negative view on many social policies as they see them as undermining the traditional nuclear family. They are particularly critical of welfare benefits that are given to single-parent families as they believe they encourage young women especially to become pregnant, knowing the state will look after them and their child. They believe that the single-parent family should be discouraged and the nuclear family encouraged. One way to do this would be to reduce or eliminate the benefits given to single parents whilst making the nuclear family and marriage more financially attractive. The New Right are also critical of divorce laws as they believe divorce is too easy, and people need to be encouraged to work at their marriage and not take the 'easy option' of divorce.

Feminist views on social policy

Feminists support benefits for single parents because most single parents are women. Feminists argue that most women do not want to be single parents, but may have left abusive or empty shell marriages and should be supported by the state. They also argue that if benefits for single parents are reduced then the children will suffer. Feminists are also in favour of the divorce laws because they enable women to free themselves from patriarchal control, and would welcome the recent civil partnership law which enables gay couples to gain similar legal rights to heterosexuals. They would obviously welcome the laws against domestic violence, but often question how useful they are if the police are sometimes reluctant to become involved.

Feminists also argue that many social policies are sexist and stereotypical. One example is maternity leave which although on one level favours women also supports patriarchy. This is because maternity leave is far more generous for women than paternity leave is for men. This encourages the assumption that women will want to look after the child while men would rather be back at work. Child benefit is also normally paid to the women, which again assumes that they are the primary carer.

Fig. 2.7 *Karl Marx suggested that there is an inequality between capitalists and the working class*

■ Marxist views on social policy

Marxists focus on the inequalities that exist in society between the bourgeoisie or capitalists (owners of factories and businesses) and the proletariat or working class (everyone else). The relationship between these two groups is not equal as the working class are forced to sell their labour to the capitalists in return for money. The capitalists make a profit as they pay the workers less than the value of what they produce. The role of social policies in all this is complex and not all Marxists agree with each other. For some Marxists social policies such as free education, health care and the welfare state are the result of class struggle. In other words the working class have 'won' these benefits from the capitalist class who were afraid of the consequences if they did not give the working class a better quality of life. For other Marxists social policies are just 'smokescreens' to make life appear better. Education and health care are free, for example, but are inferior to the private education and health care enjoyed by the capitalist class. Health care is also only provided free to enable the workers to get better as quickly as possible so they can get back to work ready to be exploited all over again! Welfare benefits are kept as low as possible to force people back to work, and only exist to prevent conflict and possible revolution. State pensions in particular are very poor as elderly people are no longer of any benefit to capitalism and no longer have a purpose.

■ Summary questions

17 Why do functionalists have a positive view on social policy?

18 Name two New Right views on social policy.

19 Name two feminist views on social policy.

20 Name two Marxist views on social policies.

Chapter summary

Further resources

F. Engels, *The Origin of the Family, Private Property and the State*, Lawrence and Wishart, 1972

The film *Pleasantville* (1998) is an excellent illustration of the functionalist view on the family. In this film two modern teenagers enter a world of the 1950s when men went to work and women stayed at home and baked.

- Functionalists and the New Right see the nuclear family as performing vital functions for society, and argue that other types of family are not as beneficial.

- The New Right are particularly critical of single-parent families.

- Feminists are more accepting of family and household diversity and are often critical of the nuclear family.

- Radical psychiatrists and Marxists are also critical of the nuclear family.

- Social policies are laws passed that can affect family life, and these change over time and vary from country to country.

- Social policies can be seen positively or negatively, depending on the theoretical approach taken.

2.3 Marriage, divorce and cohabitation

Marriage, divorce and cohabitation

Learning objectives:

- Describe marriage, divorce and cohabitation patterns in the UK.

- Evaluate variations in divorce rates between social groups.

Fig. 2.8 *It is difficult to get statistics on the number of empty shell marriages there are*

Hint

There is a lot of information to be absorbed in this chapter, so do not get bogged down in too many statistics or percentages – it is overall trends and patterns that are important, not exact measurements.

Summary questions

1. What is meant by the term 'empty shell marriage'?

2. What is meant by the term 'cohabitation'?

3. Name two variations in divorce between social groups.

4. Name two changes in marriage that have taken place in the last 30 years.

Divorce patterns

What have Elvis Presley, Albert Einstein and Lady Diana Spencer got in common? They all got a divorce, as will about 40 per cent of all people that marry in the UK. In 1931 less than 4,000 people got divorced. In 2004 it was over 165,000!

Variations in divorce rates between social groups

- Teenage marriages are twice as likely to end in divorce.

- There is a higher rate of divorce for couples in the first five years of marriage.

- Older people now divorce more. Couples married for more than 30 years are twice as likely to divorce as they were 10 years ago.

- The working class has a higher rate of divorce than the middle class.

- Asians have a far lower rate of divorce than whites.

- Childless couples are more likely to divorce than couples with children.

- Those who marry partners of a different social class, ethnicity or religion are more likely to divorce.

Empty shell marriages and separation

Divorce statistics tell us nothing about empty shell marriages, where the couple stay together but no longer love each other. They could stay together 'for the sake of the children', to avoid embarrassment, or for religious, cultural or financial reasons.

Separation normally refers to a married couple who separate but have not divorced. Some go on to get a divorce, but others will try to 'try again'. Obtaining statistical information on separation is difficult. A couple might go to a magistrates' court to obtain a 'legal separation order' but not always.

Marriage and cohabitation patterns

In the 1970s there were about 400,000 first marriages, and today it is about half that. Almost half of all marriages today are remarriages. Most people will eventually get married, and far more than before will remarry after divorce. The average age for a man to marry in the mid 1960s was 25, for both men and women now it is nearer 30.

Cohabitation means living with someone and having a sexual relationship with them, without marriage. Today there are about two million cohabiting couples. About 60 per cent of first-time cohabitations turn into marriage.

The increase in divorce

Learning objective:

■ Understand the reasons for the increase in the divorce rate.

Fig. 2.9 *People are more likely to avoid divorce because of religious teachings*

Divorce has increased steadily since the 1970s, and the reasons suggested for this increase are as follows.

■ Legal changes:

In the UK divorce has been possible for many years. The three most important divorce laws in the UK are as follows:

1 The Divorce Law Reform Act 1969, which came into effect in 1971. With this Act you no longer had to prove one partner 'guilty' of a matrimonial offence. You just had to show that the marriage had 'irretrievably broken down'. If the couple had been separated for at least two years, this demonstrated that the marriage had irretrievably broken down.

2 The Matrimonial and Family Proceedings Act 1984. This allowed couples to get a divorce after only one year of marriage.

3 The Family Law Act 1996, which came into effect in 1999. This increased the amount of time before a divorce could proceed to 18 months. It also introduced compulsory marriage counselling sessions in an attempt to slow the divorce rate.

■ The impact of feminism: about three-quarters of divorce petitions are from women. Women have become far more independent.

■ The welfare state: state benefits help divorced women, particularly those with children.

■ Changing social attitudes: divorce has lost its social stigma partly because there is so much of it. In the past divorce was rare and seen as scandalous.

■ Secularisation: secularisation is the decline of the influence of religion in society. People are less likely to be influenced by religious teachings when considering divorce.

■ Rising expectations of marriage: functionalists argue that people find the reality of marriage disappointing. In the past people would often marry for economic reasons, today most people marry 'for love' and happiness.

■ Increased life expectancy: if you marry in your late twenties you can expect to live for another 50 years. This may mean that people are more prepared to divorce if they fall out of love. In the past they may have been prepared to stay in a loveless marriage as they would have fewer years to spend together!

Summary questions

5 When was the Divorce Law Reform Act introduced?

6 What percentage of divorce petitions are from women?

7 What is meant by the term 'secularisation'?

8 Name four reasons why divorce has increased.

Declining marriage/increasing cohabitation

Learning objective:

- Evaluate reasons why marriage is losing its appeal and why cohabitation is increasing.

Link

This area links to education and helps to explain why girls are now doing so much better than boys at school – their priorities have changed and they are far more focused on gaining qualifications and careers.

Fig. 2.10 *The average cost of a marriage in the UK is now well over £15,000*

Reasons

Marriage is less popular today than it has been for many years and cohabitation more popular. There are many reasons for this.

The impact of feminism

In the past, women would have to marry to gain financial security. With women earning their own living, this is not the case any more. Sue Sharpe (1976, 1994) has conducted some interesting research into this area. In the first edition of her book *Just Like a Girl* (1976), the girls she interviewed talked about their future plans, to fall in love, get married and have children. A career was not seen as a high priority. When she repeated her research in the 1990s girls' priorities had changed; the careers came first and marriage and children were less important. Women now have far more choice and opportunities compared to the past. They may choose to marry after a career, but are likely to cohabit first.

Fear of divorce

An ever-increasing number of people have seen those around them getting a divorce. This will have put some off marriage, particularly if their own parents went through a 'messy' divorce. Cohabitation is one 'solution' to avoiding divorce at a later stage.

Secularisation

People are less religious in the UK today, so are able to cohabit without feeling they are 'living in sin'. The church is less likely to condemn people who cohabit. If people are not religious there is no reason why they would not cohabit.

Changing social attitudes

Cohabitation is seen by most people today as socially acceptable. It is very rarely criticised. The media portrays cohabiting couples and married couples in the same way. It is seen as normal for couples to cohabit before marriage, or not to marry at all.

The expense of marriage

The average cost of a marriage in the UK is now well over £15,000. Cohabiting is a cheaper option, and will allow the couple to save for a wedding or not marry at all.

Summary questions

9   How does Sue Sharpe argue girls' priorities have changed since the 1970s?

10 What is the average cost of marriage in the UK?

11 Give three reasons why marriage has lost its appeal.

Theoretical views

Families and households

- Understand New Right views on marriage, divorce and cohabitation.

- Understand feminist views on marriage, divorce and cohabitation.

The New Right

The New Right are in favour of marriage and against cohabitation and divorce. Functionalists would also share many of their views. Their reasons are as follows:

- Marriage between two heterosexual people is the cornerstone of a civilised and ordered society. This is how it has been and how it should be in the future.

- Cohabiting couples are far more likely to split up than married couples. If they have children, this will lead to a single-parent family. Single-parent families cannot socialise children as well as married couples.

- Divorce is far too easy to obtain these days, and should be made more difficult to ensure that people work at their marriage and do not take the 'easy' option. In the past when divorce was not so easy couples had to focus on their relationship and make it work for their own and their children's sakes.

- In the 'golden olden days' most children lived with their married parents and society was stable. Now there is family breakdown and society suffers. High crime rates are linked to family breakdown, as are drug and alcohol abuse.

- The government should do whatever it can to encourage marriage and to discourage cohabitation and divorce. Religious organisations such as the Church of England should also play a part in this, and should not be afraid to encourage marriage and condemn divorce.

Feminism

Feminist views are very different to the views of the New Right:

- Feminists are not necessarily against marriage, but they do generally see marriage as favouring men more than women. Radical feminists in particular focus on inequalities with regard to housework and childcare, and also on domestic violence. Feminists are also more in favour of divorce than the New Right.

- Feminists argue that before divorce was legal in the UK many women were trapped in violent or empty shell marriages. Divorce now allows women to leave such marriages and start again. The fact that most divorces are initiated by women shows that women are no longer prepared to put up with poor marriages.

- Feminists are also more accepting of cohabitation than the New Right. They would argue that for women it gives them a chance to 'check the man out' and to make sure that he is not an old-fashioned sexist male but a 'new man'. Feminists also argue that for gay couples cohabitation is the only choice they have as they cannot get married, although now they do get legal recognition and protection with a civil partnership.

Summary questions

12 Why do the New Right dislike cohabitation?

13 Why do the New Right like marriage?

14 Why do feminists tend to support divorce?

15 Why do feminists tend to support cohabitation?

Chapter summary

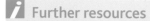 **Further resources**

www.fathers-4-justice.org – A pressure group that is often in the news which campaigns for fairer custody arrangements so fathers can see their children.

The film *Kramer vs. Kramer* (1979) is a very well-made film that tells the story of a divorce and its impact on the couple involved and on their young son.

- Fewer people are getting married overall.
- People are marrying later.
- More people are getting remarried.
- Divorce and cohabitation have increased.
- Sociologists have examined a wide range of reasons to understand these changes.
- The changes that have taken place can be seen positively or negatively, depending on which theoretical approach is taken.

2.4 Childhood

Childhood as a social construct

Key term

Social construct: the idea that an apparently objective phenomenon is created by society or its institutions, rather than being a natural occurrence.

If you were asked to describe 'a child' you might say something like 'A child is a person who is not yet an adult. They are biologically immature'. Whilst this is clearly true, for sociologists there is more to it than this because being 'a child' is not just about biological definitions, but also about sociological definition, as the next section shows.

When do you stop being a child in the UK? Perhaps at age 16 when you can marry with your parents' consent. However, there are certain things you cannot do until you are 18 (buy alcohol) or even 21 (become a member of parliament), so does childhood stop at these ages and adulthood begin? Is childhood today the same as it was in the past? Is childhood in the UK the same as childhood in other parts of the world? Clearly the answer to these questions is no, which is why sociologists argue that childhood is a '**social construct**'. This means that ideas about what childhood is varies according to time and location. It is a relative and not an absolute concept. Each individual society effectively defines childhood and decides how children are to be treated.

Your experiences

The idea of childhood being a social construct can be illustrated by thinking about your own lives. Many of you reading this will be 16 or 17 years old. You will be students and in a way are very lucky! Fifty years ago most of you would be working full time, and the opportunity of going to university was very small. If you happened to be born and spend your childhood in a developing country, you could have been working full time for the last 10 years!

A privileged time?

Although you might not feel privileged, in a way you are. You are protected by a whole range of laws, you receive free schooling and there are plenty of professionals in society 'looking out for you'. However, your experience of being a child will have been influenced by your class, gender and ethnicity, so none will have experienced childhood in exactly the same way. Some of you will have experienced very happy childhoods, and others less positive. Also, some of you may feel that you are over-protected and that you are no longer a child but rather a 'young adult' (another social construct!).

Summary questions

1 What is meant by the term 'social construct'?

2 What can you do at 21 that you cannot do at 18?

Childhood in the UK

Learning objective:

- Describe the historical development of childhood in the UK.

History and development

The history of childhood in the UK can be divided into three stages: pre-industrial (pre-1760), industrial (1760 onwards) and modern (1960 onwards).

Childhood in pre-industrial times

Before the industrial revolution children worked on the land alongside their parents. As soon as they were physically able they would be labouring in the fields. They were a useful resource. Leisure time would be short and life was hard. One of the major writers to study childhood is the French sociologist Phillipe Aries (1962).

Phillipe Aries argues that 'childhood', as we understand it today, is a relatively recent invention. In the Middle Ages (10th–13th centuries) childhood did not exist. Children were not treated any differently to adults. They wore the same type of clothes, ate the same food, went to work and were punished (harshly) for crimes in the same way as adults.

The question that needs to be asked, though, is how does Aries know this? And this raises a big concern in the history of childhood – that of research.

Researching childhood

All historians face the same problem – how do you find out about the past? For sociologists investigating childhood this is particularly difficult, as apart from writings about the children of emperors and kings, little evidence exists which relates to 'normal' children. They could not (on the whole) write. Photographs and videos of them do not exist, so you face a serious research problem. Aries partly overcame this by using paintings of the period. These showed little difference between adults and children. In the paintings children and adults are shown hunting, eating and working together.

A criticism here is that this is clearly not primary (first-hand) research. Aries has to rely on the original artist to be 'telling the truth' about what he painted. Another problem is that most art was paid for by the rich and paintings of the poor are rare. A final problem is paintings can only tell us so much – what about the emotional bonds between parents and children – were they close? Some historians have argued that parents did not feel the same love towards their children as (most) parents do today. High infant and indeed child mortality rates encouraged indifference and neglect. However, other historians have questioned this viewpoint and point to the developing world – infant mortality rates are clearly higher than in the West, but parents still love and care for their children.

The gradual emergence of childhood

'Childhood' did not happen overnight. Aries claims that it began to emerge from the 13th century onwards. First, public (fee-paying) schools were opened to educate the children of the rich; secondly, children were increasingly seen by the church to be 'different' to adults and in need of special discipline and protection.

Children in industrial times

With the industrial revolution (1760 onwards) the position of children changed, although not for the better. Children were still working, but no longer on the land. They were employed in factories and coalmines and up chimneys. They were not protected by any laws and were simply useful at bringing in vitally needed income. Gradually laws were passed to protect children, and there was a shift towards what has become known as a child-centred society.

Childhood today

'Child-centred' means that children are valued, loved and protected. This 'child-centred' society probably started to emerge in the 1950s. It is normally a good time to be a child:

- Children go to school from five to at least 16.
- Children have their own doctors, teachers, social workers and other professionals to care for them.
- Children have toys, books, magazines, TV programmes and films made especially for them.
- Special foods and drinks exist for children (not always healthy ones).
- Children are protected by a range of laws covering working hours to the age of consent, all of which are designed to protect them.

Why might childhood today not be a positive experience?

Although many argue that the UK is a child-centred society, this view can be challenged:

- Child abuse exists. This can be physical, sexual or emotional. It is obviously very difficult to measure the extent of child abuse as it generally goes on behind closed doors. It is certainly an area that is more out in the open and discussed today, but this does not necessarily mean that the amount of child abuse has increased. Organisations like Childline are taking an increased number of calls from children, but again this could be because public awareness of child abuse has increased.
- Bullying takes place in many schools.
- Divorce has increased and many sociologists, particularly functionalists and the New Right, argue this has a very negative effect on children.

Fig. 2.11 *Children in industrial times were put to work and had no laws to protect them*

AQA Examiner's tip

It is important when discussing childhood to present a balanced and cautious view. Although for most children in the UK childhood is a positive experience, for others it is an unbearable one because of abuse.

Summary questions

3 What does Aries mean when he says that children were treated as mini-adults?

4 What was Aries' research method?

5 How were children employed during industrial times?

6 Why is society today often described as 'child-centred'?

Changes in the position of children

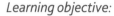

Learning objective:

- Describe reasons for changes in the position of children.

Link

This area links to education, and the idea that the school leaving age may even be raised to 18 in the near future.

How did the position of children change from being the invisible, 'mini-adults' of the past to being the centre of society today? The following reasons have been suggested:

- As the infant mortality rate declined, families were able to invest emotionally and financially in their children. In the past it was expected that some children would die, but with improvements in public health and medical knowledge, more children survived. As such, each child could be valued more and nurtured. Parents could afford to love each child and spend time with it, knowing that there was a very good chance of the child surviving.

- From 1880 all children were made to attend school from five until 10. With children going to school they could no longer work from such a young age, and it was possible to see them as different from adults. Gradually the school leaving age was raised to 12 in 1889 and 14 after the First World War, and it is now 16. Many children now stay on until 18 and then go to university. This has increased the amount of time children are dependent on adults. They are kept as children for longer, and forced to be economically and often emotionally dependent on their parents.

- Laws were passed to protect children, such as the Prevention of Cruelty to Children Act 1889 and more recently the Children Act 1989. The type of work children could do was gradually restricted, as was the number of hours they can work. Children stopped being economic producers and became consumers, dependent on their parents to provide for them.

- People now work fewer hours than in the 19th century, so have more time to spend with children. The family has become increasingly child centred, and families spend leisure time together.

- Age restrictions exist to separate children from adults. Children cannot work part time until they are 13 or full time until they are 16. Children cannot buy cigarettes or alcohol until they are 18. The age of consent is 16.

- The growth in the idea that children have rights, and that their opinions are useful and should be sought in custody cases for example.

- The impact of the mass media. Children now have access to information in the same way as adults using such things as the internet. In many ways they are better at accessing and using information than adults, who no longer have the power to withhold information from children.

Summary questions

7 How does the decline in infant mortality affect how children are treated?

8 Name two Acts that have protected children.

9 Name four reasons why the position of children has changed.

Children in different cultures

Learning objective:

■ Compare how childhood in other cultures differs to childhood in the UK.

The idea of childhood differs over time. It also differs between countries, especially between the Western world and developing nations.

In many ways children in developing countries are experiencing the same type of childhood as children in the UK did in the past – they are working on the land or in factories. In many countries they are not protected by labour laws and experience long hours, low pay and exploitation as well as child poverty.

■ Child poverty in the developing world

A major study in this area is by the Townsend Centre for International Poverty Research (Townsend *et al.*, 2003). This used data from 46 developing countries and the final sample includes data on nearly 1.2 million children. Its main findings make depressing reading.

■ Over one-third of the world's children, 674 million, suffer from **absolute poverty**.

■ Over one-third of all children in the world have to live in dwellings with more than five people per room or which have mud flooring.

■ 134 million children aged between seven and 18 have never been to school.

■ Over 375 million children are using unsafe water sources or have more than a 15-minute walk to water.

■ Many children live in countries affected by civil wars which make an already difficult life almost impossible.

Key term

Absolute poverty: poverty defined by the minimum requirements necessary, such as food, clothing and shelter, to lead a healthy existence.

Fig. 2.12 *An example of childhood in the developing world*

Fig. 2.13 *In some parts of the world children are trained to become soldiers and made to fight*

■ Infectious diseases

Children in the developing world are also far more at risk from infectious diseases such as typhoid and malaria due to lack of clean water, poor waste disposal and lack of medical techniques such as vaccination and immunisation. In some counties one in five children die before their fifth birthday. Every day 3,000 people die from malaria, three out of four of them are children. In the time it has taken you to read this sentence, another child has died from an infectious disease.

■ Child soldiers

'I would like to give you a message. Please do your best to tell the world what is happening to us, the children, so that other children don't have to pass through this violence.' This is from a 15-year-old girl who escaped from the 'Lord's Resistance Army' in Uganda, as reported on the Amnesty International website. Worldwide, more than half a million children under 18 have been recruited as child soldiers. It is probably impossible for children from the rich West to imagine the sights they witness and the physical and psychological damage it does to them.

■ Link

This area links to world sociology and demonstrates the differences that exist between the affluent West and the much poorer south.

■ Summary questions

10 What is meant by the term 'absolute poverty'?

11 How many children in the world suffer from absolute poverty?

12 Why are children in the developing world far more likely to die of an infectious disease?

The future of childhood

Families and households

Learning objectives:

- Evaluate the positive view and the conflict view of childhood.

- Understand the death of childhood argument.

The positive view and the conflict view

The positive view on the future of childhood, sometimes called the 'march of progress' view, argues that over time the lives of most children have improved, and that Western society is 'child centred'.

The conflict view is a more negative view which focuses on two types of inequalities – inequalities among children and between children and adults.

Inequalities among children

Many children suffer deprivation. Material deprivation is lack of income. Some children in the UK will experience relative poverty or homelessness. Cultural deprivation is lack of parental encouragement. Some children are deprived of stimulation from books and toys, and parental attention. Research shows that middle-class children are read to more and that working-class parents are more likely to smack children.

Boys tend to be given more freedom. Parents, especially fathers, spend more time with their sons playing sport, and more time with their daughters reading to them.

Asian girls tend to be given even less freedom than white girls, and children from Asian backgrounds will generally spend more time in religious activities.

Inequalities between children and adults

'Child liberationism' focuses on the controls placed on children by adults, especially their parents. This includes:

control over children's time and space;
where children can play and who they can play with;
use of discipline;
what they wear;
what they eat;
what are appropriate standards of behaviour.

This has been criticised because children need to be guided by their parents who should know best!

The death of childhood

Neil Postman (1994) is a key writer in the 'death of childhood debate' – that children are growing up too quickly and losing their innocence. Evidence could be:

underage sex, drinking and smoking;
teenage pregnancies;
children wearing older clothing;
children watching adult TV, films and playing violent computer games.

Postman argues that television and the internet are readily available and children can access 'adult' material and grow up too quickly. However, it could also be argued that with the correct parental supervision children can still remain children longer.

Summary questions

13 What is the 'march of progress' view of childhood?

14 What is meant by material deprivation?

15 Name two controls that parents place on children.

16 Name three ways in which childhood can be seen as dying.

Chapter summary

Further resources

www.childline.org.uk – A charity which provides a free and confidential helpline for children.

www.Amnesty.org – An organisation that seeks to help oppressed people around the world, including an increasing number of children.

- Childhood is a social construct.
- Being a child in the UK today is very different to being a child in the UK in the past.
- Sociologists have examined the reasons for the changes in childhood.
- Children will experience childhood differently depending on what country they are born in, and what class, gender and ethnicity they belong to.
- The future of childhood can be seen positively or more negatively.

Domestic labour and gender roles

Domestic labour and gender roles

Learning objectives:

- Outline key concepts that are relevant to domestic labour and gender roles.

- Understand functionalist and New Right views on domestic labour.

Domestic labour is simply the sociological name for housework and childcare. Feminists have conducted most of the studies in this area, and have shown that most housework and childcare is done by women. They have also shown that most women do not enjoy housework and that it can even cause depression. They use a number of key concepts when looking at this area.

Patriarchy

This refers to male domination in society. In the family it refers to men controlling women, making key decisions and not doing their share of housework or childcare.

Joint and segregated conjugal roles

Conjugal roles simply mean roles within marriage, and some of the earliest research in this area was conducted by Elizabeth Bott (1957). She argued that there are two types of conjugal roles: segregated and joint. Segregated conjugal roles are where the couple have separate roles. The man would be out at work (the breadwinner role) and the woman the housewife. This was the typical relationship throughout most of the 19th and 20th centuries. Joint conjugal roles are where the couple share housework and childcare, a relationship which has become more common since the 1970s.

The double shift and the triple shift

The double shift refers to women having paid work and also doing most of the housework. They in effect have two jobs, but only get paid for one! The triple shift takes this one step further, and adds emotional work to women's responsibilities. This refers to women taking care of the emotional needs of the family. Women are the ones who provide the love and care needed to make a family happy, including organising birthdays, buying the type of food everyone wants, dealing with friendship issues and generally providing a 'shoulder to cry on' for everyone in the family.

Feminists argue that these responsibilities are unfair burdens on women, and that men need to take more responsibility for housework, childcare and employment too. Other theorists such as functionalists and the New Right, though, take a different approach.

Functionalist and New Right views on housework

Functionalist and New Right writers often argue that it is 'natural' for women to be housewives and men breadwinners. They argue that both jobs are important and that it makes sense for women to be housewives and mothers because of their nurturing characters. Men are more suited to the world of work. In this sense both husbands and wives only have responsibility for one shift, and this makes them both fulfilled.

AQA Examiner's tip

These key concepts can be, and should be, included in any question on domestic labour. They demonstrate to the examiner that you understand key concepts and can use them to answer questions.

Summary questions

1. What does the term 'domestic labour' mean?

2. What does the term 'patriarchy' mean?

3. What is the difference between joint and segregated conjugal roles?

4. What are the three parts of the triple shift?

Domestic labour and gender roles – research

Some of the earliest research was conducted by Young and Willmott in their 1973 book *The Symmetrical Family*. They felt that by the 1970s roles in the family between husbands and wives had become more symmetrical. From their sample they found that 72 per cent of men did housework other than washing up during the week. Characteristics of joint conjugal roles include the following:

■ Husbands and wives both do housework.
■ Husbands and wives both look after the children.
■ Husbands and wives both have paid jobs.
■ Husbands and wives spend leisure time together.

Young and Willmott take what has been called a 'march of progress' view to relationships between husbands and wives. They take an optimistic view on relationships in the family, a view not shared by most feminist sociologists.

Feminist views of housework and childcare

The radical feminist Ann Oakley (1974b) disagrees with Young and Willmott and argued the figure of 72 per cent proves very little. Oakley's research showed 15 per cent of husbands had a high level of participation in housework, and only 25 per cent had a high level of participation in childcare. Her sample was based on 40 married women, so may not be representative.

Other later research by feminists such as Boulton (1983), has tended to confirm Oakley's findings. She found that fewer than 20 per cent of the husbands took a major childcare role. A more recent study by Ferri and Smith (1996) showed that women are still more likely than men to be responsible for childcare. The man was the main carer of children in only 4 per cent of the families studied.

A study by Gillian Dunne (1999) showed equality in lesbian households. She examined 37 cohabiting lesbian couples and found that they were more likely to share housework and childcare responsibilities. Often both partners would try to spend equal time with the children.

The British Social Attitudes Surveys

One problem with the research conducted by Oakley, Boulton and Dunne, is that it is based on small samples. Studies with larger samples of over a thousand people have been undertaken as part of the British Social Attitudes Surveys of 1984, 1991 and 1997 edited by Jowell. These show that women do most of the housework and childcare, and men are more likely to do household repairs than the ironing, but they do show a trend over time of men doing more, especially with childcare. The surveys fit in more with Young and Willmott's 'march of progress' ideas about the symmetrical family.

Hint

There are a lot of studies to deal with in this chapter. One way to learn them could be to write key prompt words about each study on a separate piece of paper and get other people to test you on them.

Summary questions

5 According to Young and Willmott, what percentage of men did housework other than washing up during the course of a week?

6 Why is Ann Oakley not impressed by this?

7 In Oakley's research, what percentage of men had a high level of participation in housework?

8 What group did Dunne focus her research on?

The impact of paid work

Learning objective:

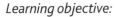 Compare research into whether women working has had an impact on domestic labour.

Several studies on housework and childcare were conducted in the 1970s and 1980s when many women were full-time housewives. Today about three-quarters of married or cohabiting women have paid jobs. Sociologists are interested in whether this means men are doing more housework. Research in this area has been conducted by the following sociologists.

Lydia Morris (1990)

Lydia Morris studied families where the husband is unemployed and the wife works. In such families you would expect men to compensate for the fact that they are not working by doing the housework and childcare. However, Morris found that the unemployed men in her sample did little more housework than before they lost their jobs because they felt that their masculinity was threatened by being unemployed, and to do housework would further emasculate them.

Jonathan Gershunny (1994)

Like all other studies, Gershunny found that women are still responsible for the majority of housework and childcare. Wives who work full time, though, do less housework than housewives. Men do compensate for the fact that their wives are working by doing more around the house, but it is still a long way from symmetry or equality. Again it can be seen as a 'march of progress' idea, confirmed by a later study conducted by Gershunny and Laurie in 2000. This again showed husbands taking on more housework and childcare over time, especially when women work.

Man-Yee Kan (2001)

A study by Man-Yee Kan conducted at Oxford University found similar results to the previous research. Even though most women are now working, they still do the majority of housework and childcare. Women in full-time employment spent nearly 12 hours a week on housework and were responsible for 65 per cent of the household chores. She did find that the more a woman earned the less housework she did. Every £10,000 increase in the woman's annual salary reduced her weekly housework time by nearly two hours. She also found that if both the partners had university degrees there was more equality than less-qualified couples.

Overall these studies show that women working has not had a huge impact on the levels of housework and childcare carried out by men who 'help out' rather than doing an equal share. Men are doing more work than in the past, but not an equal share.

Summary questions

9   Why did the unemployed men Morris studied do little housework?

10 Why does Gershunny take a march of progress view?

11 According to Man-Yee Kan, what makes a difference to how much housework a woman does?

Power relationships/domestic violence

Learning objectives:

- Examine decision-making and power relationships in the family.

- Examine issues of domestic violence.

AQA Examiner's tip

Balance is needed when writing about domestic violence. Do not write that all men attack their wives or that all women are victims, as this is clearly not true.

Fig. 2.14 *Dobash and Dobash (1980) argued that female victims of domestic violence do not report it to the authorities out of fear*

Summary questions

12 What group did Edgell look at?

13 What did Edgell find out?

14 Give two reasons why men tend to dominate decision-making.

15 Who has conducted research into domestic violence?

Decision-making

Some of the earliest research in this area was conducted by Edgell (1980). He found men are far more likely to make the important decisions, for example moving house and finances, and women the less important decisions. A more recent study by Hardill *et al.* (1997), showed some evidence of more equal decision-making taking place between middle-class couples.

Financial control

Pahl (1989) interviewed 102 couples who both earned. She found out that in most couples (39 of them) money was shared, but the husband had financial control. She called this 'husband-controlled pooling', most likely in higher-income households. Another common arrangement (in 27 couples) was 'wife-controlled pooling' where money was shared but the wife controlled spending. The least likely arrangement was when the woman controlled spending (14 couples). Pahl did not find any real evidence of symmetry when it comes to financial equality; more recent studies agree.

Why do men tend to dominate decision-making?

- Men tend to earn more money than women.
- For some ethnic minority groups, traditionally men make decisions.
- Men may feel that their masculinity is threatened if they do not make decisions.
- Some feminists argue that women are socialised to be passive.

Domestic violence

The radical feminists Dobash and Dobash (1980) interviewed female victims of domestic violence who had left their abusive partners and had escaped to a refuge. Dobash and Dobash argued women do not report most incidents out of fear.

The Home Office (www.homeoffice.gov.uk) states domestic violence accounts for 16 per cent of all violent crime; has more repeat victims than any other crime (an average of 35 assaults before a victim calls the police); claims the life of two women each week and 30 men per year; is the largest cause of morbidity (sickness) worldwide in women aged 19–44; and will affect one in four women and one in six men in their lifetime.

Kirkwood (1993), argued that domestic violence causes psychological damage too. This includes low self-esteem, depression, anxiety and stress.

Radical feminists argue that domestic violence exists because society is patriarchal and will only stop when women become equal. Some men themselves may be victims of domestic violence from their wives. Men may be more unwilling to report attacks than women because of embarrassment and fear that they will not be taken seriously.

Chapter summary

🔆 Further resources

www.womensaid.org.uk – A national charity working to end domestic and sexual violence.

Shirley Valentine (1989) is a film that is a good example of segregated conjugal roles and what may happen to men if they do not contribute to housework!

 ■ Domestic labour is the sociological term for housework.

■ Feminists in particular have conducted much research in this area.

■ Feminists are generally critical about the amount of domestic labour carried out by men.

■ Other sociologists take a march of progress view and argue that, gradually, men and women are becoming more equal in the home.

■ Sociologists have examined the impact that women going to work has had on men's contributions.

■ As well as looking at housework and childcare, sociologists have also investigated power relations in the family. Particularly domestic violence.

☑ Read Items 1(a) and 1(b) below and answer parts (i) to (v) that follow.

1   (a)   The stereotypical image of Asian families, often reinforced by the media, is that of the extended family. In reality only about a quarter of Asian households in the UK are extended, and these tend to be mainly Sikh and East African Asian. The rest are mainly married couples or nuclear families, with about 10 per cent being single parent. Having said this, although the nuclear family is the most typical family form, most studies show that extended family ties remain strong in most Asian families, and many Asian families live close to each other and maintain regular contact for both emotional and financial support.

African-Caribbean families are more likely to be single parent than other ethnic groups and whites. Fifty per cent of black families with dependent children are lone parents, compared to 25 per cent in the population as a whole.

(b)   Women are having fewer children today than in the past. In the 1870s women would have on average six children. In the 1960s the average was about 2.7, and today the average is about 1.6. More women are also choosing to remain childless, and those that do have children are having them later on in life. In the 1970s most women had their first child in their mid twenties; today it is nearer 30. Another change is the increasing number of children being born to unmarried couples. About 40 per cent of all children are now born outside of marriage.

Source: adapted from Families and Households, Chapter 1 of this textbook

(i)   Explain what is meant by 'household' (Item 1(a)).   (2 marks)

(ii)   Suggest two ethnic differences in family patterns in the UK (Item 1(a)).   (4 marks)

(iii) Give three possible reasons why same-sex families have increased   (6 marks)

(iv)   Examine the extent of and reasons for family diversity in the UK today   (24 marks)

(v)   Using material from Item 1(b) and elsewhere, assess the reasons for changes in birth rates in the UK since 1900   (24 marks)

Read Items 2(a) and 2(b) below and answer parts (i) to (v) that follow.

2   **(a)**   Families and households have taken different forms at different times and places. According to Talcott Parsons, for example, the extended family was typical of pre-industrial society, whereas the rise of the nuclear family accompanied that of modern industrial society. Parsons argued that this is because the nuclear family meets the needs of modern industrial society.

There is also variation in the roles and relationships within families in terms of the tasks each member is expected to perform and their control over the household's resources. However, despite these variations, radical feminists argue that the family is inevitably patriarchal. For example, studies show that the more important a decision, the more likely it is that the husband rather than the wife makes it.

(b)   According to Ulrich Beck and Elisabeth Beck-Gernsheim (1995), individuals today are increasingly required to make choices about how they live. They argue that this trend has important consequences for the stability of marriage. In the past, individuals had little choice: everyone was expected to marry and, once married, the gender division of labour fixed their roles. Though unequal, such marriages offered security and stability.

Nowadays, however, both society and marriage are more equal, especially in terms of gender. This may create conflict, for example as husband and wife each seek to pursue their individual careers. One partner may have to sacrifice their opportunities for the sake of the other. In a society based on individualism, this may lead to resentment and divorce.

(i)   Explain what is meant by the 'patriarchal' family (Item 2(a)).   *(2 marks)*

(ii)   Identify two criticisms made of the radical feminist view of the family (Item 2(a)).   *(4 marks)*

(iii)   Suggest three reasons why husbands may be more likely to make the more important decisions (Item 2(a)).   *(6 marks)*

(iv)   Examine the reasons for changes in the position of children in the family and society.   *(24 marks)*

(v)   Using material from Item 2(b) and elsewhere, assess sociological explanations of the increase in the number of divorces since the 1960s.   *(24 marks)*

AQA, 2006

Wealth, poverty and welfare

Introduction

Link

For more information on governmental policy on poverty between the 1940s and the 1970s see Chapter 4 Social policy since the 1940s.

Key term

Self-empowerment: taking control of your own life and giving yourself the power to make the important decisions affecting you. Looking after yourself, rather than relying on others (e.g. the government) to do it for you.

💡 Differences of income and wealth between social groups is an important and sometimes controversial subject for sociologists. We live in a society where these differences are large and, in spite of a wide variety of government reforms and social policies over the last 60 years, this problem has not disappeared. In fact, it could be argued that although we have all experienced a rise in living standards in the last century, and few people living in the UK now die from starvation or malnutrition, the gap between the rich and the poor continues to widen.

One of the problems in studying this area is that a valid measurement of the number of people living in poverty is difficult to achieve because there are a number of different definitions and ways of measuring poverty in existence. Simply comparing the UK with the developing world would make it appear that we have few problems. However, many people in this country do suffer from poverty: for example, the lack of a decent education or a safe and comfortable place to live. The effects of this type of poverty may be more difficult to see than those of starvation and malnutrition, but the impact on the lives of those affected can be painful and damaging.

There have been many attempts by successive governments to try and deal with this problem, as well as ever-changing views on exactly what the problem is. The introduction of the welfare state in the 1940s was an attempt to remove poverty altogether by providing state help and assistance to those in need. Contrastingly, in the 1980s and early 1990s, the government view was that social inequality was a natural and healthy aspect of a competitive capitalist economy, and that the state should take a 'back seat', stop discouraging hard work and allow people to help themselves. It wasn't until more recently, that New Labour policies tried to combine some form of state welfare intervention with **self-empowerment** and an emphasis on individual responsibility. As Tony Blair famously stated:
'A hand up, not a hand out.'

It is clear that living in poverty brings with it a significant number of disadvantages and problems not only for the individuals concerned but also for society. A number of sociological studies and research by groups such as the Joseph Rowntree Foundation show strong links between poverty and educational underachievement, ill-health and crime. What these studies suggest is that it is more difficult for those living in poverty to be successful, and that poverty is very often passed down the generations. In other words, children growing up in poverty are significantly more likely to experience poverty themselves as adults.

Wealth, poverty …

Defining poverty

Learning objective:

- Understand the difficulties involved and the different ways of defining poverty.

One of the problems for students studying poverty is that there is no one agreed definition of what poverty means. However, in order to assess the number of people living in poverty in the UK today, it is obviously necessary to try and find a working definition which can be applied to everyone in the population.

This can be difficult because if we try to set out criteria for a person living in poverty we could, for example, use being unemployed as a determining factor. This is because it would seem that there is a clear link between not having a job and experiencing poverty. However, there may be some people, for example some members of the royal family, who are so wealthy that they do not need to have a job! Clearly these people are unemployed in the sense that they do not work but are not living in poverty.

Equally, there have been attempts by researchers to create a list of essential goods and services, and to define those who cannot afford to buy a substantial number of these as being poor. However, what are considered to be essential changes over time? Also there may be some unusual households who choose not to have a television set or DVD player for cultural reasons, not because they cannot afford them.

Finally, it might appear that compared to those who are literally starving to death in other countries, there is no real poverty in the UK: in other words, 'what have we got to complain about?' These are all important issues that need to be considered carefully when attempting to understand what is meant by poverty.

Within the context of sociology there are usually considered to be two main definitions of poverty that are most commonly used: absolute poverty and **relative poverty**.

Key term

Relative poverty: poverty within the context of the overall standard of living in any given society.

Absolute poverty

The definition of absolute poverty was introduced in the late 19th century by Charles Booth and Seebohm Rowntree, and was based on the belief that it is possible to establish a common set of requirements, such as the need for shelter, food and clothing, which could be applied in the same way to groups of people regardless of where they lived. This way of defining poverty is useful because it provides a universal definition, which can be used effectively in comparing levels of poverty between different countries and over different time periods. It also provides a relatively easy way of defining those who are poor, by deciding on a level of income required to sustain basic needs and determining that those who live below this income are living in poverty. This distinction between those who are poor and those who are not, also used when making relative poverty comparisons, is often known as the **poverty line**.

- It is very difficult to measure objectively the so-called 'essential needs' that must be met for people to survive: for example, opinions differ on what a healthy diet should include, how much food a person needs to eat in order to survive and so on.

Key term

Poverty line: an income level below which people are said to be living in poverty. In relative poverty terms, this is often 60 per cent of average income.

■ What is defined as essential in today's society may be very different from what was seen as essential in the late 19th century.

■ Relative poverty

The fact that what we would consider to be essential items changes so much over time and from country to country has led to the view that poverty is relative, and as such should be measured in terms of the standards of a particular society at a particular time with the recognition that what constitutes poverty can change.

Research study: Townsend (1979)

Townsend's study was one of the first to argue that poverty cannot be measured absolutely because the notion of 'essential needs' can change so much over time. These needs are **socially constructed** in the sense that it is society that determines what is needed to feel involved in society and that most of us compare our own living standards to those of other people when we are deciding whether or not we feel deprived.

Individuals can be said to be living in poverty when they lack the resources to obtain the types of diet, participate in the activities and have the living conditions and amenities which are customary, or at least widely encouraged or approved, in the societies in which they belong.

Townsend (1979), Poverty in the United Kingdom

So how we define poverty is not fixed, but can alter in line with changes in society and the expectations of those living within that society. Relative definitions of poverty allow a more flexible approach to measuring the numbers of those deemed to be living in poverty, and do not only base it on subsistence needs but on the ability to take full part in society as well. For example, those families who cannot afford to buy Christmas presents for their children could be defined as living in poverty as this excludes them from participation in society's customs.

Fig. 3.1 *Scotland has one of the highest rates of childhood poverty in the European Union*

■ Key term

Social construct: the idea that an apparently objective phenomenon is created by society or its institutions, rather than being a natural occurrence.

■ Summary questions

1. What is meant by 'absolute poverty'?
2. What is the belief behind the use of the definition of absolute poverty?
3. Identify one problem with the use of this definition of poverty.
4. What is the difference between absolute and relative poverty?

AQA Examiner's tip

Look carefully at any question which is asking you how poverty is defined: you need to check if it is asking you to define absolute or relative poverty.

Defining wealth and income

Learning objective:

- Understand the difficulties and issues involved in defining wealth and income.

Key term

Social survey: a form of research method used by sociologists and others, usually consisting of a list of questions which the respondent either fills in themselves or has read out to them by a trained interviewer.

Link

See pages 228–30 for more about the problems with the use of social surveys and validity of data collected.

Key term

Capitalism: a system of economic enterprise based on market exchange. 'Capital' refers to any asset which can be used to produce commodities for sale or invested in a market with the hope of achieving a profit. Nearly all industrial societies today are capitalist in orientation.

Wealth

Wealth can be defined very simply as 'the ownership of property, shares, savings and other assets'. However, in the same way that it is not very easy to define poverty, there exists a similar problem when trying to define and measure wealth in society. This is partly because the government tends to have less information about the very wealthy in society, often because they are reluctant to share the details of their income and other assets with the HM Revenue and Customs, and also because it is hard to establish what exactly constitutes property and assets.

One method that is used by sociologists to try to establish the level of wealth of individuals in society is through **social surveys**. The two main examples of this type of research are the Expenditure and Food Survey (EFS) and the Family Resources Survey (FRS).

The EFS is conducted annually by the Office for National Statistics and is carried out on a representative sample of 7,000 households in the UK. It contains details of household expenditure on housing, goods and services and analyses those in relation to household income, size and geographical location. The results can also be used to compare levels of household income over time, and are used by the government to establish levels of income inequality and the areas of the country which are the most deprived.

However, there are a number of problems with this form of data collection. First, there is the problem of low response, especially amongst the very rich who may not want to reveal details of their wealth to sociologists. Secondly, it is very difficult for sociologists to establish whether or not those who do fill in surveys are telling the truth.

Official statistics, however, tend to divide wealth into two categories:

1 **Marketable wealth** This includes any type of asset that can be sold and its value realised. This means things like land, shares, savings, homes and personal possessions such as cars, jewellery and so on.

2 **Non-marketable wealth** This includes non-saleable items such as pensions.

However, there are still some problems with these distinctions because it can be argued that having a home is an essential item for most people, so if a person sold their home then they would have more capital but would effectively be homeless, and would therefore not necessarily be defined as more wealthy. There are also clearly issues about what is defined as essential in terms of housing: for example, a family of three living in a seven-bedroom mansion clearly has more than is needed, whereas a family of seven living in a three-bedroom flat may be considered to have less.

Ownership of shares is also an important aspect of wealth, especially as share ownership has increased and become more widely distributed since the 1980s and the Conservative government's privatisation programme. This may give the impression that wealth – and particularly ownership of the means of production, which is very important to Marxists in terms of defining power in **capitalist society** – has become more equally distributed. However, in reality, the very small number of shares held by large numbers of the population has not really changed wealth distribution a great deal, mainly because the majority of small shareholders sell their shares within the first year of buying them.

Fig. 3.2 *Ownership of shares is an important aspect of wealth*

■ Income

Income is also somewhat difficult to define easily; however, in general it can be measured in two main ways: gross income and disposable income.

Gross income is a measure of all sources of income before any deductions for income tax and National Insurance. This may include earned and unearned income, for example child benefits or tax credits etc., whereas disposable income is defined as gross income minus the above deductions.

However, once again this definition is made on the basis that everybody pays taxes and National Insurance and that may not necessarily be the case. People who work 'cash in hand' may not pay tax and the very wealthy also tend to find ways of avoiding large tax bills as well.

There is also a difference between earnings and income. Earnings refer to one aspect of an income for a person or household that is received from paid work. However, there are also other sources of income, such as savings and investments, government benefits and pensions, which can provide households with additional income.

Evidence suggests that for the majority of households, earnings account for most of their income. The EFS 2006 found that 93 per cent of the total income received by those paying income tax was earned income. However, income from investments is more likely to be received by those in the higher income brackets: 70 per cent of investment income is received by those earning above £20,000 per year.

This therefore suggests that those who have higher earnings potential also have other ways of boosting their annual household income, and is useful to take note of when measuring levels of inequality.

AQA Examiner's tip

Make sure you understand the difference between gross and disposable income and are aware of the difficulties of measuring income and wealth.

■ Summary questions

5 Why is it difficult for sociologists to collect data on wealth with the use of social surveys?

6 Explain in your own words the difference between the two types of wealth used by official statistics.

7 Why do you think that the majority of new shareholders tend to sell their shares within a year?

Measuring poverty, wealth and income

Learning objective:

- Evaluate the difficulties involved in measuring poverty, wealth and income.

Link

See p224 for more information on operationalising concepts.

Key terms

Operationalise: putting a concept or idea into a measurable and universally understood format.

Budget standards approach: a budget standard identifies the goods and services required to attain a given standard of living, and then prices them to arrive at the budget that corresponds to the standard.

Poverty

Clearly how poverty is measured depends on how it is defined and the ability of governments and sociologists to **operationalise** poverty.

Using an absolute definition of poverty first requires the sociologist or government to set a standard of living below which a person is then defined to be living in poverty. This is similar to the way in which Rowntree tried to measure absolute poverty in the 19th century: his initial findings showed that 33 per cent of those surveyed in his study were living in poverty, as their living standards did not meet the criteria for 'the necessaries of a healthy life'. This type of measurement is more recently known as the **budget standards approach** as it attempts to work out a basic budget required for a family or individual to live on and then to define all those living on incomes below that budget as in poverty. In this way it appears relatively easy to identify those who are poor simply by measuring their income compared to what is required for a basic subsistence standard of living.

However, absolute definitions of poverty have been criticised by those who argue that it is not possible to determine so easily what is required for a so-called 'basic standard of living', and that poverty should be

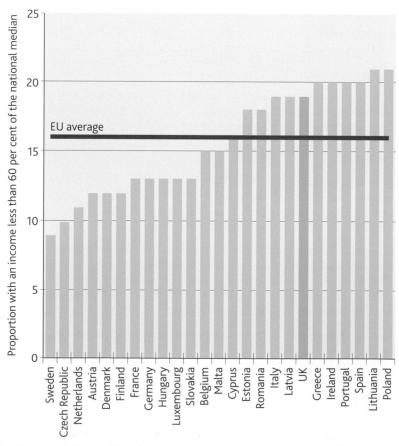

Fig. 3.3 *The UK has a higher proportion of its population in relative low income than most other EU countries*

measured in relation to the historical and social context of the person involved. They also claim it should include reference to **social exclusion** and the ability of the individual to enjoy social activities as well as be able to afford life's basic essentials.

As a result of this Townsend devised a **deprivation index**, which he used to operationalise his definition of relative poverty. The way that he did this was by identifying 12 items that he believed would be relevant to the whole population, such as the ability to take a week's holiday at least once every 12 months, having a birthday party (for children only) and having a fridge, and then calculated the percentage who were deprived of them based on a social survey (*Poverty in the United Kingdom*, 1979) including 6,098 individuals. Each household was given a score on the deprivation index: the higher the score, the more likely they were to be defined as deprived.

Using this format means that what is included on the deprivation index can change year by year, so that relative deprivation can be measured more accurately in terms of changing economic and political situations. Interestingly, one of Townsend's 12 items was having a cooked breakfast most days of the week, which today would probably be seen as unhealthy and excessive rather than an indicator of poverty. It also includes reference to eating fresh meat on a regular basis, which again might have changed more recently with the increase of vegetarianism and changing attitudes to food consumption.

Wealth and income

Measuring wealth and income is different from measuring poverty in the sense that there does not appear to be an agreed line above which people are defined as wealthy and below which they are not. Therefore, it may be more difficult for sociologists to assess the true extent of wealth and its distribution.

The most common methods used by HM Revenue and Customs are to look at the assessments of wealth made for taxation purposes when somebody dies, and the levels of earned income before and after income tax and National Insurance have been paid.

However, recent research conducted by Ian Townsend and published in September 2004 attempted to measure levels of income in the UK in a number of ways. Using data from both the Expenditure and Food Survey and the Family Resources Survey, he assessed levels of income and wealth and looked at comparisons of the distribution of marketable wealth over a period of 30 years.

He argues that marketable wealth is particularly important in measuring inequality and he also recognises that it is this type of wealth which is most difficult to measure accurately. However, according to his data, the distribution of marketable wealth in the UK has not become more equal in the last 30 years: in fact, it has become more unevenly distributed. Inland Revenues statistics show that in 1976, the top 1 per cent of the adult population owned 21 per cent of the total marketable wealth, and the top 50 per cent owned 92 per cent. In 2001, these figures have increased slightly, with the top 1 per cent owning 23 per cent and 95 per cent respectively.

Townsend claims that an important aspect of the measurement of marketable wealth is linked to housing and the increasing cost of buying a house. Property has now become a big divider between rich and poor,

Key terms

Social exclusion: the alienation of individuals or groups, who find themselves unable to participate fully in the activities and daily life of the society in which they live due to various deprivations, such as disability or poor standard of living.

Deprivation index: this measures the level of deprivation in a particular area. There are several distinct dimensions of deprivation called domain indices (things like income and employment), which are scored separately and then collated to give a total score: the higher the figure, the higher the level of deprivation.

Wealth, poverty …

with many people unable to afford to buy their own house compared to 30 years ago. On the other hand, those who do have one or more properties can make high levels of income from them. This inequality is also reflected in earnings figures and expenditure, both of which suggest that there are still large inequalities of both wealth and income in the UK.

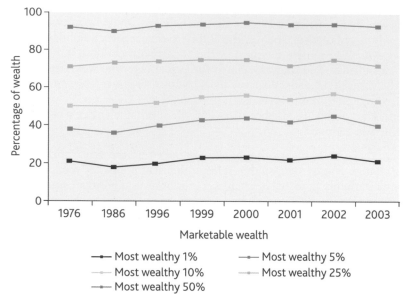

Marketable wealth

- Most wealthy 1%
- Most wealthy 5%
- Most wealthy 10%
- Most wealthy 25%
- Most wealthy 50%

Fig. 3.4 *In 2003, 1 per cent of the UK's population owned 21 per cent of the wealth. In contrast, 50 per cent of the population owned just 7 per cent of the total wealth*

Summary questions

8 Explain what is meant by the phrase 'to operationalise poverty'.

9 What types of items do you think constituted 'the necessaries of a healthy life' according to Rowntree in the 19th century?

10 What types of items would you consider necessary to your life now in the 21st century?

11 Explain in your own words what 'deprivation index' means.

12 What two methods does HM Revenue and Customs use for assessing wealth and income?

13 Suggest two criticisms of these methods.

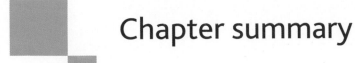

Chapter summary

Further resources

P. Townsend, *Poverty in the United Kingdom,* Penguin, 1979.

P. Trowler, *Investigating Health, Welfare and Poverty*, Collins Educational, 1995.

- Defining poverty can be difficult because it is difficult to establish what being poor actually means.

- In general, there are two main definitions of poverty: absolute and relative poverty.

- How we measure poverty depends largely on how it is defined.

- Usually measuring poverty using a relative definition suggests that there are more people living in poverty.

- Measuring wealth and income is also a complex issue. This is partly because those who are wealthy may not wish sociologists or government agencies to know about the extent of their wealth.

- Whatever measures we use, it is clear that in the UK there are large differences of wealth and income between different social groups.

Gender

Learning objective:

- Understand the way that income is distributed in relation to gender and the reasons why women are more likely to be defined as poor than men.

AQA Examiner's tip

You are unlikely to be asked to remember exact statistics but it is a good idea if you have a rough idea of the percentage or numbers of women, for example, living in poverty.

AQA Examiner's tip

Questions on this subject are likely to be asking you *why* these groups are more likely to be living in poverty.

Women and poverty

One of the issues when studying wealth distribution is being able to identify which groups are more likely to experience poverty than others and assess the reasons for this.

Women form one of the social groups in society today most likely to be experiencing poverty. According to the Equal Opportunities Commission report (2005), women are 14 per cent more likely than men to live in households with incomes that are 60 per cent of the national average, and it is argued that this is probably an underestimate of the actual number of women living in poverty due to the fact that official figures measure income by household rather than individual. Government figures actually show that almost half of all women have an individual income of less than £100 per week.

Fig. 3.5 *Jobs that many women perform tend to be less well paid than men*

What are the reasons for this?

Women and men tend to do different jobs, and the jobs that women do are often less well paid or part time.

Evidence from the Labour Force Survey (2006) found that women's average hourly rate for working full time was £11.67 and men's was £14.08, giving a gender pay gap of 17.1 per cent. Part-time women earned £8.68 on average, compared to part-time men, who earned an average of £9.81.

In terms of occupational status, the Labour Force Survey (2005) also reveals that women are more likely to be working in low-paid sectors. For example, 95 per cent of receptionists, 76 per cent of cleaners and domestic workers, and 74 per cent of waiting staff are women. In contrast, men are over-represented in the occupations categorised as high paid: 83 per cent of directors and chief executives of major organisations, 79 per cent of ICT managers, and 63 per cent of medical practitioners are men.

Fig. 3.6 *The difficulty in childcare arrangements can affect a woman's employment situation*

The fact that women are more likely to work part time also affects their ability to pay into a pension or even to be entitled to the full state pension allowance when they retire. According to figures from the Women and Equality Unit (2005), after retirement women receive a weekly income that is 47 per cent lower than that of men. Childbirth and childcare responsibilities also result in interruptions in women's employment, and the cost and difficulty in arranging childcare can force women into poorly paid part-time work.

Studies such as the Breadline Britain Survey (Gordon and Pantazis, 1997) also suggest that women and men have different attitudes towards domestic spending, and that women are more likely to deprive themselves of basic resources if there is a limited budget.

■ Link

See p50 for more on the feminist perspective of domestic division of labour.

Summary questions

1 Explain in your own words why the figure relating to the number of women living in poverty quoted by the Equal Opportunities Commission is likely to be an underestimation of the actual numbers involved.

2 Suggest why women are:

a more likely to work part-time, and

b more likely to be working in secretarial rather than management positions.

Wealth, poverty ...

Ethnicity

Wealth, poverty ...

Learning objective:

■ Analyse the reasons why those from ethnic minority groups are more likely to be living in poverty.

Key terms

Minority ethnic groups: ethnicity refers to a shared identity based on common cultural and religious factors. In the UK the majority ethnic group is white, British and Christian therefore a person is defined as belonging to a minority ethnic group if they do not share these common characteristics.

Census: this is a 10-yearly government survey, which has been conducted since 1801. It is sent to all households in the UK and it is a legal requirement to complete it.

Hint

Be careful when assessing the reasons for poverty among minority ethnic groups not to make generalisations or stereotypical comments about all minority ethnic groups as if they all share the same problems or are in some way responsible for their poverty due to their culture.

Links

See p29 for more on ethnic identity and culture, and p146 for information on cultural deprivation in the context of education.

For more on family diversity see p48.

Minority ethnic groups and poverty

The Joseph Rowntree Foundation found that people from **minority ethnic groups** are twice as likely to live in poverty than white people in the UK (2007). Statistics published by the foundation show that 40 per cent of minority ethnic people live in poverty (1.8 million people), twice the rate of white people.

However, minority ethnic groups experience varying levels of poverty, and there are different underlying reasons for each one's situation. According to the report, the Bangladeshi population is the worst affected, with 65 per cent of Bangladeshi households living below the poverty line compared with 55 per cent of Pakistanis, 45 per cent of Black Africans, 30 per cent of African-Caribbeans and 25 per cent of Indians.

A number of reasons are suggested for this, not least the high levels of unemployment among the Bangladeshi community. According to the 2001 **census**, around 15 per cent of non-retired white British men aged over 25 were not in paid work, with similar percentages for 'white other' and Indian men, whereas between 30 and 40 per cent of Bangladeshi and Pakistani men were not in paid work. This situation is reinforced by 80 per cent of all Bangladeshi and Pakistani women not being employed according to the 2001 census.

Research study: Yeandle *et al.* (2005)

This study was based on small focus groups with a number of different groups of individuals experiencing poverty in the UK, one of which was a group of Bangladeshi families living in Sandwell, near Birmingham. They were asked a number of questions about their experiences of the difficulties involved in living on low incomes or benefits. The main problems they identified were the poor quality of the (mainly privately rented) housing that they lived in, the difficulty of managing on a tight budget without getting into debt and the social exclusion experienced as a result of poverty. They also stressed that they wanted to work but that there were preventative factors, including childcare issues and language barriers.

Family type is also an important factor in relation to the high levels of poverty among both African and Caribbean households: this is mainly due to the high proportion of single-parent families in this section of the population, and also the relatively large numbers of children they have compared to the white population.

Summary questions

3 What reasons can you think of to explain why unemployment rates are higher among minority ethnic people than white people?

4 In your own words, suggest one thing that the government could do to reduce the number of people from minority ethnic groups who are unemployed.

5 What difficulties does the research above identify as being experienced by the Bangladeshi community in Sandwell due to their poverty?

Single parents

Wealth, poverty ...

Key term

General Household Survey (GHS): a multi-purpose continuous survey conducted by the government, begun in 1971. Each year, a sample of around 13,000 people are selected and interviewed about subjects like household size, income, etc.

Single-parent families and poverty

According to the **General Household Survey** (2001), 25 per cent of all families with dependent children in the UK were single-parent families, breaking down into 22 per cent families with single mothers and just 3 per cent families with single fathers. Statistical evidence also suggests that this social group is among the most economically disadvantaged in society. Evidence from the same survey indicates that 51 per cent of single-parent families had a gross income of £150 per week or less, compared with 13 per cent of married couples and 23 per cent of cohabiting couples. Recent evidence from the End Child Poverty Campaign (2006) also supports this. They claim that 48 per cent of single-parent families live below the poverty line and that 10 per cent of single parents cannot afford to buy more than one pair of shoes for each of their children per year.

What are the reasons for this?

Probably the main reason for the poor living standards experienced by single parents is the fact that they are more likely than two-parent families to be relying solely or partly on government benefits. Government figures support this, suggesting that 55 per cent of single-parent families received income support compared with just 4 per cent of two-parent families in 2001.

Part of the reason is that there is only one parent rather than two to bring in an income, but it is also often because it is much more difficult for single parents, especially mothers, to find paid employment – mainly due to the difficulty of arranging and paying for satisfactory childcare. Even the introduction of new policies (such as the working families' tax credit, which has helped a number of poorer families) has not removed the problems experienced by single mothers, such as organising work around school hours and school holidays, the length of which seems to make the assumption that there is a parent available at home to look after school-age children. However, the government has made some attempt to address these issues with the introduction of breakfast and after-school clubs, some of which also run during school holidays.

Summary question

6 Suggest in your own words the main reason why single-parent households are more likely than two-parent households to be living on government benefits.

The low paid and unemployed

Learning objective:

■ Understand the problems related to low pay and unemployment in relation to poverty.

■ The low paid

The Low Pay Commission defines the low pay threshold as two-thirds of the average male wage. This rate currently stands at £7.44 per hour, and anyone earning less than this is considered to be low paid. Male earnings are used so that the threshold is not affected by the gender gap in earnings. Certain types of work are more likely to be in this income bracket than others: for example, the Annual Survey of Hours and Earnings (2004) showed that those people working in personal service, sales and customer service, and elementary professions (jobs like childminders, carers, cleaners and catering staff) are most likely to be earning wages which would put them into the low income category. The minimum wage for workers over 22 years of age is £5.52 per hour.

The Joseph Rowntree Foundation report measuring poverty and social exclusion (Millar and Gardiner, 2004) found that low-paid workers suffer a number of specific disadvantages, such as having to work longer and more unsociable hours, which often increases childcare costs for those with children. They also lose many of the welfare benefits that the unemployed have, such as free school meals for their children, free prescriptions and housing benefit.

■ The unemployed

Evidence suggests that the unemployed experience many similar problems to the low paid. According to sociological research (Howard *et al.*, 2001) figures from 1999–2000 show that 77 per cent of people living in households where the head of the house was unemployed were living in poverty (in this case defined as 50 per cent less than the average income after cost of housing was deducted).

Those involved in the study were asked to identify how difficult they found it to exist on unemployment benefit: 61 per cent of those involved said that they found it quite difficult or very difficult, compared with 32 per cent of people employed in low-paid work. The study also highlighted various issues, such as the fact that only 32 per cent of the unemployed had been on holiday in the last 12 months, and 38 per cent had actually had to cut back on their food consumption since being unemployed.

It is suggested that those who are unemployed also experience other less-easily measured effects as a result of their economic position, such as loss of their own sense of identity and purpose, and a significant number also end up with marital problems. Evidence from the Social Change and Economic Life Initiative 1994 found that the marriage of someone who was unemployed was 70 per cent more likely to break up during a 12-month period than someone who had never been unemployed.

Fig. 3.7 *A recent study has shown how difficult it is to survive on unemployment benefit*

Summary questions

7 According to the material above, which types of jobs are more likely to be low paid and why do you think this is?

8 Suggest two reasons why it is more difficult to measure the loss of social identity and focus than it is to measure the financial effects of poverty.

Age and disability

Learning objective:

- Analyse the reasons why children, the elderly and disabled are more likely to be living in poverty.

Link

See p51 for more information about single parent families.

Key term

Cumulative: increasing in quantity of degree by successive additions, e.g. the effects of poverty on a person can worsen as they add up over time.

Children

The most vulnerable social groups experiencing high levels of poverty in the UK today are children. In a wide-ranging social survey conducted for the Joseph Rowntree Foundation (Gregg *et al.*, 1999), the number of children living in poverty was estimated at one-third of all children living in the UK – over 4.3 million in total. Although this figure has decreased in the last 10 years, in 2004 it was estimated to be 28 per cent, which is still a large proportion.

This figure rises when we take into account other factors, such as living in a single-parent family or with one or more parents who have disabilities. Two-thirds of children with single parents are estimated to be living in poverty compared to a quarter of children with two parents; and 38 per cent of children living with one or more disabled parents are living in poverty, although this figure has also decreased from 45 per cent in 2000. The highest risk of all, however, is experienced by disabled children living with one or more disabled parents, although this group only makes up 4 per cent of all children in the UK. This disadvantage appears to increase into adulthood, with evidence suggesting that by the age of 18, young disabled people are three times as likely to be unemployed in comparison with the non-disabled, and this figure increases to four times by the age of 26. Those who do work tend to earn at least 11 per cent less than non-disabled people of the same age, according to figures from the Department for Work and Pensions (2005).

Evidence suggests that the effects on children of living in poverty are widespread and can be **cumulative**, especially in relation to educational performance. The National Child Development Study found that those with disadvantaged backgrounds were likely to earn less than those from non-disadvantaged backgrounds, and were also more likely to experience unemployment in adulthood. Men were more likely to have been involved with crime and have spent time in prison by the age of 23, and women were more likely to become single parents. The study also stated that family poverty is one of the most important factors in poor childhood development: coming from a single-parent family was found to be much less of a disadvantage if that family was not poor.

The elderly

In relation to the influence of age on poverty, the other social group identified as having a high risk of poverty is the elderly. However, this risk varies quite significantly when comparing old people totally reliant on state pension with those living on private pensions or other sources of income. There are also variations in relation to gender, marital status, ethnicity and previous occupational status to take into account alongside the age factor.

Evidence suggests that widowed and divorced older people have the lowest levels of material resources, particularly those women who have been widowed for a considerable length of time, who may have been involved in part-time or low-paid work, and who have not contributed to a private or state pension themselves. As the majority of old people in the UK are women (currently 113 to every 100 males in the 65–74 age group and 259 women to every 100 men in the over-85 age group), this is clearly linked to the overall high levels of women experiencing poverty.

In terms of occupational status, evidence suggests that taking early retirement or redundancy can be closely linked to old-age poverty, especially in men. However, this varies depending on their previous occupation prior to retirement. Researchers for the Social and Economic Research Council gathered data throughout the 1990s and found that having a low income after the age of 60 was strongly related to occupational group and continuity of employment between the ages of 20 and 60. Both men and women who worked continuously in managerial, professional and clerical occupations were less likely to be poor than those involved in manual or caring professions.

Summary questions

9 What reasons can you think of why the number of children living in poverty has decreased in the last 10 years?

10 Why do you think that being poor has such a negative impact on educational performance?

11 According to the data above, which group of old people are most likely to be living in poverty?

12 In your own words, explain why this might be the case.

Chapter summary

Further resources

O. Gough, 'The Impact of the Gender Pay Gap on Post Retirement Earnings', *Critical Social Policy*, 21(3), 311–34, 2001

L. Hancock, 'The Care Crunch', *Critical Social Policy*, 22(1), 119–40, 2002

D. Mason, *Race and Ethnicity in Modern Britain*, Oxford University Press, 2000

D. Sainsbury, *Gender, Equality and Welfare States*, Cambridge University Press, 1996

- Evidence suggests that some social groups are at more risk of living in poverty than others.

- Gender is an important factor related to poverty. Women are far more likely to live in poverty than men. There are a number of key reasons for this linked to the nature of paid work done by women.

- Ethnic background is another key factor related to poverty, with various minority ethnic groups suffering high levels of poverty.

- Single-parent families are more likely to have to rely on claiming government benefits than two-parent families. This is due largely to there only being one parent rather than two to bring in an income as well as the difficulties in finding paid employment to fit around childcare arrangements.

- Those who are unemployed or defined as low paid also risk being in poverty.

- Age is another major factor related to poverty, with children and the elderly most at risk.

- Poverty is not equally spread out over the social structure: some groups are more at risk than others.

3.3 The persistence of poverty

Dependency-based explanations

Learning objectives:

- Understand differing and competing explanations for the continuation of poverty in contemporary society.

- Analyse dependency-based explanations and society-based explanations.

Link

This topic links to the topic of Crime and Deviance at A2.

Key term

Dependency-based explanations: explanations which claim that the causes of poverty in modern society are to do with the over-reliance of some social groups on financial help and assistance from the government, and a lack of self-help and independence.

One of the biggest problems for governments and sociologists over the last 50 years has been the persistence of poverty and social inequality in the UK, despite living standards as a whole rising and a variety of government reforms designed to help eradicate poverty, particularly in the last 10 years. A report called 'Monitoring Poverty and Social Exclusion' produced by the Joseph Rowntree Foundation (Howarth *et al.*, 1999) made the following discoveries:

- The gap between the average and the poorest levels of income increased during the period 1995–99.

- The number of individuals aged between 25 and retirement currently defined as being on low pay increased, as did the number of premature deaths of adults in this age group.

- The number of children who were permanently excluded from school also rose, as did the number of young adults, aged 16–24, with criminal records.

This type of information clearly indicates that poverty and its effects are still a problem in contemporary society, there are a number of different sociological explanations for this. This section looks at **dependency-based explanations**, which tend to see the causes of poverty as most likely to be found within certain individuals or groups in society.

The common assumption behind these explanations is that the blame for being poor can usually be applied to the individuals or groups involved. This view is linked to the 19th-century sociologist Herbert Spencer, who was known for his harsh and uncompromising views of poverty and its causes. He once claimed that the poor were 'good for nothings and criminals', and suggested that those who were too lazy to work should not be allowed to eat. This view was strongly linked to **social**

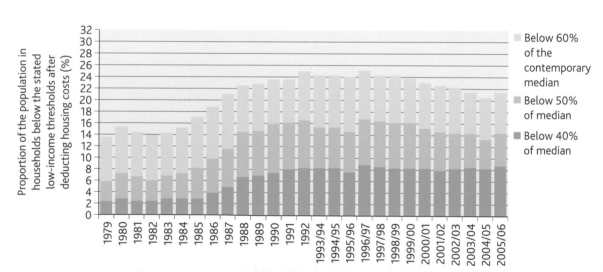

Fig. 3.8 *The proportion of people in the UK on low incomes started to rise again in 2005/06 after six years of decline*

evolutionary theories and Darwinism's idea of 'the survival of the fittest'. The belief was that social inequality and poverty were of benefit to society because they provided incentives to work hard.

More recently, this kind of view has been linked to the **New Right** and the political views of Margaret Thatcher and John Major, both of whom were strongly influenced by the work of Charles Murray (1990) and David Marsland (Marsland and Segalman, 1989; Marsland, 1996), who have criticised the welfare state for undermining the incentive to go out and seek work when effectively you can receive a number of benefits from the government without leaving your bed!

Marsland argues that for most people defined as living in poverty, this is as a result of an over-generous welfare system. He contends that the provision of universal welfare benefits has created a 'culture of dependency' in which there is an expectation that society and the government will look after us. This is also linked to the idea that a culture or 'subculture of poverty' exists within which individuals 'learn to be poor' and the experience of being poor is passed down through generations; therefore, it is frequently the case that if your parents are poor, you will also be poor.

Murray goes even further than this by claiming that there is a growing class in Western society which is distinct and separate from the rest of the society: the so-called 'underclass'. Although Murray does not believe that all those who are poor are part of this underclass, he does claim that its numbers are increasing and that it represents a real threat to the stability and well-being of society.

Hint

Remember that these explanations are based on sociological theory and are not necessarily factually correct. It is often useful to start a sentence with 'it can be argued' or 'it has been suggested'. Also, do not forget to be evaluative.

Key terms

Social evolutionary theories: a discipline of evolutionary biology that is concerned with social behaviours, which suggests that competitiveness is a natural and healthy aspect of society. The 'survival of the fittest' occurs – i.e. those who are the most successful, succeed – because they are most suited to the context.

New Right: a political movement associated with functionalist thought, which emphasises the importance of 'tradition' and the 'proper function' of social institutions (together with the importance of the free market).

Link

This issue is relevant for A2 Crime and Deviance: Subcultural Theory.

Wealth, poverty …

Fig. 3.9 *Some argue that we live in a 'culture of dependency', in which we expect society and the government to look after us*

Murray identifies three major indicators that support his claims:

1 **Illegitimacy** Murray argues that rising rates of illegitimacy in the UK indicates an undermining of the traditional two-parent family unit and the growing tolerance for children being born to unmarried mothers. This is a danger, according to Murray, because children born outside of marriage are more likely to be undisciplined.

2 **Rising crime rates** This is another social problem linked to the development of the underclass, according to Murray. Rising rates of property crime produce fragmented and broken-up communities, leading to lack of trust among neighbours and the breakdown of stability and social order.

3 **Unemployment** Murray claims that attitudes towards work have changed and that being unemployed is no longer socially unacceptable, especially among young men. This is potentially very bad for society as it will lead to large numbers of young men out of work, unable to support their family and quite happy to live on government benefits.

These points are reinforced by Marsland, who also claims that unemployment benefit gives people an incentive to remain unemployed and removes the incentive for individuals to improve themselves through higher education. His solution is to remove benefits from all but the most needy in society, those who are either too sick or disabled to support themselves. He estimates this to be around 5–8 per cent of the population. This, Marsland claims, will not only reintroduce a strong incentive to find work, but will also strengthen family ties through the need for mutual help and support, and save the state large amounts of money, which could be redistributed into investment in industry.

Marsland also criticises organisations such as the Joseph Rowntree Foundation for exaggerating the extent of poverty in society. He claims that absolute poverty has been virtually removed from Western societies, and that relative definitions of poverty serve to make the problem appear greater than it is. His view is that poverty in contemporary society has been confused with social inequality, which is an entirely different situation, and a necessary incentive to hard work and competition.

Summary questions

1 Explain in your own words how poverty and social inequality can be 'good for society'.

2 Why does Marsland see the welfare state as acting as a disincentive to going out to work?

3 According to Marsland, how will the removal of benefits from the majority of those claiming them improve society?

Society-based explanations

Society-based explanations for the causes of poverty tend to see the individual as less in control of their own situation and view poverty as something more related to the structure of society. In fact, certain social groups and individuals can be said to benefit from the continuing poverty of others; therefore it is in their interests to maintain a society based on social inequality.

This view is often associated with the Marxist perspective: Marxists argue that the existence of poverty in capitalist societies can be explained in terms of how it benefits the **ruling class**. Marxists claim that poverty exists because its existence directly benefits those who control the means of production. It allows them to maximise their profits and exploit the labour of those who have to work for them.

Fig. 3.10 *Marxists claim that poverty exists because it benefits those who control the means of production*

Marxists also argue that a capitalist economy requires a highly motivated workforce, who can see the value of putting in a hard day's work. In order for this to take place, those who do not work (for example, the elderly, sick and unemployed) must not be seen to be better off than those who do: therefore, welfare benefits are deliberately kept at a low level in order to encourage hard work. This directly contradicts the view of dependency theory, which claims that welfare benefits are, in fact, too high. Another point made by Marxists is that capitalist society is based on individualism and competition: workers compete with each other for pay and status, therefore a large number of workers on low wages helps to keep all wage demands down, as most workers will be satisfied with a relatively low standard of pay as long as someone else is still earning less than them. The Marxist analysis would conclude that poverty is inevitable within the context of a capitalist society, and that there is no real prospect of poverty declining unless there is a revolutionary transformation of society.

This view that one group of people use their position of power to actively keep another group in poverty is also supported by feminists, who argue that in a patriarchal society men use their position of dominance to keep women in a inferior position. Often this is linked to the financial dependence of women on men, especially after having children, when they may be unable to work or may be restricted to working in part-time, poorly paid jobs. Marxist feminists in particular draw attention to the powerless position of women in capitalist society where the work that they do in the home is unvalued and unpaid. This situation, they claim, is of benefit to the ruling class, as it reduces the bargaining power of the male breadwinner because his whole family is dependent on his wage.

It is also important to be aware that not all structural, society-based explanations are based on the view that society is essentially exploitative and unfair. Some functionalist sociologists, such as Davis and Moore (1967), also share the view that it is the structure and nature of society which is responsible for inequality and poverty. However, this situation is seen as reasonable and inevitable because it is based on the assumption that society is **meritocratic**, and that those who are unable to be successful fail due to their own lack of talent and ability. There will always be those who are relatively poor compared to others, simply because the functions that they perform for society (for example, cleaners) are less difficult and require less skill and training than others (for example, doctors) who therefore deserve to be paid more highly.

Functionalists would conclude that it is not possible to have a completely equal society; social inequality and its consequences are a natural and functional part of all societies.

Key term

Meritocracy: a social system in which rewards are based on talent and effort rather than social background.

■ Wealth, poverty ...

■ Summary questions

4 Explain in your own words why capitalist societies need social inequality and poverty.

5 Do you agree with the view that welfare benefits for those who cannot or do not work should not exceed the lowest-paid worker? Give reasons for your answer.

6 Can you think of any other ways that employers could motivate their workers other than through rates of pay?

Social exclusion

Learning objective:

■ Understand the concept of social exclusion and its impact on certain groups in society.

The term social exclusion has been used with more frequency since 1997, especially by the current New Labour government. It is often used to describe the social conditions of a group of people, or as an explanation for certain types of anti social behaviour. The government describes social exclusion as 'what happens when people or places suffer from unemployment, discrimination, poor skills, low incomes, poor housing, high crime, ill-health and family breakdown', although this definition does not really explain how social exclusion affects those groups. Gordon *et al.* (2000), in their study *Poverty and Social Exclusion in Britain*, define it as 'a lack or denial of access to the kinds of social relations, social customs and activities in which the great majority of people in British society engage'.

Social exclusion, therefore, is about more than simply being defined as living in poverty, although being poor certainly increases an individual's chances of experiencing social exclusion. It is also possible for a group to be socially excluded even if they are not defined as being in poverty. People who are currently referred to as 'socially excluded' are not only the financially poor but also from social groups whose ethnic background, cultural values and social identity have little influence in the important decision-making areas of society. They are likely to be the least well educated (and so excluded from the opportunities of higher education or university), the most likely to be unemployed or casually employed, and the least likely to be involved in any form of participation politically.

The term 'social exclusion' is also often applied to whole communities and areas of the country (usually inner-city urban areas, often largely or wholly made up of council estates), leading to a 'concentration of disadvantage' in which the whole community becomes labelled as a no-go area, further increasing the chances of its members becoming more removed from the opportunities that they might have living elsewhere.

Gordon *et al.*'s study (2000) identifies a number of factors associated with the chances of an individual or community becoming socially excluded. Individual factors include: unemployment, dependence on state benefit, debt, poor health, low educational achievement, and loss of **primary integration**. Community factors include: high levels of unemployment, poor local authority services, poor community resources, poor housing, poor public transport and high levels of crime.

These indicate that it is possible to identify certain factors which can increase the chances of an individual or community experiencing social exclusion, and Gordon argues that there is a cumulative effect; in other words, the more of these factors that are present, the greater the risk of becoming socially excluded.

Link

This section links to the functionalist perspective on education and the importance of the education system as an agency of secondary socialisation to be found on p132. It also links to Power and Politics at A2.

Key term

Primary integration: the feeling of belonging to a social group within society. Those individuals who are socially excluded therefore do not experience a feeling of social solidarity and belonging and as a result may be more prone to committing crime or being involved in anti social behaviour.

Wealth, poverty …

Research study: Barry (2002)

This study explores the relationship between poverty and social exclusion, and the ways in which experience of poverty can lead to individuals or groups being socially excluded. Barry found that lack of money is a major factor in preventing participation in the wider society. He used the example of the ability to get a fair trial in a court of law, which he claims is very difficult without the funds to pay for a high-quality lawyer. However, he also argues that although personal financial circumstances are very important, so too is the provision of public services, without which social exclusion becomes more likely. As in the example above, without a publicly funded legal aid system, not having enough money to pay for a good lawyer becomes even more of a problem. Therefore, he concludes that the less the government intervenes to remove social inequality, the more likely social exclusion will continue to be a problem for large groups of people in contemporary society.

Fig. 3.11 *It is argued that social exclusion can be used as an explanation for high unemployment, poor housing and crime*

Summary questions

7 What types of anti social behaviour do you think the government is particularly concerned about?

8 Suggest three types of social customs and activities that the majority of British people might engage in.

9 Why do you think that lack of involvement politically (for example, not bothering to vote in elections) is an important aspect of social exclusion?

Chapter summary

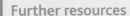 **Further resources**

F. Field, *Losing Out: The Emergence of Britain's Underclass*, Blackwell, 1989

K. Mann, *The Making of an English Underclass*, Open University Press, 1992

W. Hutton, *The State We're In*, Cape, 1995

- There is a debate about the reasons for the continuation of poverty in contemporary society.

- Dependency-based explanations tend to blame the individual for their own situation: they see the removal of poverty as something which the government should not really be involved in and take the view that people should help get themselves out of poverty.

- Society-based explanations tend to see the individual as less in control of their own situation and view poverty as something more related to the structure of society.

- More recent research has also included the concept of social exclusion and the detrimental effects both on the individuals concerned and on the wider society caused by relatively large numbers of people who are unable to participate or feel part of the society as a whole.

The social democratic approach: 1940s–1970s

Wealth, poverty …

Learning objective:

- Understand the introduction of the welfare state and the implications of this policy on poverty rates.

Key terms

Social solidarity: a sense of community and a feeling that you belong in society.

Means-tested benefits: benefits which are allocated based on levels of income, size of family, etc. as opposed to universal benefits.

Fig. 3.12 *The evacuation of poor working-class children opened many eyes towards a level of poverty that many had not previously realised existed*

AQA Examiner's tip

To answer questions you may be required to name policies and have a good idea of when they were implemented. If you cannot remember exact dates and names, you should describe the policy and what effect it had as closely as possible.

💡 The introduction of the welfare state

Provision of more state welfare began to take place in the UK before the start of the Second World War. However, it was the Beveridge report in 1942 that is often credited as the birth of the welfare state as we know it today. The acceptance of this social policy is often linked to the sense of national identity and **social solidarity** created by the sacrifices of the war taking place at that time. Also, the large-scale evacuation of poor working-class city children to the countryside brought home to many middle-class families the degree of poverty being experienced by many of the population, of which they had not previously been aware.

Beveridge identified what he referred to as five 'giant evils' that the government should fight in order to eradicate poverty: these were want, disease, ignorance, squalor and idleness. His 'social plan' consisted of a number of key changes to be implemented to help reduce not only poverty but also disease, lack of education, poor housing and long-term unemployment.

So, how was this to be achieved?

- First, on Beveridge's recommendation, the post-war Labour government developed a universal system of National Insurance, to which all working adults would contribute. This would help to alleviate temporary poverty during times of sickness or unemployment, and also provide money for after retirement.

- This would be backed up by national assistance, which was a **means-tested benefit** for those who could not claim National Insurance or were unemployed or sick for a long time, although the general assumption was that this situation would only apply to a tiny number of people.

- A universal family allowance was introduced for all families with more than one child. This benefit was paid directly to the mother in order to ensure that it was spent on the children, which is still the case today with child benefit. The amount allocated was supposed to be in line with the actual cost of raising a child, although this was not the case.

- The National Health Service was created in 1948 to provide free health care for all, including dental care, maternity services and prescriptions. The emphasis on health was also reinforced by the provision of free school milk for all pupils under 18 in 1946. This policy was not designed specifically to alleviate poverty but to improve the standards of health amongst the population, and may have contributed to increased life expectancy and decreased rates of infant mortality in the latter part of the twentieth century.

■ How well did it work?

Initially it appeared that the introduction of the welfare state had significantly reduced the number of people living below the poverty line: Rowntree's third study of York (Rowntree and Laver, 1951), based on the use of a **representative sample**, indicated that whereas in 1936 a total of 17.7 per cent of the population was living below the poverty line, it was only 1.6 per cent in 1951.

Rowntree claimed that this was due to Beveridge's social reforms. However, this claim has been disputed by other research using Rowntree's figures. Townsend (1979) found that 5.4 per cent of households were actually in poverty at that time and Atkinson and Bourguignon (1982) reanalysed Rowntree's data and found that 14.4 per cent of working-class households should have been judged as poor.

Other criticisms of Beveridge's policies included the fact that the amount of insurance paid out to those in need was based on a flat rate. As Glennerster and Evans (1994) point out, this did not take into account the diversity of rent levels in different parts of the country. Another problem was that although single women were treated as contributors to the insurance scheme, married women were treated as dependents and were covered by their husband's contributions. This provided little incentive for married women to work, and made them financially dependent on their husbands.

Despite this, however, it was generally assumed during the 1950s and 1960s that the best way to alleviate poverty was through state-organised welfare provision. Both Conservative and Labour governments continued the work begun by the Beveridge report, although during the 1970s policies began to be more targeted towards the worst-off in society and became more closely linked to income.

The Conservative government in 1970 introduced the family income support scheme. This was a tax-funded benefit aimed specifically at low-income families: a group who had not really been helped by the introduction of National Insurance. This financial support for families was further developed by the Labour government of 1974, which introduced a more comprehensive version of the family allowance called child benefit. It was more generous and also included the first child, which the family allowance did not.

Another significant development in the 1970s was the introduction of disability benefits: again, targeting a group who had not really been helped specifically by Beveridge's report. The attendance allowance was introduced in 1972, followed by a mobility allowance for those who had difficulty getting about and an invalid care allowance in 1976, for those responsible for looking after the sick and disabled.

■ Key term

Representative sample: a sample of people who have been selected as having social characteristics that are typical of the total population being studied. A representative sample can be used to make generalisations about the total population.

Fig. 3.13 *From 1946, all pupils were provided with free school milk to address the concerns regarding low income and the links to malnutrition and underachievement*

Wealth, poverty ...

■ Summary questions

1 Summarise, in your own words, the main reforms introduced by Beveridge.

2 According to the evidence above, how significant was the introduction of the welfare state in reducing poverty?

3 How were the policies introduced by the Conservative and Labour governments of the 1970s different from the original policies introduced in the 1940s?

The New Right approach: 1979–1997

Learning objective:

■ Evaluate the changing direction of social policies on welfare from 1979 to 1997.

■ A radical change

The election victory for the Conservatives under the leadership of Margaret Thatcher in 1979 saw the beginning of a radical change in government policies towards welfare and the removal of poverty. Instead of being viewed as having a positive role, the welfare state became 'part of the problem', often viewed as acting as a disincentive to self-help and hard work, and also as a huge expense to the state. Therefore, two of the main policies of the Conservative government of the 1980s were to reduce public spending and improve incentives to work. As a result of these policies unemployment went up to nearly 5 million. Many researchers today view this social experiment of the Thatcher years as a failure.

Policies to reduce poverty and social inequality were not given high priority. The Royal Commission on the Distribution of Income and Wealth set up by the previous Labour government was wound up and poverty was no longer considered a real social problem. As the Social Security Secretary John Moore claimed in 1989, 'it's the end of the line for poverty': he argued that it was both 'false and dangerous' to discuss the view that large numbers of the British population were in need on the basis of poverty lines that moved in line with national prosperity.

■ A new policy direction

The New Right followed a policy direction aimed at reducing government spending on welfare and the responsibility of the state to assist those defined as poor. The assumption was that by reducing spending, more money would be released to create a more healthy and competitive economy: this would trigger a rise in living standards for everybody and help reduce the so-called 'dependency culture', which made people too reliant on state benefits.

These policies included:

1 **An increase in selectivity and means-tested benefits.** In contrast to Beveridge's universal benefits, things like free eye tests, prescriptions and dental treatment became subject to means testing; only those on the lowest incomes (usually the unemployed) and the over-65s were eligible to receive these. Supplementary benefit was replaced by income support, and loans were introduced for those claiming this benefit, which they could apply for from a social fund. Loans were only given to those who could afford to pay them back, which meant that those in most need did not get any help. This system was designed to make claimants more responsible and to manage their budgets more effectively.

2 **Benefit freezes and changes.** Those benefits that already existed were rarely actually cut, but were not increased in line with inflation. For example, child benefit and housing benefit were frozen at the same level for three years in the late 1980s, although in contrast to this, in 1988 the family income support scheme was re-named family credit and was increased with the emphasis on helping the poorest families. Unemployment benefit was also 'adjusted' many times in the 1980s.

Atkinson and Micklewright (1991) recorded 38 changes to the system of benefits for the unemployed in the 1980s, all of which resulted in reductions of entitlements. One such change was the introduction of jobseeker's allowance in 1996, which meant that those claiming unemployment benefit had to sign a jobseeker's agreement, showing details of how they intended to find work. The time allowed to claim this benefit was also reduced from one year to six months. Another similar 'name change' was the replacement of invalidity benefit with incapacity benefit in 1995: under the new system, individuals had to prove that they were genuinely 'unfit for work', which was not only more difficult but also potentially humiliating.

3   **The introduction of the Child Support Agency.** Introduced in 1993, the aim of the CSA was to cut the extensive social security budget by making 'absent parents' support their children financially instead of the state. In a social sense, this reform also reinforced the New Right view of the responsibilities of the family (and, in particular, men towards their children) which they claimed was lacking. It may also have served as a disincentive to single mothers to claim the benefits available to them for fear of being 'tracked down' by the Child Support Agency and has been massively inefficient at making payments. More recently, the organisation has also come in for heavy criticism from many fathers, who have argued that it unfairly targets those men who are already paying child support and ignores whether or not they have a second family to support.

■ Criticisms of the New Right policies

Many critics argue that the policies of the New Right did not reduce poverty or bring greater prosperity to the whole country. It actually increased poverty and hardship for the poorest sections of the population. In fact, John Hills (1996) shows that during the period 1979–86, the income of the poorest 20 per cent of the population fell by 6 per cent whereas the income of the richest 20 per cent rose by 26 per cent. It can also be argued that the increased use of means-tested benefits led to more stigma being attached to being poor, and in some ways increased the **poverty trap**, whereby reliance on state benefit leads to the inability to get off benefits and back into work.

■ Key term

Poverty trap: a situation in which an increase in income results in a loss of benefits so that you are no better off.

■ Link

See p59 for more information about the New Right.

■ Summary questions

4   Why was the welfare state viewed as a cause of poverty by the New Right?

5   Explain in your own words what John Moore meant when he referred to the danger of using poverty lines that moved in line with 'national prosperity'.

6   Identify one advantage and one disadvantage of the introduction of the Child Support Agency.

Wealth, poverty ...

The New Labour approach: 1997–present

Learning objective:

■ Evaluate the approach to welfare of the New Labour government.

Link

This section links with the discussion of education policies implemented since 1997 (e.g. the introduction of Education Action Zones, etc.) on p161.

Key terms

Gross Domestic Product (GDP): the market value of all final goods and services produced within a country in a given period of time.

New Deal policy: similar to the Youth Training Scheme, the policy was introduced by New Labour in 1998. It targeted young people between the ages of 18 and 24 who had been unemployed for six months. Benefits were cut, and employers given a subsidy to take these candidates on as trainees.

■ The pledge to end poverty

Tony Blair, at a lecture to commemorate Beveridge in March 1999, stated: 'Our historic aim will be for ours to be the first generation to end child poverty. It is a 20-year mission but I believe it can be done.' In September 1999, the New Labour government published a report called 'Opportunity for All'. It dealt with what the government saw as the main problems linked to the persistence of poverty in the UK and looked at ways of combating problems such as social exclusion (especially for the younger generation), inequalities in health care and pensioner poverty.

One of the main reasons for the social exclusion of young people was suggested to be the lack of access to a good education, and government spending on education has increased under this government. It has introduced policies such as Sure Start, designed to try and combat poverty-related disadvantages at pre-school age. One of the initiatives of the Sure Start programme has been to increase the number of pre-school nursery places available and to introduce parenting support classes for those who need them. An attempt has also been made to make school hours more flexible, with the introduction of breakfast and after-school clubs in most state schools in England and Wales. The aim of these schemes is to allow working parents to have somewhere safe for their children to go when they are at work, and by doing so widen participation in the workforce, especially for single mothers. These policies can be seen as attempts to relieve, or compensate for, the effects of poverty without involving direct financial help. The educational opportunities and achievement of the poorest sections of society are seen by this government as an important way of improving their chances of social mobility.

Child benefit has also been increased and the introduction of the child tax credit in April 2003 was specifically aimed at low-income families with young children using registered nurseries or child minders. In terms of national expenditure, spending on child-related benefits rose from 1.38 per cent of the **Gross Domestic Product (GDP)** in 1997/98 to 2.04 per cent in 2002/03. Statistical evidence does suggest that these policies have had some impact on child poverty, and that the number of children defined as living in poverty has fallen since 1997.

■ Other New Labour policies

One of the early actions of the New Labour government on election in 1997 was the introduction of the **New Deal policy**. The money for this scheme was partly funded by the so-called 'windfall tax' on the profits of the privatised utilities, such as the gas and electricity companies, which can be seen as an attempt to redistribute the large profits made by these companies to those in financial need. This was designed to get unemployed young people off benefits and into work or work-related schemes. The system 'kicked in' for anyone under 25 who had been on unemployment benefit for more than six months: at this point, they were required to take part in a job-related training scheme, go back into education or even undertake voluntary work. If they refused to take part, they would lose their entitlement to any benefits. This idea of 'welfare to work' was also applied in the New Deal for lone parents, which had a similar aim: to get single mothers back into work and off benefits.

Wealth, poverty …

This type of policy can be seen to reflect New Labour's attitude to the provision of welfare, which in some ways reflected the New Right approach. Tony Blair claimed that state welfare benefits should represent a 'hand up not a hand out'; in other words, the emphasis should be on providing the help required to make people self-reliant rather than dependent on government welfare. This view was reinforced by the Home Secretary of the time, David Blunkett, who stated that government provision of welfare should 'empower individuals to seize control of their future' and that 'paid work is the key to productive and fulfilling lives'.

The launch of the Social Exclusion Unit in December 1997 was another example of an attempt by the New Labour government to reintegrate into society those individuals who had become socially excluded. The unit was designed to concentrate on targeted areas of extreme deprivation in the UK, and to deal with issues such as truancy and drug dependency, which are seen as being particular examples of anti social behaviour. Again, this is not a policy specifically designed to alleviate poverty but to deal with the effects of extreme deprivation and social exclusion, not only for individuals but for whole neighbourhoods.

However, both Blair and Blunkett also remained committed to the idea of social justice and fairness in terms of income distribution. This can be seen by the introduction of the minimum wage in 1997, and by the fact that one of the first things the New Labour government did was to sign up to the Community Charter of Fundamental Social Rights as part of the 1991 Maastricht Treaty. This aspect of the Treaty had been dismissed as a 'socialist charter' by the two previous prime ministers, John Major and Margaret Thatcher.

Therefore, it can be argued that the New Labour policies have been more about the prevention of poverty rather than the relief of poverty, and seem to be about making individuals as far as possible responsible for their own welfare and self-improvement, mainly via better educational opportunities resulting in a reasonably paid job. Whether or not these policies have made a genuine impact on the levels of poverty and income inequality in the UK is difficult to assess: the number of children defined as living in poverty has gone down in the last 10 years, although not to the degree that Tony Blair predicted in 1997. However, Page (2002) argues that New Labour policies have generally begun to make a significant difference. He particularly draws attention to those policies designed to improve the lives of those in poverty through self-improvement, such as educational reforms like the introduction of literacy and numeracy hours in schools and Working Families Tax credit, which has made it easier and more affordable for single parents and those on low incomes to get off income support and into work.

Hint

Think here about the difference between policies designed to prevent poverty and those designed to relieve poverty. Which do you think are the most useful?

Summary questions

7 Describe briefly two of the policies introduced by the New Labour government designed to get rid of child poverty.

8 Explain in your own words what Tony Blair meant by 'a hand up not a hand out'.

9 Give one example of a New Labour policy which illustrates this approach.

Chapter summary

Further resources

T. Cole, *Whose Welfare?*, Tavistock Press, 1986

P. Dunleavy, *Developments in British Politics*, Macmillan, 1993

S. Kane and M. Kirby, *Wealth, Poverty and Welfare*, Blackwell, 2003

- There have been a number of key social policies aimed at reducing poverty in the last 60 years.

- The aim of the introduction of the welfare state was to abolish poverty and 'want' altogether. It was partly successful in this aim.

- The New Right changed the nature of social provision of welfare and saw the welfare state as a disincentive to hard work and self-reliance.

- New Labour policies have followed a different approach, attempting to help those worst affected by poverty by giving them ways to get back into work and take responsibility for themselves.

The roles of public and private welfare provision

Learning objective:

- Evaluate the changing nature of welfare provision since 1979 and the increasing involvement of the private sector in the provision of welfare.

💡 The birth of private health care

As discussed previously, government policy towards the provision of welfare varied relatively little in the period between 1945 and 1970. The general consensus was that it was the responsibility of the government to ensure a decent standard of living for its citizens, including provision of health care, education and financial assistance during times of economic hardship, for example unemployment, and that on the whole the welfare state should be universally available to all regardless of income.

However, it must also be remembered that state intervention in the provision of welfare services actually began much earlier, with the Poor Law Act 1601, which made local parishes responsible for the welfare of their members. This involvement increased during the 19th century, with the introduction of compulsory education and various Public Health Acts.

It is also important to note that other agencies such as charities played an important role in providing welfare, especially in relation to health care and schooling for the poorest sections of society. There has always been a mixed economy of welfare provision; what has changed is the balance in terms of the amount of welfare provided by the state and the amount provided by other agencies.

From 1979, the consensus established by Beveridge started to be challenged by the Conservative government, influenced by New Right ideology, who argued that universal welfare benefits acted as a disincentive to hard work and family values and individual responsibility. The New Right were also concerned about the rising cost of the welfare state: the phrase a 'crisis of welfare' was frequently used to suggest that the welfare budget was out of control and that the UK economy could no longer afford to fund such a generous provision of welfare.

Fig. 3.14 *Private-health providers emphasise the higher standards and shorter waiting lists they can offer compared with the NHS*

AQA Examiner's tip

The emphasis of the section is on contemporary society, so make sure that the material you include in your answers reflects this.

■ Key term

Monopoly: a persistent market situation where there is only one provider of a product or service; in other words, a firm that has no competitors in its industry. Monopolies are characterised by a lack of economic competition for the product or service that they provide and a lack of viable substitute goods.

■ Link

See p165 for more on private school education and the assisted places scheme.

■ Summary questions

1 Why were some individuals encouraged to make use of private health care? What were the benefits for (a) the government, and (b) the consumers?

2 Why do you think the New Labour government got rid of the assisted places scheme in 1997?

One of the solutions to this problem was seen to be a movement towards changing the balance of welfare provision: welfare was still to be part-funded by the government, but also increasingly via private companies, in order to encourage those people who could afford to do so to use private providers of services rather than the state provision. A good example of this is in the case of health care, whereby individuals were encouraged by the government to pay for private medical insurance through companies like BUPA or to pay for private beds or rooms in National Health Service (NHS) hospitals. The assumption made by the Conservative government, and certainly reinforced in the advertising campaigns of the private companies today, was that private health care is of a higher standard and that the waiting lists for private hospitals are shorter than those for the NHS.

■ The end of the NHS monopoly

The view held by many New Right politicians seems to be that under a fully state-funded system, there is no incentive for the provider to attract customers as they have a **monopoly** on the service available. Therefore, the NHS can effectively offer its users a poor service simply because they have nowhere else to go. The New Right wanted to use a more market-based approach to the provision of welfare, seeing users of the services as 'consumers'.

The same type of view can be seen in their policies towards education and housing: the Conservative government introduced a scheme to provide financial assistance, usually in the form of scholarships, to 'bright' children who could not afford the fees of independent schools, thereby filtering money from the state education budget and allocating it into the private sector. However, this scheme was removed by the New Labour government in 1997 and, in fact, the numbers of children in private education in this country has not varied greatly in the last 50 years, remaining fairly steady at between 7 and 10 per cent of the population at secondary age and slightly less in the primary age range.

The removal of state funding from education has also been one of the more controversial policy decisions of the New Labour government with the introduction of tuition fees for university students in 2001. Many critics of this policy see it as effectively removing the possibility of university for many of those from poorer sections of the population.

Another area which has seen the impact of private involvement is pensions: since the 1980s, those people who work for employers and who can afford to do so have been encouraged to opt out of the state pension scheme paid for by National Insurance contributions and general tax contributions and instead to pay their contributions directly into a personal or work-related pension scheme, to which their employer would also contribute. This has proved very popular with a large number of employees, and Department of Social Security statistics show that by 1995 approximately 8 million people were contributing to an occupational pension scheme as opposed to just under 6 million still contributing to the state-related pension scheme. Again, the incentive to take part in a private pension scheme is seen to be a higher return on your savings and a more competitive system.

Voluntary and informal welfare provision

Learning objective:

- Analyse the role of voluntary and informal welfare provision in contemporary society.

Key terms

Voluntary welfare provision: welfare provision by independent organisations such as charities which do not seek to make a profit from their services.

Informal welfare provision: care which is provided for those in need by their families or friends.

Industrial revolution: the process during the 18th and 19th centuries in the UK whereby societies moved from agricultural production in rural environments to industrial manufacturing in urban environments.

Extended family: a family group consisting of more than just a couple and their children, either living in the same household or in a close relationship with each other.

Link

See p50 for more information on extended families.

Key terms

Community care: welfare services, such as meal on wheels, paid for or provided by the local council for those who require it: for example, elderly people, those with an impairment or illness, or someone who looks after a child or adult who can't look after themselves.

Geriatric ward: a hospital ward specialising in care for the elderly.

The effect of the welfare state

Before the introduction of the welfare state and the changing attitude towards the provision of welfare in this country, despite a number of social reforms discussed earlier, the vast majority of **welfare provision** was based on a **voluntary** and **informal** basis. Prior to, and even during, the immediate aftermath of the **industrial revolution**, the family was largely responsible for the welfare of its members. This is why many sociologists argue that the **extended family** was the most prominent type at this time. The argument follows, therefore, that after the introduction of the welfare state, the family had many of its welfare responsibilities removed and so the evolution into the smaller nuclear family units that we have today, which had already begun by this point, accelerated mainly because the family no longer had to perform these functions.

However, there is now evidence to suggest that the family and other agencies, such as voluntary organisations and charities, are becoming more and more involved in providing help and support, and that this situation has been encouraged by recent governments. Voluntary organisations are those that have been formed by individuals who join together for a common cause, usually through experiencing a particular type of situation or hardship themselves. These include organisations such as Shelter, MIND, the NSPCC, and self-help groups, such as Alcoholics Anonymous. As well as providing help and support to those in need, they often also lobby the government and act as pressure groups to try and bring about changes in the law.

A return to voluntary and informal welfare provision?

Why would the government encourage voluntary and informal welfare provision? First, there is the economic incentive for the government to save money by encouraging 'community care'. This can be illustrated in the implementation of the Community Care Act 1990. Government statistics in 1996 suggest that the cost of keeping an elderly person in a **geriatric ward** for one week would be over £395, whereas if this person was cared for by their relatives or neighbours, the cost would be more like £100–£150 for a week. This is of particular concern in relation to the elderly, as statistics show that there are now more people in Britain over 60 than there are under 16, which potentially will put a great strain on government spending on welfare. It has been estimated that to keep someone in a care home for one year costs £24,000. This explains why the government is so keen on the involvement of other agencies, family, or (for those who can afford it) private care homes in care for the elderly. Using the voluntary sector is also cheaper than state provision, as charities tend to rely on unpaid volunteers and may also have less in the way of bureaucracy and administration costs.

Secondly, supporters of community care policies argue that being allowed to remain in the community is beneficial for the individuals involved as they can retain as close a normal way of life as possible and be taken care of by people who care about them. There will also be less of a stigma

Wealth, poverty …

attached if they are disabled or suffering from a mental illness compared with what they might experience if placed in an institution. This view is backed by Goffman's Asylums study (1968b) in which he demonstrated that institutional care often had a detrimental effect on those placed in it and made it more difficult for them to re-enter society after treatment.

Thirdly, it has been argued recently by government figures like John Hutton, Work and Pensions Secretary (2006) that involving local communities in providing their own welfare and making them responsible for their own self-improvement would be a better solution to social exclusion than state intervention. Hutton claimed – after a visit to Harlem in the US where an independently run organisation called Harlem Children's Zone has apparently 'transformed schools, cut student absences and reduced illnesses such as asthma' – that 'harnessing the spirit of local involvement ... will be crucial to us in the UK if we are to succeed in tackling poverty and deprivation.' This view is again closely linked to the New Labour belief in self-motivation and empowerment which we looked at previously.

So, how much welfare provision is being delivered in this way? It is difficult to estimate accurately the number of people who are being cared for by informal means. However, statistics from the 2001 census suggest that as many as one in seven adults in Britain (estimated at around 6 million) are responsible for looking after children and adults who are unable to look after themselves. The economic value of these 6 million carers is suggested to be between £15 billion and £24 billion per year.

These large numbers are also reflected in the increasing number of agencies particularly involved in voluntary health care. Estimates suggest that the number of registered charities has doubled since 1970, and that the total income of these voluntary organisations, which includes work with drug addiction, HIV/AIDS patients, the elderly and children, is around £12.7 billion. This income is also often boosted by government funding and money from the National Lottery.

Summary questions

3 Identify and explain in your own words the three advantages associated with the use of informal care as opposed to care provided by the government.

4 Why do you think that it is more difficult to estimate the numbers of people involved in informal care provision?

The issues and problems with a mixed economy of welfare

Learning objective:

- Consider the issues and problems in contemporary society related to having a mixed economy of welfare.

Criticisms of private provision

There are a number of criticisms that have been made of the changes to the provision of welfare in Britain in the last 30 years, in particular in response to the move from an emphasis on state provision to the emphasis on private provision we have now.

Criticisms of the introduction of more privately funded forms of welfare provision tend to form the view that private welfare provision is only available to the most wealthy and powerful in society, therefore creating a two-tier system of welfare, in which those who can afford to do so can access a better standard of care. For example, private schools tend to have better facilities, smaller class sizes and may appear therefore to be superior to state-funded schools, and the same analogy could be applied to private health care.

This can also be seen as a problem in relation to the increasing investment in private pensions by those who can afford it, leading to large inequalities of income at retirement age. Those who have invested in a private pension scheme are often much better provided for than those who rely solely on the state pension. Again this issue is closely linked to gender and income inequality: women are far less likely to be able to afford to make contributions to a private pension than men. This goes some way to explaining the large number of elderly women living in poverty. It also goes against the Beveridge vision of welfare provision, which was that it should be universal and applied equally and fairly to all.

The other criticism of the increasing use of private welfare provision, such as private pension schemes, is that this behaviour will lead to a change in attitudes to the provision of welfare by the state, and that support for free welfare will gradually be eroded and replaced by a more individualistic attitude similar to that in America, where everyone pays

Wealth, poverty …

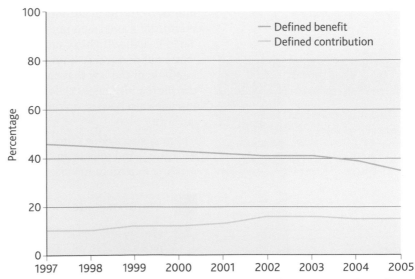

Fig. 3.15 *In 2004/05, 39 per cent of the working age population were members of a private pension scheme; more men than women were members*

125

for themselves. However, recent opinion surveys such as the British Social Attitudes Survey (2005) suggest that this is not the case, and contend that even among users of private schemes, support for state welfare provision is still high.

■ Criticisms of voluntary and informal provision

Critics of the growth of informal care tend to point out that the real reason for the government encouraging more focus on 'care in the community' is to save money, not to improve community relations or give a better service for the recipients. A study by the Equal Opportunities Commission (1990) stated that 'Whilst this policy may be expedient for the local authorities, its implications can be severe for families caring for dependents who, without adequate support, may find it difficult to cope.' The report goes on to suggest that care in the community is, in fact, 'care on the cheap'.

This criticism is also reinforced by feminist sociologists, who claim that the majority of informal care is provided by women who are rarely paid or supported by the government for this work, which is often done in addition to working outside the home. This may also be a reason why the number of women defined as living in poverty is so high. Carers may be paid an allowance for their support by the government, but critics argue that this in no way compensates them financially for the number of hours involved or the difficulty of the work. A study by the Equal Opportunities Commission (2000) found that three times as many women as men were looking after elderly and disabled relatives.

Problems are also identified for those in receipt of voluntary care. Scull (1984) argues that there is in reality very little real 'care in the community', and that those who are no longer looked after by government-run institutions are often neglected, and may pose a danger both to themselves and others. Problems have also been identified with the organisation and efficiency of voluntary organisations in delivering good-quality welfare provision.

This is also an issue in relation to private welfare provision for the elderly, where the standards of care received are not closely monitored by the government. Even when residents are placed in privately run care homes by the local authorities, they are still treated as being privately run institutions and so do not have to be inspected by government bodies. The Disability Rights Commission have complained about this, stating 'Nine out of ten care homes are privately run. It is therefore a serious loophole in the law that the most fundamental of legal provisions (under the Human Rights Act) do not extend to a commercial company that provides a service in accordance with arrangements made with a local authority'.

There is also a wide range of voluntary organisations, some of which are very small and reliant on contributions from the population or lottery funding to remain in existence.

Fig. 3.16 *Feminist sociologists claim that the majority of informal care is provided by women, who are rarely paid and supported for this work*

Link

See p81 for more information on domestic labour and gender roles.

AQA Examiner's tip

If the criticisms are made by a particular sociological theory (for example, feminism), then make sure that you show this in your answers.

Summary questions

5 Identify and explain in your own words the two main criticisms of the provision of private welfare.

6 Why are feminists so critical of the use of informal welfare provision?

Chapter summary

 Further resources

P. Dunleavy, *Developments in British Politics*, Macmillan, 1993

G. Lauder, 'Taking Care with Welfare', *Sociology Review,* September 2003

J. Morris, *Independent Lives? Community Care and Disabled People,* Macmillan, 1993

M. Powell (ed.), *Understanding the Mixed Economy of Welfare,* Policy Press, 2007

www.odpm.gov.uk – This is a website which gives information on services for children, the elderly and disabled people in different areas of the country.

www.helptheaged.org.uk

www.mind.org.uk

www.shelter.org.uk

- There has been a change in the provision of welfare in the UK in the last 30 years.

- The balance of our 'mixed economy' of welfare, in which state provision is accompanied by a mixture of private and informal welfare provision, has changed, placing more emphasis on privately funded provision.

- There has been a 'blurring of the boundaries' between the provision of welfare by the different agencies. This is based on the view that the final service provided to the individual will be improved as the different agencies complement each other.

- There are both benefits and problems with this type of welfare provision.

Wealth, poverty …

☑ Read Items 1(a) and 1(b) below and answer parts (i) to (v) that follow.

1   (a)   Members of minority ethnic groups on average have both a lower income and less wealth than the majority population of Britain. For example, in 2000, only 18 per cent of white people fell in the bottom fifth of the income distribution, as against 26 per cent of black Caribbeans, 32 per cent of Indians and 61 per cent of Pakistanis and Bangladeshis.

As a result, members of minority ethnic groups are more likely to be in poverty and to be receiving means-tested benefits. For example, compared to white people, about twice the proportion of black Caribbeans are in receipt of income support and housing benefit. Despite this, there is evidence that members of minority ethnic groups face greater difficulties in accessing the benefits system. For example, a study by the Commission for Racial Equality in Manchester (1995) found that Asian claimants were asked for supporting evidence more often, and fraud officers were called in more frequently, than in the case of non-Asian claimants.

(b)   We can distinguish between two broad types of explanation of poverty. On the one hand, 'victim-blaming' theories see the cause of poverty as lying within the poor themselves. For example, in the 19th century, Herbert Spencer argued that the poor were often in poverty because of individual inadequacies such as laziness, low intelligence or wastefulness. However, more recent victim-blaming theories tend to see the culture of the poor as the root of the problem, rather than the inadequacies of individuals.

The other broad type of explanation blames poverty on the structure of society. These are 'conflict' theories. They see poverty as the result of an unequal society in which there exist conflicts of interest between different groups. In these conflicts, some groups have less power and it is these groups who are most likely to find themselves in poverty. Some conflict theories, such as Marxism, see poverty as the inevitable outcome of the stratification system.

(i)   Explain what is meant by 'means-tested benefits' (Item 1(a)).   *(4 marks)*

(ii)   Explain the difference between 'income' and 'wealth' (Item 1(a)).   *(4 marks)*

(iii) Suggest two reasons why members of minority ethnic groups are more likely than the majority of the population to be in poverty (Item 1(a)).   *(4 marks)*

(iv) Examine the contribution of voluntary, private and informal providers to the welfare of the population.   *(24 marks)*

(v)   Using material from Item 1(b) and elsewhere, assess conflict theories of poverty. *(24 marks)*

AQA, 2005

Read Items 2(a) and 2(b) below and answer parts (i) to (v) that follow.

2   **(a)**   Child benefit, which is paid to everyone who has children, and the National Health Service, which was intended to provide health care for all citizens free at the point of need, are examples of universal benefits and services. When the modern welfare state was created in the 1940s, many people saw a universal system of welfare, publicly funded and run by the state, as the most effective way of meeting people's needs.

                In recent decades, however, there has been a trend away from a comprehensive state welfare system based on universal benefits and services. Instead, we have moved towards a more selective, means-tested system of state benefits and services, together with a greater role for non-state welfare providers. These include not only informal providers, but also voluntary organisations, which are mainly charities, and the private sector, which is made up of business organisations.

    (b)   Poverty is an important and divisive social problem. To remedy it with appropriate policies, we first need to understand what poverty is and how much of it there is.

                Unfortunately, there are disagreements among researchers as to how to define poverty. For example, should we use an absolute or a relative definition? Should we define it purely in material terms, or as 'social exclusion'? And who should do the defining – the researcher, or the poor themselves?

                There are further disagreements when it comes to measuring poverty. Researchers often draw up lists of items whose possession is considered essential to keep out of poverty. They then calculate the cost of these items in order to establish a poverty line. However, researchers disagree about which items should be included on such a list and even about who should draw it up in the first place.

(i) Explain what is meant by 'informal providers' of welfare (Item 2(a)). *(2 marks)*

(ii) Suggest two advantages of 'universal benefits and services' (Item 2(a)). *(4 marks)*

(iii) Suggest three advantages of voluntary organisations as providers of welfare (Item 2(a)). *(6 marks)*

(iv) Examine the reasons for the continued existence of poverty in society today. *(24 marks)*

(v) Using material from Item 2(b) and elsewhere, assess the problems involved in defining and measuring poverty. *(24 marks)*

AQA, 2005

Introduction

Key terms

Informal education: education delivered by non-specialised institutions such as the family, work or religious groups.

Formal education: education delivered by specially created institutions such as schools, colleges and universities.

Structuralist sociologists: those who examine society as a system, exploring how institutions such as education, the family and religion operate together to make society 'work'. They argue that these structures shape individuals, leading them to behave in certain ways.

Interactionist sociologists: those who examine social contexts at the level of individuals, exploring how they negotiate meanings and power relationships, and form identities.

Official curriculum: that which is taught within school according to its stated aims.

Social mobility: the ability to move up or down from the social class one is born into.

Equality of opportunity: the ideal that everyone has an equal chance to succeed in education. This notion is different from 'equality of outcome', which implies that everyone should leave education with the same rewards.

Education seems to be common to all societies. In some, it is an **informal** process, provided through non-specialised institutions – often the family and religious organisations. In others, such as our own, it is a more **formal** process, and is delivered through specialised institutions such as schools, colleges and universities. Regardless of its medium of delivery, however, education is an important social institution – and its nature and effects are consequently of interest to sociologists. This interest is wide-ranging, and is certainly not confined to the study of schools. Instead, sociologists are interested in education as it occurs throughout life, and across various social contexts.

In practice, a number of distinct areas of focus have emerged in the sociology of education and this chapter examines each in turn:

■ At the broadest level, **structuralist sociologists** are interested in why education is important and the functions it performs for both the individual and society.

■ **Interactionist sociologists** focus instead on what goes on inside the school building. They explore the exchanges between students, teachers and the curriculum, particularly the power relations, meanings and roles which are negotiated within the classroom. Both groups of sociologists explore what is taught in school not just in terms of the **official curriculum**, but also those things learnt incidentally through the rules, regulations and relationships of the school (known as the hidden curriculum).

■ Some sociologists have focused on specific social problems relating to education, such as why some groups seem to systematically underachieve. They attempt to identify and explain patterns of attainment by class, gender and ethnicity.

■ Finally, some sociologists have studied the impact of the education policies created by governments, evaluating their effects on **social mobility**, **equality of opportunity**, and the experiences of those within the school walls.

The sociology of education is a particularly useful unit of study, in that it demonstrates a wide range of skills used by sociologists. The two opening topics, for instance, involve perspective-taking and the application of theory to real-world institutions. In studying differences in achievement, the emphasis is on developing explanations for social problems, and applying empirical evidence to support and refute these theories. Finally, the chapter on educational policy involves placing a familiar institution in an historical context, and demonstrates the importance of sociological thought in the evaluation of initiatives and policies.

Please note that there is a certain amount of cross-over between sub-topics: for instance, the 'relationships and processes' part of the specification is also touched upon in the chapter 3 sub-topic, 'The influence of the school', as well as throughout chapter 4.

Education

Learning objectives:

■ Explore the ways in which education teaches children to behave in certain ways.

■ Examine positive and negative interpretations of this function.

■ Outline ways in which this line of argument has influenced social policy.

Key terms

Consensus perspectives: these examine society in terms of how it is maintained for the 'common good'.

Functionalism: a body of theory routed in the work of Emile Durkheim, and formalised by Talcott Parsons, which examines institutions in terms of how they contribute to the smooth running of society.

Anomie: a state of chaos, in which society lacks a shared set of norms and values to guide behaviour.

💡 Education is present in all societies – and many spend large amounts on schooling – raising a fundamental question: what makes the institution so important? Structuralists have focused on this question, highlighting two themes in the functions that education performs for society.

One theme is that education continues the job of the family, ensuring that children think and act in acceptable ways. In other words, that education is an agency of secondary socialisation.

At its most basic, this argument is that schools instil society's norms and values, using mechanisms of social control to ensure that these are followed. Theorists have noted that education does this in ways which are different to the family. Schools provide a 'society in miniature', allowing pupils to practise behaviours and interactions expected of them outside the family.

Some also note the importance of education in producing citizens and enabling them to engage in democratic processes. Furthermore, schools foster belonging and identity, making people 'feel' like citizens.

■ Consensus perspectives

Functionalists emphasise positive aspects of schools. Emile Durkheim, for instance, noted the importance of education in preventing **anomie**. He also emphasised the role of subjects such as history in teaching children their shared heritage, promoting integration and solidarity.

Fig. 4.1 *Going to school extends children's experiences of adults beyond the 'parental'*

Education

Functionalists have also noted ways in which education teaches children to interact outside their families. Durkheim argued that whilst the family is based on **affective relationships**, society is based on **instrumental relationships**. As children progress through school, their experience with adults becomes increasingly formal, easing them across this transition. Talcott Parsons develops this idea, arguing that education teaches children to value **achieved status** rather than that **ascribed** by the family. Furthermore, school rules acclimatise children to **universalistic standards** rather than the **particularistic standards** of the family.

Finally, Parsons argues that education instils values of competition, equality and individualism. These are crucial to the functioning of capitalism – but the family, based as it is on cooperation and **collectivism**, struggles to teach them.

Conflict perspectives

Where functionalists emphasise the positive role of education, **conflict perspectives** are more critical. Marxists and feminists argue that education operates as an ideological tool – manipulating people to think in certain ways to **legitimise** exploitation by the ruling class and inequality.

For Marxists, schools render the **proletariat** passive and resigned to their fate, crushing any rebellious instinct. The French neo-Marxist Louis Althusser argued that education operates as an 'ideological apparatus', i.e. controlling people by 'brainwashing' (in contrast to a 'repressive apparatus', which controls through force). Applying Althusser's idea to schools, it could be argued that the hidden curriculum transmits values such as obedience and respect for authority, whilst free thought is met with punishment. At the same time, the official curriculum portrays capitalism as sensible and natural, and other social systems as irrational or dangerous.

Research study: Bowles and Gintis (1976)

In *Schooling in Capitalist America* the authors argue that the organisation of the school mirrors the workplace. They contend that this 'correspondence principle' prepares children to fit easily into their future exploitation as part of the proletariat. They emphasise a number of dimensions, including the following similarities:

- The school and the workplace are based on a strict hierarchy and the same patterns of obedience and power.
- Each shares the same values, such as punctuality, hard work and appropriate dress.
- External rewards are emphasised in both – grades in education, pay in work – rather than the intrinsic reward of enjoyment.
- Fragmentation and alienation are present in both: in schools and workplaces, individuals are split (by form group, subject, department, job function, etc.).

They also argue that education transmits a myth of meritocracy, presenting an illusion of social mobility and blaming the working class for their inevitable failure.

Whilst feminists emphasise gender rather than class inequality, their fundamental argument mirrors that of Marxists. Therefore they also argue that education legitimises inequalities. In particular, feminists

Key terms

Affective relationships: such as those in the family, in which people help one another out of love and affection.

Instrumental relationships: are based on mutual self-interest – for instance, shop assistants help customers because their wages are dependent on people buying things.

Achieved status: that earned through performance or ability.

Ascribed status: that assigned to individuals on the basis of biological or family characteristics.

Universalistic standards: a set of rules which is applied uniformly to all members of a social group.

Particularistic standards: a set of rules which is specific to an individual within a group.

Collectivism: emphasis on the social group as more important than the individuals within it.

Conflict perspectives: a group of theories – including feminism and Marxism – which emphasise the way in which society is maintained to the benefit of one group, and at the expense of another.

Legitimation: the process of making inequalities and exploitation seem fair and just.

Proletariat: in Marxist theory, this is the majority of the population who do not own the means of production (i.e. those who are not part of the Bourgeoisie, the ruling class).

Education

maintain that the ways in which boys and girls are treated sends subtle messages about appropriate behaviours and aspirations. All of these create the illusion that patriarchy is reasonable.

■ Influence on social policy

Education's socialisation function has had influence on the government policies. Most notable is the introduction of Citizenship as a compulsory National Curriculum subject in 2002. There have also been recurrent demands that schools teach students 'core British values' and the 'British way of life'. Finally, this theme has had particular influence on **liberal** traditions of education which attempt to produce rounded, critical individuals.

■ Research study: Osler and Starkey (2003)

The authors argue that citizenship education has been based on a 'deficit model', which sees young people as dangerous but politically apathetic. The result is programmes of study which do not match with students' interests, and therefore alienate them. They argue that minority ethnic children have been perceived as suffering a dual deficit: first as young people, and then in terms of the labels associated with their ethnicity. Through interviews with children in Leicester, however, the researchers demonstrate that these children have sophisticated identities in which they can combine complicated notions of ethnicity and nationality in ways that do not cause conflicts.

■ Summary questions

1. Outline two ways in which education performs a socialisation function.

2. Give three ways in which education 'bridges the gap' between the family and wider society.

3. Identify the key difference between consensus and conflict perspectives on education's socialisation function.

4. Outline the main difference between Marxist and feminist perspectives on education's socialisation function.

5. Give two ways in which the theme of 'education, socialisation and citizenship' has influenced social policy.

Education and the economy

Learning objectives:

■ Examine the ways in which schools prepare and select people for jobs and careers.

■ Understand the positive and negative interpretations of this process.

■ Outline the ways in which this theme has influenced educational policy.

One idea at the centre of structural analyses of education is its role in socialisation and citizenship. A second is the link between the institution and the economy; that education equips students with skills and values needed in later employment.

In addition, functionalists, feminists and Marxists have argued that education performs a 'sorting' function, assigning individuals to jobs. As individuals progress through education, they pass through a variety of 'filtering' devices – ability grouping, examinations and so on – each directing them into differing levels of qualification and career paths.

Consensus perspectives

As noted previously, functionalists focus on the ways institutions benefit society – and it is this framework they apply to education's economic functions. Theorists such as Durkheim pointed to the importance of education in meeting economic needs, not only providing a grounding in the skills needed by employers, such as literacy and numeracy, but also in the general values which make 'good workers', such as punctuality and hard work. Education is perceived as crucial in producing the 'kinds' of employees needed by businesses. In turn, this not only makes individuals more employable, but gives society a healthy economy, driving up standards of life.

Research study: Human capital theory

The idea of 'human capital' was proposed by Theodore Shultz (1962) and Gary Becker (1993). It argues that economic growth occurs not just because of investments in infrastructure (e.g. better machines) but also through investment in expertise and skill. This idea has influenced international development policy, where education is emphasised alongside investment in modern technologies. It is argued that, whilst machines lose value (or depreciate), the value of education is cumulative as better-educated parents pass on skills and expertise to their children.

Talcott Parsons extends this basic principle, highlighting that schools are important in assigning people to jobs which match their abilities. He sees education as meritocratic – a neutral filtering device in which the most talented and hard-working are able to succeed in particular subjects and qualifications. Education is crucial in ensuring that the right people are assigned to jobs which, in modern society, are increasingly specialised.

Conflict perspectives

Whilst conflict perspectives agree with these basic principles, they disagree on their nature. Rather than operating in a neutral way, they argue that education **reproduces inequality** – 'locking' individuals into existing positions in the **stratification** system, maintaining exploitation and privilege.

For Marxists, the key to this sorting process is not ability but social class. They argue that education ensures that the proletariat are filtered into jobs of low status and pay, whilst the children of the rich retain prestige. They

Key terms

Reproduction of inequality: the process of filtering individuals into their existing place in the society's stratification system.

Stratification: the way in which individuals in society are divided into 'levels' of status (or strata), such as in the class system.

Education

also note that education ensures that rebellious students are kept away from jobs where they might cause a problem, ensuring that such children fail (unlike their compliant peers) and even excluding them completely.

■ Research study: Cultural capital theory

The French neo-Marxist Pierre Bourdieu outlines one mechanism through which working-class failure is ensured (Bourdieu and Passeron, 1973). He argues that the curriculum draws on primarily middle-class cultural capital (his term for experiences, social networks and understandings). As a result, working-class children are disadvantaged. Whilst their culture is as valid as their richer counterparts, it is not recognised and given status by the school (or society more widely).

Fundamentally, feminists agree with the arguments of Marxists that education sorts individuals by social characteristics and not ability. Where Marxists emphasise class, however, feminists note that schools recreate gender inequalities in their sorting function. Historically, this was accomplished through **formal mechanisms** – with restrictions placed on what and where girls could study. Girls were frequently barred from studying 'academic' subjects, and prevented from sitting examinations or entering university. In recent years, reforms have removed many of these biases. Feminists argue, however, that gender inequalities persist through **informal mechanisms** – girls and boys are 'encouraged' into gender-specific careers through peer and teacher pressure and the 'packaging' of subjects.

■ Research study: Hamilton (2003)

The author demonstrated how messages about 'appropriate' aspirations were sent by work-experience placements. Examining statistics from the Scottish careers advisory service, she found that boys and girls were still undertaking overwhelmingly stereotyped placements. She acknowledged that the mechanisms which produce this are complex: combining children's free choices, availability of placements and assumptions held by teachers and employers.

■ Influence on social policy

The economic function has shaped educational policy in substantial ways. For instance, the origins of state schooling in the late 19th century lay largely with economic need rather than with concern for creating a fairer society. The industrial revolution had transformed society and Britain required a skilled workforce. The family, previously responsible for education, was not equipped to accomplish this function.

Economic needs continued to shape education throughout the 20th century. This influence intensified from the 1980s onwards, with the advent of a movement called **New Vocationalism**. This sought to improve education's service to the economy by more closely matching its needs. As a result, the Conservatives – and the New Labour government that followed – introduced and rebranded vocational qualifications in order to give them higher status, and integrated work-based learning into the heart of compulsory education.

■ Key term

New Vocationalism: movement from the 1980s onward which aimed to focus the school curriculum to better meet the needs of business and industry.

■ Summary questions

6 Outline the two main ways in which education serves the needs of the economy.

7 According to functionalists, Marxists and feminists, on what basis does education perform its 'role allocation' function?

8 Outline two ways in which this function has influenced social policy.

Chapter summary

Further resources

BBC, 'Citizenship Lessons "Inadequate"'. http://news.bbc.co.uk

S. Bowles and H. Gintis, *Schooling in Capitalist America: Educational Reform and the Contradictions of Economic Life*, Routledge & Kegan Paul, 1976

M. Cole, *Bowles and Gintis Revisited: Correspondence and Contradiction in Educational Theory*, Falmer Press, 1988

B. Francis, J. Osgood, J. Dalgety and L. Archer, 'Gender Equality in Work Experience Placements for Young People', *Occupational Segregation Working Papers*, 2007, from http://www.eoc.org.uk

P. Freire, A.M.A.J. Freire and D. Macedo, *The Paulo Freire Reader*, Continuum, 1998

J.F. Lane, *Pierre Bourdieu: A Critical Introduction*, Pluto Press, 2000

A. Osler and H. Starkey, *Changing Citizenship: Democracy and Inclusion in Education*, Open University Press, 2005

T. Parsons, *The Social System*, Routledge, 1991

J. Shepherd, *What Does Britain Expect*, 2007, from http://education.guardian.co.uk

- Structuralist sociologists are interested in the role of education as part of the social system.

- One of their core arguments is that education takes over from the family as an agent of secondary socialisation – ensuring that children internalise a set of norms and values, and become effective citizens.

- For functionalists, this is a positive function – as it prevents society from breaking down and ensures that children can interact outside of the family.

- For Marxists and feminists, the function is negative – transmitting ideologies which justify inequality and 'keep people in their place'.

- A further theme in this type of analysis is that education serves the needs of the economy, by sorting people into jobs and equipping them with necessary skills and values.

- Again, functionalists are positive about this function. They argue that education is based on meritocracy, sorting the most talented people into the most important jobs.

- Marxists and feminists, by contrast, argue that education simply 'reproduces inequality'; ensuring that people stay in their existing position in the stratification system.

Teacher–student interactions

Learning objectives:

- Understand the process through which teachers label students.

- Examine some of the implications for a student of being labelled.

Key term

Labelling theory: a body of sociological theory which examines how the identity and behaviour of individuals is shaped by their categorisation by significant social others.

Link

The studies on this page and p165 show how some teachers label students based on class, gender and ethnicity.

Structuralists are interested in education in terms of its functions as part of the broader social system. Interactionists are focused on the processes which occur inside educational institutions – and, in particular, schools – on the negotiation of meanings, roles and power within the classroom.

The most influential aspect of interactionist thinking on education concerns how teachers 'pigeonhole' students – part of a body of argument called **labelling theory**. It highlights the ways in which teachers make judgements about the 'types' of students they are dealing with, and attach mental 'labels' to them.

Fig. 4.2 *Teachers can make judgements about students, leading them to mentally attach labels to them*

Research study: Hargreaves, Hester and Mellor (1975)

This research was based on overt participant observations and unstructured interviews in two schools in Northern England – urban and suburban. It revealed how teachers label students through three distinct steps:

- Speculation: teachers begin to make guesses about students – based on their appearance, enthusiasm, relationships and so on.
- Elaboration: teachers test their hypotheses, which are gradually confirmed or contradicted.
- Stabilisation: the teachers' hypotheses solidify – becoming fixed and stubbornly attached to the child.

At the end of this process, teachers will feel that they know what makes a student 'tick', interpreting all behaviour in terms of a label.

Teachers might find labelling useful as it helps them to 'pigeon-hole' types of student and quickly form a sense of what their classes are 'like'. However, a number of studies show that teachers base labels on stereotypes rather than evidence.

Sociologists have also shown that, once attached, labels can be 'sticky' and difficult to lose – and they can have real consequences for a student's education. For instance, teachers might 'screen out' behaviour that contradicts their expectations, making it difficult for a student to escape a negative label. Furthermore, labels can impact on the types of experiences children gain from education; whether they are allowed on school trips, their assignment to sets or exam tier and so on. Perhaps most damagingly, the student might start to believe the label; internalising it as part of their identity. According to interactionists, these processes risk creating a **self-fulfilling prophecy**.

Research study: Rosenthal and Jacobson (1968)

This classical piece of research demonstrated that self-fulfilling prophecies could occur. The researchers administered IQ tests to students in a California school. Twenty per cent of the student population was then selected at random, and teachers informed that these students could be expected to show rapid intellectual growth. A year later, the IQ tests were re-administered and it was found that the children labelled in the first part of the study showed greater gains in IQ. Other documents, such as report cards, showed that teachers also believed that these students had made greater progress.

Summary questions

1 Outline three stages through which teachers label students.

2 Give three processes through which labels might become self-fulfilling prophecies.

Key term

Self-fulfilling prophecy: the phenomenon by which, through a range of processes, labels attached to students become true – regardless of their accuracy.

Education

Student subcultures

Learning objectives:

- Examine the different types of school subculture identified by sociologists.

- Understand the ways in which different social groups form school subcultures.

Key terms

Anti-school subculture: groups of students who actively oppose the norms and values of the school.

Pupil adaptations: Peter Woods' term for the attitudes to school held by different subcultures.

Fig. 4.3 *Some sociologists believe that anti-school subcultures form when students have no legitimate means of gaining status in the school*

Summary questions

3 Explain what is meant by 'anti-school subculture' and 'pupil adaptation'.

4 Give one explanation of the emergence of anti-school subcultures.

5 Identify two studies which have examined the subcultures formed by different social groups.

Teacher–student relationships are not the only interactions of interest to sociologists. Those between students and their peers are arguably as, if not more, important in constructing the sociology of the classroom.

Sociologists are interested in understanding the nature of **anti-school subcultures**, groups of students who oppose the authority of the school.

Research study: David Hargreaves (1973)

Based on interviews with boys in inner-city secondary-modern schools, Hargreaves argues anti-school subcultures are formed as a response to negative labelling, which allows individuals access to only the lowest status in the school. As a result, students subvert the culture of the school to gain access to higher status – for instance, by attaching prestige to the disruption of lessons.

Not all student subcultures oppose the school in such dramatic ways, and Peter Woods (1981) argues that the division between pro- and anti-school subculture is simplistic. Instead, he identifies eight different **pupil adaptations** or responses to the culture of the school. These range from wholehearted subscription to the school's norms and values (ingratiation) through to open rebellion. In between are a number of more subtle adaptations, for instance, conforming to the schools norms, but without subscribing to its goals and values – such as attending college only to obtain Educational Maintenance Allowance (EMA) payments.

Sociologists have also studied the subcultures formed by different social groups – with a particular focus on class, gender and ethnicity. A common theme in this research is the idea that subcultures emerge as a coping strategy for the constraints placed on different groups – both within the school and in wider society.

Research study: Valerie Hey (1997)

In *The Company She Keeps*, Hey examined the sociology of schoolgirls' friendships, using a methodology which combined overt participant observation, unstructured interviews and analysis of the notes passed by girls in class. She uncovers a complex dynamic in these interactions, and many mechanisms of informal social control which serve to 'prop up' a dominant ideology of the female role. In particular, she points to the practices of bitching, falling out and rituals of exclusion – all of which see girls re-inscribing a socially constructed female stereotype, and marginalising those who do not conform.

Similar findings were made by Paul Willis (1977), demonstrating that working-class boys form subcultures as a response to their limited opportunities. Ultimately, however, these are self-defeating strategies as they effectively lead to disengagement from education, and underachievement.

The curriculum

Learning objectives:

- Examine the impact of the curriculum biases on student experience and attainment.

- Understand the influence of role models and the hidden curriculum on students' experiences.

Key terms

Curriculum: everything which is taught within the school in terms of knowledge, skills, understandings a\nd values.

Vertical segregation: workplace inequalities according to position in the management and responsibility structure.

Horizontal segregation: inequalities in the workplace according to job function or sector (in the school, this might relate to subjects taught).

Link

See also the discussion of Bourdieu on p136.

Summary questions

6 Identify three different types of curriculum bias.

7 Identify two effects that curriculum bias might have on students' experience and attainment.

A third set of educational relationships of interest to interactionists are those between students and the **curriculum** – the concepts, understandings and values taught in school.

The official curriculum

One strand of this argument is that the content of the official curriculum suffers from cultural biases. In particular, it seems to draw heavily on cultural capital more familiar to white, middle-class students.

As a result of this bias, some groups may identify more strongly with the school, whilst others are left feeling like 'outsiders'. In this context, subcultures are created not as an act of defiance, but because some groups are systematically marginalised. Furthermore, curriculum biases can have a direct impact on the achievement of students. As some students are more fluent with the culture of the curriculum, they have a head-start. Others are left in a constant attempt to 'catch up'. As such, curriculum content offers one explanation of the underachievement of some children.

Research study: Joseph George Ghevarughese (1987)

Ghevarughese argues colonialism rewrote history to exclude the contributions of non-European societies to maths and science – a legacy which remains at the heart of the curriculum. He notes a linear assumption that knowledge has developed from the Ancient Greeks, through to renaissance and modern Europe. This ignores significant developments in Mesopotamia, Egypt, China, the Americas, India and Arabia. Greek thinking, he maintains, owed a significant – and ignored – debt to the ideas of most of those cultures.

The hidden curriculum

Interactionists are also interested in the relationship between students and the hidden curriculum. On the one hand, the emphasis here might be on the way in which subjects are 'packaged' to appeal to certain groups. For instance, there is a gender bias in the types of activities and examples used in subjects – making them more appealing to either males or females. Alternatively, interactionists might point to the attitudes of teachers to social groups, and the ways in which these translate into differential treatment.

Finally, theorists in this perspective emphasise role-models in the school. They point to both **vertical** and **horizontal segregation** of staff by gender and ethnicity. Women, for instance, are over-represented in primary school (reinforcing the 'motherly' role) and under-represented in management. Similarly, all minority ethnic groups are under-represented in schools, and where they are present they are rarely in management positions. Interactionists would highlight that these tendencies send messages to students, not only about whether they 'belong' in school, but also about appropriate aspirations.

Education

Chapter summary

Further resources

D. Hargreaves, *Social Relations in a Secondary School*, Routledge & Kegan Paul, 1973

D.H. Hargreaves, S. Hester and F.J. Mellor, *Deviance in Classrooms*, Routledge & Kegan Paul, 1975

V. Hey, *The Company She Keeps: An Ethnography of Girl's Friendship*, Open University Press, 1997

R. Rosenthal and L. Jacobson, *Pygmalion in the Classroom: Teacher Expectation and Pupil's Intellectual Development*, Crown House, 2003 (originally published in 1968)

P.E. Willis, *Learning to Labour: How Working-class Kids Get Working-class Jobs*, Saxon House, 1977

P. Woods, *Schools and Deviance*, Open University Press, 1981

- Interactionists are interested in what goes on inside the classroom – the sociology of the interactions between students, teachers and the curriculum.

- They note the power that teacher expectations can have on the experiences of children, through the processes of labelling and the production of self-fulfilling prophecies.

- In addition, they study the way in which children interact with each other and the institution of education, with a particular focus on the formation of school subcultures.

- Finally, they are concerned with the interactions between students and the hidden and official curricula, their responses to the role-models in the school, and to the content of subjects.

Education

Patterns of achievement

Learning objective:

- Examine the patterns of educational achievement and underachievement by class and ethnicity.

Link

In this chapter, we focus primarily on achievement by class and ethnicity. Sociologists are, however, also interested in the impact of gender on underachievement, see pp153–8.

Hint

You might want to think a bit more critically about official statistics as a source of evidence. Might they be biased, or conceal a hidden figure? Do they tell us everything about what students 'get' from education?

Link

There is further information on official statistics on 172.

Key terms

Correlate: to show the relationship between two variables; may be positive or negative.

Affluent: wealthy.

Link

See pp159–69 for further detail on education policies.

The nature of, and solutions to, social problems is an important aspect of sociology. In the context of education, the most pressing is underachievement. This implies more than just low attainment – inevitably, some will take more from education than others. Instead, it suggests a systematic failure of certain social groups to realise their full potential and talent.

In attempting to measure underachievement, sociologists draw on a range of official statistics. These usually take the form of exam results or rates of participation in post-compulsory education.

Social class

The **correlation** between attainment and class is well established – poorer children achieve less well than their more **affluent** counterparts at every key stage and level of education, and are significantly under-represented in post-compulsory education. Furthermore, the effects of early disadvantage appear to be cumulative and, as children progress through school, the gaps between social classes widen.

Whilst various education policies (not least the introduction of free state education) have improved the attainment of poorer students, the achievement of more affluent children has also risen. As a result, the gaps between rich and poor have actually widened over the past century. According to the Office of National Statistics, for instance, 77 per cent of children from professional backgrounds attained 5 A*–C grades at GCSE in 2002 – double that of those whose parents had manual occupations (32 per cent). This has a knock-on effect of participation in post-compulsory education; at 17 years, 87 per cent of children from professional backgrounds are still in education, compared to 58 per cent of those from manual backgrounds.

Ethnicity

In exploring patterns of achievement across ethnicities, it is important to first note that not all ethnic minorities tend to underachieve. Many groups do extremely well; in particular, Indian children outperform their white counterparts, as do those of Chinese heritage. Some ethnicities do, however, tend towards underachievement, and sociologists have focused particularly on students of Pakistani, Bangladeshi and black Caribbean ethnicities. Each group does significantly worse in examinations compared to their white peers and each is under-represented at university. Furthermore, black Caribbean students, in particular, are more likely to be involved in the discipline and punishment regimes of school – and are consequently nearly three times as likely to be excluded.

Education

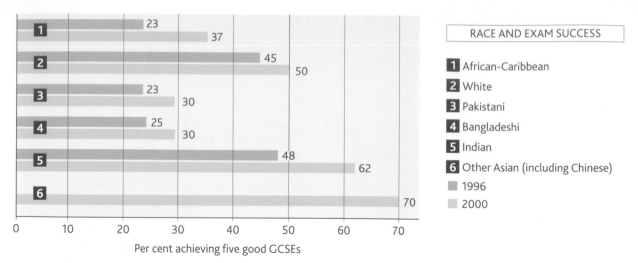

Fig. 4.4 *Ethnicity and exam success*

We should also note that class and ethnicity can combine to produce very specific patterns of underachievement. In this respect it has been noted, with increasing volume, that white working-class boys have a higher rate of underachievement than their black Caribbean counterparts.

Summary questions

1 Explain the trend in differential achievement of rich and poor students as they progress through school.

2 Identify two ethnicities which achieve well in school.

3 Give three ethnicities which tend to underachieve significantly.

The influence of the home

Learning objectives:

- Understand the influence of poverty on educational prospects.

- Examine ways in which parental attitudes and values might affect attainment.

- Evaluate the links between language use and achievement.

Key term

Material deprivation: a technical name for poverty and its effects on educational attainment.

Fig. 4.5 *Some sociologists emphasise the influence of the family in explaining differential achievement*

Link

The work of Callender and Jackson on p168 gives one contemporary example of the impact of material deprivation – as does that of Gibbons and Machin on p163.

Some sociologists have focused on the family as a cause of underachievement. They argue that the financial and cultural resources available in the home have a bearing on a child's potential to make the most of their talents.

Material deprivation

One branch of this argument holds that poverty, or **material deprivation**, is a key influence on attainment – both directly and indirectly. Poorer parents may be unable to provide educational toys, computers or books, or buy into the catchment of a successful school. More subtly, poverty might lead to cramped housing – an environment with no space for homework, and in which illnesses spread quickly. Children from poorer backgrounds are also more likely to need part-time jobs, and to finish school at the earliest opportunity.

Research study: Harker (2006)

In a review of evidence commissioned by the housing charity Shelter, Lisa Harker documents the links between poor-quality overcrowded housing on educational achievement. She notes a number of distinct negative effects:

- Less space to play, impairing cognitive development and leading to higher rates of depression or aggressive behaviour.

- Less space to study.

- Increased bullying in school, leading to increased truancy.

- Greater disruption because of moving from house to house.

- Hazards to health including damp and lead contamination, not only producing more days lost to illness but also, in the case of lead, possibly impairing brain development.

- Higher rates of stress and mental illness in parents, who are therefore less supportive.

This review demonstrates that the impact of poverty occurs on many levels, and can conspire to affect attainment in overwhelming ways.

There is also some evidence to suggest that those ethnic groups who tend to underachieve tend also to have low incomes. The Joseph Rowntree Foundation (Platt, 2007), for instance, estimate that 70 per cent of Bangladeshi and over 50 per cent of Pakistani children grow up in poverty – compared to 20 per cent of the white population and 30 per cent of Indians. We should, however, note that there are inconsistencies in the data. Black Caribbean children, for instance, have a similar rate of poverty to those of Indian heritages – but the two groups have very different rates of attainment.

■ Hint

The implication here is that ethnicity, in itself, is not a cause of underachievement. Rather, it suggests that ethnicity and social class tend to be closely related.

■ Key terms

Cultural deprivation: inadequacies in the socialisation process, and the impact that these might have on achievement.

Fatalism: to be resigned to one's fate, and seeing little chance of social mobility. This would translate in a low emphasis on the importance of education.

Deferred gratification: the practice of 'putting off' rewards in order to attain greater ones in the future.

Immediate gratification: emphasis on taking rewards at the earliest opportunity (for instance, leaving school to start earning money).

Linguistic deprivation: inadequacies and limitations in a person's use of language that might undermine their educational success, such as the inability to use 'standard' English.

■ Hint

Linguistic deprivation is technically an aspect of cultural deprivation theory. It is, however, substantial enough to merit an independent overview.

■ Cultural deprivation

An alternative possible source of underachievement is the socialisation experience of children; the values, expectations and norms transmitted in the home. In short, this approach blames poor parenting for failure.

One area of focus has been on child-raising practices and the impact of family structure. For instance, Driver and Ballard (1979) argue that high achievement in some Asian groups might be linked to the presence of close-knit extended family. Conversely, Pryce (1979) highlights a high rate of matriarchal single-parent families in black Caribbean communities – which might explain both underachievement in this ethnicity, and why girls do better.

In addition, theorists exploring this explanation have examined the values transmitted by the family. Some theorists suggest that lower social classes tend to be more **fatalistic** – and this translates into low aspirations and low expectations. Furthermore, because they are more oriented to the future, middle-class children are more comfortable in **deferring gratification** than their working-class counterparts – who are more likely to emphasise **immediate gratification**.

Finally, cultural deprivation theorists have argued that the experiences and cultural emphases in some families fail to prepare children well for school. Thus, they might argue that middle-class parents are more likely to take their children to museums, and might emphasise the importance of literature, rather than television. Similarly, New Right thinkers have argued that some ethnic minority groups underachieve because they cling to their historical roots and fail to embrace British culture.

■ Linguistic deprivation

The ability to use appropriate language is an important factor in educational success. Given the importance of the family in this respect, it has become a further point of focus.

Research study: Bernstein (1971)

Based on interviews with children of different classes, Basil Bernstein distinguished two patterns (or codes) of language use:

- ■ Restricted code is used casually. It is characterised by limited vocabulary, simple grammar, and is context bound (the listener must be aware of the topic for it to make sense).
- ■ Elaborated code is used in formal situations. It has far more sophisticated grammar and vocabulary, and can be understood regardless of whether the listener knows the topic of discussion (so it is context free).

Bernstein argued that, whilst middle-class children are able to switch between these codes, children of working-class backgrounds are limited to restricted code, meaning that they are disadvantaged in education, where language use is formal.

In the context of ethnicity and differential achievement, emphasis on language use has focused on the proportions of children with English as an Additional Language (EAL). Wilson *et al.* (2005) note a particularly high incidence of EAL amongst Pakistani (93 per cent) and Bangladeshi (97 per cent) families. They also note, however, a high rate amongst those of Indian heritage and a very low rate amongst black Caribbean families. This seems to contradict the explanation as these groups perform at opposite extremes to that which the theory would predict.

Summary questions

4 Explain what is meant by material, cultural and linguistic deprivation.

5 Outline three ways in which poverty might affect attainment.

6 Give three ways in which upbringing and socialisation might affect attainment.

7 Identify how the working class and some minority ethnic groups might use 'inferior' forms of language.

Wider social constraints

Learning objective:

■ Examine the way in which wider social processes might shape values, aspirations and attitudes to education.

Key terms

Situational constraint: (or social constraint) the argument that underachievement occurs because the child's position in society produces particular values and attitudes.

Culture of poverty: Oscar Lewis's name for the patterns of norms and values which evolve in those who occupy the margins of society, and help them cope with their environment.

Absolute aspirations: career aims judged in terms of their absolute position in the stratification system.

Relative aspirations: career aims judged in terms of the number of 'jumps' up the stratification system from the child's starting point.

Summary questions

8 Give two examples of values which might operate as a protection mechanism for the working class.

9 Illustrate the difference between absolute and relative poverty.

10 Give two reasons why a child might not feel connected to education as an institution.

For some theorists, attitudes that children bring to school are not necessarily a product of the family, or of 'bad parenting', as is implied by cultural deprivation theorists. Rather, they are born of the family's position in society, and the **situational constraints** under which they exist.

Values

One dimension to this argument is that values such as immediate gratification and fatalism are born out of the experience of poverty – and not taught by the family. Oscar Lewis (1966) proposed the idea of a **culture of poverty**: a set of norms and values that help individuals to cope at the margins of society. So, those growing up in poverty might emphasise immediate gratification because rewards are rare, and thus important to grasp. Similarly, children might sometimes seem 'rough and ready' because this enables them to survive their environment.

Aspirations

For cultural deprivation theorists, some students have low ambitions through lack of parental encouragement. Social constraint theorists, however, argue that to understand these aspirations, we need to appreciate the individual's origins in the stratification system.

Olive Banks (1971), for instance, drew the distinction between **absolute** and **relative aspirations**. She noted that, in absolute terms, children may appear to have low ambitions – for instance, to be a bank clerk rather than a lawyer. However, if we consider the jobs undertaken by their parents, this might involve considerable social mobility. In terms of relative aspirations, therefore, the move from cleaner to bank clerk is much greater than that from teacher to lawyer.

Relationships to formal institutions

A final aspect of this argument focuses on how students relate to formal institutions. Lewis, for example, argues that the culture of poverty involves a disconnection from these agencies and a focus on informal, illegitimate alternatives (such as cash-in-hand work).

In terms of ethnicity, this branch of argument explores how groups react to racism running through society and into each of its institutions – and the way in which each response translates into differing educational outcomes. Some research suggests, for instance, that black Caribbean boys tend to react angrily and reject white-dominated institutions (e.g. O'Donnell, 1991; Mac an Ghail, 1988). Girls of the same ethnicity attempt to work within racist institutions to disprove negative stereotypes (e.g. Fuller, 1982; Mirza, 1992). These varying responses may help to explain differing levels of attainment within one social group.

Education

Home–school interactions

Learning objective:

- Understand how underachievement might be produced by a mismatch between the culture of the home and school.

Key terms

Cultural difference hypothesis: the argument that underachievement is produced by the mismatch in cultures between the home and the school.

Marginalisation: the process by which individuals or groups are pushed to the edge of, and sometimes excluded from, mainstream society.

Mediate: to intervene in a dispute to bring about an agreement or reconciliation.

Link

The content on p141 provides further context for this page, exploring how the curriculum might impact on the experience of students.

The studies outlined on p163 provide some contemporary empirical evidence on these factors.

Summary questions

11 Give two ways in which the content of the official curriculum might be biased.

12 Outline two effects of a lack of role models on the attainment of children.

13 Identify three ways in which the school admissions system might produce underachievement.

Sociologists have also explored how home and school interact to influence attainment. Families of underachieving students are not seen as deficient – and the school is not seen as malign – rather, it is a mismatch of the two which breeds underachievement.

Curriculum content

One important argument in this branch of theory is the **cultural difference hypothesis**. The approach disagrees with cultural deprivation theory, arguing that the cultures which some children bring to school are not deficient. It is simply that they are not recognised by the curriculum.

Research study: Labov (1973)

Labov is a key critic of Bernstein. He interviewed black working-class children from Harlem using a range of different interviewers with different linguistic styles. Labov found that, when allowed to converse in language with which they were comfortable, the children could express sophisticated ideas. This suggests that children are disadvantaged if they are forced to 'fit in' with the dominant model of language use.

The impacts of these forms of bias are twofold. First, some students are less able to transform their cultural capital into achievement (for instance, the right answer in the wrong form of language). Secondly, they are less likely to identify with the school – retreating into anti-school subcultures.

A second dimension in this argument focuses on the role models available within the school, who are predominately white and middle class. Once again, there are two lines of impact stemming from this bias. Students of other backgrounds have less to identify with in the school and so feel **marginalised**, whilst messages are sent about the appropriateness of low aspirations.

Access to schools

We could, in this context, also consider families' engagement with the admissions policies around which education is organised. A child's ability to make the most of their talents is **mediated** by their access to good schools – and their parents' ability to ensure this. Two key processes might bias this:

- The financial ability of parents to move into the catchment area of successful schools.
- Parents' possession of the experiences, education and confidence necessary to make informed choices about schools – and to appeal, ensuring that these choices are respected.

In both of these cases, certain social groups might be systematically prevented from accessing schools which would enable them to make the most of their talents.

The influence of the school

Learning objectives:

- Examine the ways in which teacher expectations might impact on student success.

- Explore the impact of subcultures in the school in producing success and failure.

Key term

Differentiation: the process of providing differing work to match differing aptitudes in a mixed-ability classroom.

Link

The studies outlined on p138 and p139 give a theoretical basis to this content.

Together with the family, the school is the institution which most obviously influences achievement. As such, some sociologists have examined how processes inside the school might facilitate or inhibit success.

Teacher influence

A central aspect of this argument focuses on the power of teachers in shaping progress, mediating experiences and in limiting what students achieve from the education system. Teachers, for instance, are responsible for **differentiating** work, assigning students to sets and exam tiers and for a range of powerful mechanisms of praise and punishment. The impact of teachers in shaping students' self-concepts and educational outcomes has led some sociologists to argue that the kinds of labels they apply may produce self-fulfilling prophecies.

Studies suggest that teachers label students based on prejudices, which may explain patterns of achievement and underachievement across social groups. Early forms of this research focused on stereotypes according to social classes – with a common finding that teachers underestimated children from poorer backgrounds.

Research study: Becker (1971)

This classic study was one of the first to explore the class-biased stereotypes of teachers. Becker interviewed 60 Chicago high-school teachers, asking them to describe their notion of an 'ideal student'. He found that his participants emphasised many characteristics (conduct, attitude, language, appearance, etc.) before they got to ability. He concluded that it was much easier for middle-class students – who were better dressed and spoken – to match this ideal than it was their working-class counterparts.

Thus, working-class children are less likely to be perceived as 'academic' and this will, inevitably, have an impact on the opportunities afforded to them in the school.

There is also evidence that some teachers harbour prejudices on ethnicity, suggesting that schools are institutionally racist. Much of this research has related to black Caribbean boys, who tend to be perceived as unruly and threatening (for example, Wright, 1987; Gillborn, 1990; Mac an Ghaill, 1988). Work focusing on students of Asian heritages have found a different – but equally damaging – set of labels. They may, for instance, be perceived as lacking skills in English or even a commitment to British culture. Further research shows that teachers demonstrate little sensitivity to the cultures of these groups, for instance in mispronouncing names (Wright, 1987). A final common finding is that, whilst boys of this background are perceived as 'industrious', girls are seen as 'passive' and 'docile' (for example, Brah, 1992).

These forms of teacher prejudice can have wide-ranging effects on the experiences and attainment of students. Negatively labelled groups may, for instance, be much less likely to be identified as 'gifted and talented' or placed in high sets and exam tiers. Gillborn and Youdell (2000) identified a disproportionate number of black students entered for foundation tiers at GCSE, limiting their attainment to C grades and effectively keeping them from A-level study.

At the most extreme, some students might be more likely to be excluded from school – particularly black Caribbean boys – thus removing the educational opportunity entirely. Most precarious of all – and difficult to measure – is the impact of teacher expectations on students' self-confidence. It is difficult to ascertain how many, in response to constant negativity from teachers, give up on education completely.

Research study: Sewell (1997)

This research was based on a detailed study of two schools given the pseudonyms of 'John Caxton School' and 'Township School', using a range of methods including non-participant observation and unstructured interviews. In both, he found that whilst teachers saw themselves as progressive and non-racist, black Caribbean boys were significantly disadvantaged (for instance, accounting for 85 per cent of all exclusions, despite making up only a third of the population). Teachers in his study tended to be stricter and more controlling of these students, thus escalating conflicts, and tended to explain any problems in terms of home background and lack of male role models. In practice, Sewell argues that black Caribbean students were in trouble more simply because they were around more. Disenchanted white students simply elected to play truant from school; however, when black students did the same, the police were more likely to stop them – and hence they opted to stay in school.

Fig. 4.6 *Teachers have great power in shaping the opportunities open to students, their aspirations and self-concepts*

Link

The work of Osler and Starkey on citizenship education has relevance here. See p134.

School subcultures

Structures and processes within the school might also push some students into subcultures which prevent them from making the most of their education. As outlined previously, these might be formed as a reaction to negative labelling, or because the school systematically excludes some students from the mainstream culture.

Research study: Sewell (1997)

In the research described above, Sewell notes some of the dynamics of anti-school subcultures. He found that some of his participants, disenchanted by the school, turned to anti-school subcultures as a protection mechanism and a means of gaining status. Others, however, distanced themselves from this group and, indeed, their ethnicity. They avoided street culture and made friends from other groups. The result was a dual punishment; not only were they still the object of negative and excessive punishment from teachers, but also scorn from their peers – who labelled them 'battymen' (or homosexuals). This clearly illustrates the complex and combining pressures – originating from completely different directions – which might push certain students towards educational failure.

Link

The content on p140 gives some theoretical background to this section, examining the ways in which anti-school subcultures might be formed.

Summary questions

14 Identify four ways in which low teacher expectations might affect a student.

15 Give three examples of ways in which teachers might apply negative labels to social groups based on their prejudices.

16 Outline two negative effects of anti-school subcultures.

Education

Chapter summary

ℹ Further resources

Crown, National Statistics Online, 2007, from www.statistics.gov.uk

N.G. Keddie, *Tinker, Tailor: The Myth of Cultural Deprivation*, Penguin Education, 1973

B. Sugarman, *Social Class, Values and Behaviour*, Penguin, 1970

UCAS, Admissions Statistics, 2007, from www.ucas.ac.uk

Explore the most current data on education for yourself at www.statistics.gov.uk

Read Lisa Harker's study in full at http://england.shelter.org.uk

- Sociologists have noted that class and ethnicity has an effect on educational achievement.

- Students from poorer backgrounds underachieve in education, as do those of some ethnicities (particularly those of Bangladeshi, Pakistani and black Caribbean heritages).

- Some theorists argue that the home contributes towards this underachievement. They emphasise both a lack of money (material deprivation), inadequate upbringing (cultural deprivation) and inappropriate language use (linguistic deprivation).

- Others highlight that the values, aspirations and relationships to school found in some families are not a product of bad parenting, but of their position in society (situational constraint).

- Others have looked towards the school for producing underachievement, due to low teacher expectations and structures which encourage the formation of anti-school subcultures.

- A final group emphasises the interactions between the home and school – arguing that underachievement is produced by a mismatch between the two. They focus on the content of the curriculum, role models in the school and the impact of admissions policies.

Why have girls improved?

Learning objectives:

- Examine the changing patterns of achievement by gender.

- Understand reasons for the improvement in girls' attainment.

💡 In this topic, we continue to explore achievement. However, we must deal not just with differences, but also with a changing trend. Historically, boys outperformed girls, but this situation has shifted. Within three generations, girls have overtaken boys at all levels, and males are now up to seven years behind females in attainment by the end of secondary school. This pattern occurs across ethnicities and is amplified by class, with working-class boys the group most likely to underachieve. This raises a distinct set of sociological questions, the most fundamental of which is why girls have achieved this improvement. Potential explanations might be organised along three interrelated themes.

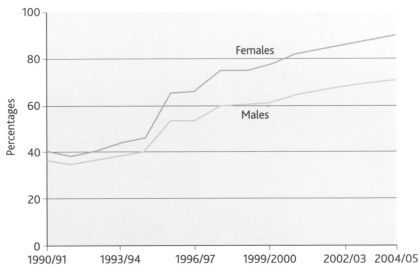

Fig. 4.7 *Since the 1980s, girls have overtaken boys at all levels of education – and the gap is getting wider*

Links

Look at pp159–69 to explore some of the reforms made to the British education system.

Some evidence, such as that on pp155–6, indicates that parents now have higher aspirations for girls than boys.

Legal and policy reforms

Recent reforms have opened opportunities to women – most notably the Sex Discrimination Act 1975, which made gender discrimination in employment illegal. They have also had an impact on schools, for instance, by making illegal the practice of filtering students into subjects by gender. This was reinforced by the introduction of the National Curriculum in 1988, which made certain subjects mandatory for all students. Some theorists have also argued that education now caters more for the learning styles of girls.

Education

■ Shifting expectations

With broadening opportunities for girls, it could also be that more is now expected of them. The messages sent during primary socialisation in the home, for instance, may now be that they can achieve academically, and gain a career.

These messages are also reflected in a more aspirational presentation of women in the media and, crucially, in the attitudes of teachers. Sociological research from the 1950s to 1970s (Stanworth, 1983; Spender, 1983) had found that girls were marginalised in the classroom and that this was particularly marked in 'traditional' subjects like the sciences (Goddard-Spear, 1984). It is likely that these expectations have now changed.

■ Changing aspirations

Finally, in response to wider social shifts, the aspirations of girls may have also increased. Thus girls now may have their sights set on university and a career – and this may translate into increased engagement with school. Sociological research has, in fact, charted an upward trend in the aspirations. In 1976, Sue Sharpe interviewed working-class girls in London, finding aspirations centred solely on family and motherhood. When she repeated her research in 1994, however, girls were far more career oriented – and took for granted the rightness of equal opportunities.

Fig. 4.8 *In just three generations girls have overtaken boys at all levels of education*

Summary questions

1. Describe how patterns in gender and achievement have changed.

2. Identify three legal and policy reforms which might have widened opportunities for girls.

3. Outline two ways in which expectations of girls might have increased.

4. Explain how rising aspirations might have led to increased attainment amongst girls.

Boys: the new underachievers?

Learning objective:

■ Examine a range of reasons why boys' attainment might be lagging behind that of girls.

■ **Hint**

Boys' results have not declined; rather girls have improved much more rapidly – leaving their peers behind.

The improvement in girls' attainment has led some sociologists to suggest that boys are the 'new underachievers'. This has triggered what Weaver-Highertower (2003) calls the 'boy turn' in educational research – generating various explanations for their lower attainment.

■ The structure of the economy

Some sociologists argue that it is impossible to understand the lower achievement of boys without situating it in wider economic contexts. They argue that the increase in opportunities and shifts in identity found amongst girls has not been matched for their male counterparts. This, coupled with the decline in traditional masculine manufacturing industries in Britain has, according to Mac an Ghaill (1994), created a 'crisis in masculinity'. Whilst the aspirational horizons of girls have widened, with the rise in the number of service sector jobs, boys have seen career opportunities become more limited. The result is that increasing numbers have low (or no) aspirations, seeing education as irrelevant and retreating into anti-school subcultures.

■ The feminisation of education

Some commentators have argued that those changes to education which have benefited girls have, in fact, gone further and 'feminised' education, with more emphasis on discussion, creativity and slow-and-steady work (rather than high-stakes examination) to the detriment of boys. Melanie Phillips (2002), for instance, argues that:

> Society tells boys at every turn that its values have turned female, and that if boys want any place in it they must do so too ... male characteristics are derided ... Authority is oppressive. Chivalry is a joke. Competition creates losers – taboo in education, where everyone must be a winner. Stoicism is despised; instead, tears must flow and hearts be worn on sleeves at all times.

Phillips (2002)

The results of this, according to Phillips, are that boys find education less easy to engage with and that they associate educational success with feminity (and, therefore, failure with masculinity). This leads to an upsurge in anti-school subcultures, and the bullying of those who conform. As Arnot *et al.* (1999) state: 'Schoolwork and academic scholarship have been portrayed by some boys as feminised and in conflict with emergent masculinities.'

■ Role models

Another dimension is that the role models of a male academic achiever are either absent or negatively stereotyped in the media. In addition, some New Right commentators have highlighted the increase in single-parent families as a cause of male underachievement, suggesting that female-led families mean that boys lack a strong male role model.

Fig. 4.9 *Some commentators argue that education has become 'feminised', which means that boys find it less easy to engage with*

■ Link

The content on p149 provides theoretical context for this argument, in terms of the way labels are formed and the effects that they can have.

A source of role models is schools themselves. Primary schools, in particular, are female dominated and the number of male teachers across compulsory education is in decline. However, female dominance of teaching is not new and is on its own a poor explanation of changing trends. But, combined with the other processes, it might imply that education is 'not for boys'.

■ Expectations of boys

A third process which might influence the underachievement of boys is the expectations of them held by significant others. In the home, for instance, parents may have fewer aspirations for their sons to achieve academically, and this might translate into less pressure to work hard and less support provided.

■ Research study: Kirkland Rowell (2007)

A survey of 500 secondary schools across Britain, comprising 137,000 students and 280,000 parents, was conducted and found a marked difference between parental aspirations for boys and girls: 67 per cent of parents with daughters wanted them to go on to university, compared to 62 per cent of those with sons. The survey also suggested that these expectations had been transmitted to the children themselves; 80 per cent of girls aspired to university, compared to 75 per cent of boys (cited in Milne, 2007).

NB: Kirkland Rowell is a polling company, not a person.

The expectations held by teachers may also be important in determining achievement and may lead to differing treatment of boys and girls – both in terms of direct academic opportunities (ability grouping, entry to exam tiers), and also in a higher tolerance for disruptive behaviour from male students, further undermining their attainment. Ultimately, the labels which teachers create based on these expectations may become self-fulfilling prophecies.

■ Research study: Myhill and Jones (2006)

The authors conducted semi-structured interviews, asking 144 students ranging from years 1 to 10 for their perception of whether teachers treated boys and girls differently. Overwhelmingly, participants indicated that boys were treated more negatively than girls – sometimes identifying very subtle forms of bias, such as tones of voice used.

■ Attitudes of boys to education

Finally, let us consider the attitudes of boys themselves. There is evidence to suggest that girls enjoy education more than boys (e.g. Keys and Fernandes, 1993; Arnot *et al.*, 1999), and this may breed male subcultures which are oriented away from educational achievement. As Sukhnandan (1999) puts it, '… an anti-intellectual, anti-educational and anti-learning culture among boys'.

This might undermine the attainment not only of those boys involved directly, but also those who are penalised by their peers for attempting to succeed.

■ Summary questions

5 Explain how changes to the economy might have stunted the attainment of boys.

6 Give three examples of ways in which the education system has become 'feminised'.

7 Outline two ways in which negative teacher expectations might affect the attainment of boys.

8 Suggest four reasons why boys might be more likely to form anti-school subcultures than girls.

Do girls still lose out?

Learning objectives:

- Explore patterns of subject choice by gender.

- Understand explanations of the gendered nature of subject choice.

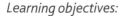

Hint

The suggestion here is that the 'feminisation of education' has been far from uniform, and is confined to those subjects which are not traditionally 'masculine'.

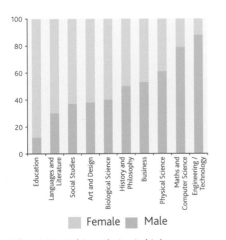

Fig. 4.10 *Subject choice in higher education remains notably gendered*

Summary questions

9 Identify four examples of the gendered nature of subject choice.

10 Outline two examples of the ways in which early socialisation might have an impact on career aspirations.

11 Explain two ways in which the school might contribute to the gender nature of subject choice.

12 Identify two ways in which biases in the workplace might lead to gender-specific subject choices.

Some sociologists are dubious of prematurely shifting the focus away from girls. They highlight that, whilst girls have improved *overall* attainment, we must also consider achievement in individual subjects.

When examined in this way we find traditional, stereotyped patterns. Boys are over-represented in mathematical and scientific subjects (with the exception of biology), whilst girls' attainment is weighted towards communicative, creative and caring subjects. This pattern intensifies through education, setting girls on a career trajectory which will earn them lower pay and status.

Early socialisation

One explanation of these patterns in subject achievement focuses on the family. It could be that the messages received in the home 'pre-load' children with gendered aspirations, interests and aptitudes. In particular, the different toys given to boys and girls shape aspirations, and allow practice in different abilities – differences which might then play out in the school (Kelly, 1987).

The school

The school might further reinforce gender-specific pathways. Early research shows that, in subjects such as maths and science, teachers have lower expectations of girls than boys – and more recent studies (Shakeshaft, 1995) have suggested that this persists.

Research study: Goddard-Spear (1984)

In this field experiment, Goddard-Spear gave secondary science teachers work to mark – telling some that it was produced by a girl and others that it was by a boy. She found that teachers would consistently assign lower grades when they thought that a girl had produced it.

Some sociologists have argued that some subjects appear 'packaged' to appeal to genders – with lessons and textbooks drawing on gender-specific examples, or theorists who are exclusively male (e.g. Kelly, 1984; Culley, 1986). Boaler and Staples (2005) further this argument, highlighting that the teaching approaches in different subjects are also gendered. In particular, they argue that the conventional method of teaching mathematics appeals more to male learning styles – explaining their greater achievement in the subject.

The structure of the economy

Finally, some research suggests that continuing biases in the workplace have an impact on the subject choices. Most obviously, that some professions are still dominated by men signals to girls 'appropriate' career aspirations. Furthermore, Marks and Houston (2002) produce evidence to suggest that girls chose courses and careers with a different set of priorities to boys – particularly, the need for flexibility to have a career break in order to start a family.

Education

Chapter summary

Further resources

Crown, National Statistics Online, 2007, from www.statistics.gov.uk

B. Francis, J. Osgood, J. Dalgety and L. Archer, 'Gender Equality in Work Experience Placements for Young People', *Occupational Segregation Working Papers*, 2007, from www.eoc.org.uk/PDF/wp27.pdf

M. Phillips, *The Sex-change Society: Feminised Britain and the Neutered Male*, Social Market Foundation, 1999

UCAS, Admissions Statistics, 2007, from www.ucas.ac.uk/figures/index.html

- Sociologists have noted a complicated and changing relationship between gender and achievement.

- Historically, boys have outperformed girls – but, over the past three decades, girls have become the higher attainers.

- This rise might be driven by a range of broader social changes – including legal and policy reforms, changing expectations held by parents and teachers and shifting aspirations of girls themselves.

- Because boys have fallen behind girls in attainment, some sociologists have attempted to explain their status as 'new underachievers'.

- They have pointed to many different factors, including the decline in traditional 'male work', the ways in which education might have become 'feminised', role models in the school, changing expectations of boys and the attitudes of boys themselves.

- Other theorists have argued that looking at overall attainment hides the degree of gender-bias within individual subjects. They have, in particular, attempted to explain the lack of girls in mathematical, scientific and technical courses.

- In explaining these patterns, they emphasise that girls' aspirations are shaped by early socialisation through toys, expectations in the school and opportunities available in the workplace.

4.5 Educational policy

Historical context

Learning objective:

- Examine the historical context of the education systems of England and Wales.

The sociological arguments and processes explored previously are framed by the way in which the school system is organised. Sociologists are, therefore, interested in the nature and effects of educational policies introduced by governments. Here, we briefly consider the history of such policies before moving on to explore the debates which underpin them.

Whilst state-funded education in England and Wales developed earlier than other public services, such as health care, it has a remarkably short history of little over a century.

Forster Act 1870

State education did not really exist prior to the 20th century and whilst private education had long existed, these schools were accessible only to the wealthy. Lucky children from poorer backgrounds might receive limited education in church schools, but most would learn only from their families.

Fig. 4.11 *The education system has changed dramatically over the past 200 years*

Key terms

Elementary schools: the original name for the sector of schooling educating five to 11-year-olds. This was later rebranded as the primary sector under the Butler Act 1944 – at which point church schools were also brought under state control.

Tripartite system: the system comprising three types of secondary school (grammar, secondary modern and secondary technical) established under the Butler Act 1944.

Eleven-plus (11+): an intelligence test which would be sat at the end of primary school, and which determined the school a child would attend under the tripartite system.

Comprehensive: a school which accepts all students, regardless of background or ability.

Catchment area: a geographical region surrounding a comprehensive school, which determines its intake of students.

Hint

GCEs, CSEs and GCSEs are different qualifications – be careful not to confuse them.

Key terms

Marketisation: the attempt to subject public services to market forces of supply and demand, in order to create competition, create choice and raise standards.

OFSTED: (Office for Standards in Education) the government agency tasked with monitoring the quality of schools and teachers in the UK.

National Curriculum: subjects and subject content which must be studied by all children in state schools – in an attempt to standardise educational provision.

At the end of the 19th century this began to change in response to new needs created by industrialisation. In 1870 the Forster Act was passed, creating **elementary schools** where no church school existed. This ensured that all could access some free education until the age of 10.

■ Butler Act 1944

The education system of England and Wales continued to evolve slowly through the early 20th century, but the next major reform did not occur until 1944. The Butler Act 1944 restructured education radically, creating a formal, state-funded secondary sector. This was known as the **tripartite system** as it consisted of three different types of school, each catering for different aptitudes:

- Grammar schools for more 'academic' students, who could sit the prestigious General Certificate of Education (GCE).
- Secondary technical schools for those with a talent in mechanical, engineering or scientific areas.
- Secondary modern schools for those not suited to the other two schools.

Students were assigned to these three types of school on the basis of the **eleven-plus**.

■ Comprehensivisation

During the 1950s, discontent grew with the way in which the tripartite system limited the opportunities available to many students. Some local authorities (such as Anglesey and Sheffield) began to rebel, dismantling their selective systems. They replaced them with **comprehensive schools**, which aimed to educate all students, regardless of background or aptitude, under one roof. Admissions were based on location or **catchment area**. The aim was to ensure that all children had access to the same level and quality of education. In 1965, the government officially began to back the move to this form of schooling. They also introduced a further qualification – the Certificate of Secondary Education (CSE) – to cater for those who did not sit the GCE.

■ Education Reform Act 1988

The next major reform came in 1988. The key principle of the Education Reform Act 1988 was an attempt to **marketise** education. Parents were given choice over where to send their children, and schools were encouraged to compete for their 'custom'. Thus, it was hoped that quality of education would rise, as schools improved in order to attract more pupils.

The 1988 Act also introduced a range of different information sources to inform choice. These included league tables and prospectuses published by schools. In addition, **OFSTED** began to produce publicly available reports on each school.

Finally, curricula and qualifications were overhauled under the 1988 Act. Most notably, it introduced the **National Curriculum** – a prescribed set of subjects and content which must be studied by all children in all state schools. In addition, SATs (Standard Assessment Tests) were introduced at the end of each key stage of schooling (introduced gradually, beginning in 1990), aiming to evaluate the performance of schools prior to final examinations. In 1986, the GCE and CSE qualifications were also combined, creating the GCSE, which would be taken by all students, regardless of ability.

Education post-1997

Following their election in 1997, New Labour's education reforms in some ways remained faithful to the 1988 Act. They retained commitment to parental choice, expanding the diversity of available schools. This included emphasis on three types of schools:

- **Specialist schools**, originally established by the Conservatives, were expanded.
- Faith Schools – whilst these have existed for centuries, New Labour were committed to expanding the number of religious schools and the faiths represented.
- **Trust schools** were introduced.

In addition, New Labour have tried to address systematic underachievement in some schools, particularly in the inner cities. In part, this has revolved around delivering extra funding through schemes such as Excellence in Cities and the creation of **Education Action Zones**. They have also attempted to foster cooperation between schools – particularly in the Beacon Schools programme, in which good schools are given money to help their less successful neighbours. Finally, OFSTED were given the power to place failing schools under special measures – under which they are re-inspected more regularly and given additional freedoms (such as the ability to attract staff with higher pay). In extreme cases, the government can close down a failing school and reopen it as a **city academy**.

Finally, the Labour government has made changes to the post-compulsory sector with a pledge that 50 per cent of young people will access some form of **higher education** by 2010. Within **further education**, structural changes were made under Curriculum 2000 – which split the A-level into AS and A2 and rebranded the vocational sector. The government also introduced the **Educational Maintenance Allowance**.

New Labour has also made significant changes to the higher education sector. This included the abolition of grants and the introduction of loans – and later, fees payable by students. They have attempted to level this financial burden by obligating universities to provide bursaries for students from less affluent families.

Key terms

Specialist schools: these receive additional funding to support a subject of expertise, and are able to select up to 10 per cent of their students on the basis of aptitude in this subject.

Trust schools: those which, with the support of local parent or business groups, have pulled out of Local Authority control. This gives them more independence over their staffing, budget and the ways in which they admit students.

Education Action Zones: inner-city areas which are targeted with additional funding, which can be spent in imaginative ways to enrich educational provision.

City academies: schools which, under New Labour, have been closed down and reopened with funding and control from private businesses.

Higher education: this occurs at university level, and includes degrees and Higher National Diplomas (HNDs).

Further education: this is post-secondary, post-compulsory education (in addition to that received at secondary school), and includes A-levels, NVQ/GNVQ and access courses.

Educational Maintenance Allowance: (EMA) a payment given to students of less affluent backgrounds to help them to continue into further education.

Summary questions

1. Identify eight types of school introduced by the British government over the last 150 years.

2. Give three ways in which the qualification system has changed.

3. Give three different ways in which children have been assigned to different schools.

Education

Admissions policies

Learning objectives:

■ Explore different approaches to admissions policy.

■ Evaluate the strengths and weaknesses of these policies.

Fig. 4.12 *Under the tripartite system, admissions were based on performance in an examination*

💡 Education reform has sparked a number of sociological debates. We begin with the debate which has provoked the most impassioned response – the ways in which children are assigned to secondary schools.

Religion

Historically, faith selection was central to schooling. Prior to 1870, poorer children could only receive schooling where it was provided by churches. When faith schools were incorporated by the state, they retained this policy and recent governments have restated commitment to faith schools.

✔ Faith schools have tended to obtain better exam results than their counterparts. Supporters point to the benefits of the atmosphere and values within them, and their links to communities.

✗ Critics are dubious of segregating children by religion and the impact this might have on communities. Furthermore, faith criteria can disguise other priorities, including ability or background.

Ability

When state secondary education was introduced in 1944, it was based on ability selection. On the basis of their eleven-plus result, students were assigned to a secondary school matched to their aptitudes. There has been a move away from this but it remains influential. Some local education authorities (LEAs) still maintain **grammar schools** where entry is based on the eleven-plus (as is the case in many **private schools**). Ability selection has surfaced in other ways – for instance, specialist schools are able to select 10 per cent of their students by ability in their subject of expertise.

✔ Advocates of this approach highlight that it tailors schooling to the needs of children – they can progress at an appropriate pace, studying subjects in which they excel.

✗ Aptitude tests have tended to suffer from biases. They draw on experiences more familiar to middle-class children, whose parents can also afford tutors. The result is a social bias in different types of school.

Key terms

Grammar schools: those schools which, under the tripartite system, admitted those students whose eleven-plus result indicated academic ability.

Private schools: fee-charging schools which are independent of the state sector.

Education

■ Catchment area

Throughout the 1960s, comprehensivisation shifted admissions policy. Rather than splitting students by ability, schools were to admit those of a range of abilities and backgrounds based on a catchment area. This remains a central influence on admissions to school.

✔ This approach aims to ensure that all children have access to the same standard of education, regardless of background or ability. It also maintains links between school and community, and parents feel connected to their children's school.

✘ Not all schools were of equal quality to begin with. As a result, many parents tried to move into desirable catchment areas, fuelling house-price rises and creating a kind of '**selection by mortgage**'. Poorer families found themselves 'priced out' of good schools. The least 'attractive' schools found themselves stuck in a downward spiral, becoming **sink schools**.

■ Research study: Gibbons and Machin (2006)

This study explored data on house sales in the south-east, with a focus on the impact of local primary schools. They conclude that 'buying into' a good catchment area can cost anything between an additional £12,000 and £61,000.

■ Parental choice

From the 1980s onwards, 'parent power' underpinned admissions. Families were able to choose their children's school, supported by data from OFSTED reports and league tables.

✔ The ideal of this reform was to empower parents and to marketise public services. Parents became consumers, able to 'shop' for a school for their child. It was thought that this would improve standards in the same way that competition between businesses can benefit customers.

✘ Unfortunately, this approach to admissions created social biases. Middle-class parents were better able to make a choice of school, and to follow through on that choice.

■ Research study: Gewirtz, Ball and Bowe (1995)

This interview study examined the ways in which parents in London made decisions over schools. They found that most middle-class parents were skilled or semi-skilled choosers with the wealth, experience and contacts to get their children into their school of choice, using appealing if necessary. Working-class parents tended to be disconnected choosers; making less-informed decisions.

■ Banding

Politicians have also tried to create admissions systems which engineer balanced intakes. One such approach is that of banding. This involves giving children aptitude tests – however, rather than assigning students

Education

of different aptitudes to different schools, each takes an equal proportion of students from high, middle and low ability bands.

✔ The strength of this approach is that it breaks the links between background, ability and quality of education. All children have the potential to access the same quality of education, and to mix with diverse peers. In short, it attempts to create schools which are, in a real sense, comprehensive.

✗ Whilst bias in the aptitude tests is an issue when banding, it is a less dramatic problem than under-selection by ability – as performance in the test is not directly linked to quality of education. However, it works against the instincts of parents, who understandably want to ensure that their children get the best start. It has therefore been met with hostility by some parents and, in extremes, it may lead to them withdrawing from the state sector completely.

Summary questions

4 Outline five different ways of organising school admissions.

5 Identify the admissions policies used under each major reform Act outlined in the previous section.

6 Give strengths of the five admissions policies.

7 Outline three ways in which admissions policies have tended to benefit the middle classes.

Non-governmental involvement

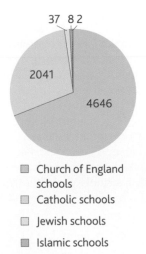

37 8 2

2041

4646

- Church of England schools
- Catholic schools
- Jewish schools
- Islamic schools
- Sikh schools

Fig. 4.13 *Religious involvement in education goes back centuries. Today's faith schools have been accused by some of being culturally divisive*

Key term

Public schools: the most prestigious, and oldest, private schools, including Eton and Harrow. So-called because they were open to all of the fee-paying public, not just those of a particular church, and because, at the time they were established, they offered the only alternative to private tutoring.

Assisted places scheme: this provided free or subsidised places at private school for children who would otherwise not have been able to afford to go, providing they scored in the top 10–15 per cent of its entry examination.

💡 Prior to the 20th century, Britain lacked state education, and any schools were managed by other agencies. Although this has changed over the past century, three key non-governmental agencies still retain a role.

Faith organisations

The church was the earliest agency to be involved in education. Priest schools existed as early as the 7th century, and by the 19th century these were the only source of education for the poor. When the state sector emerged, church schools were incorporated and, recently, the number of faiths represented has grown.

✔ Advocates of faith schooling emphasise higher results and supportive community ethos. They also argue that such schools allow cultures and religions to be preserved – ensuring that the home values are mirrored by schools. This reduces conflicts, helping minority communities to integrate comfortably without persecution.

✘ Critics argue that the negligibly higher results of faith schools is linked to their selective nature. Furthermore, they dislike segregating children, pointing to the impact that a faith school can have on the social make-up of surrounding areas. Both of these factors may undermine communities and create tensions. At the extreme of the debate, some see no place for religion in state education, arguing that children should be exposed to a variety of belief systems and allowed to form their own opinions. They are particularly critical when religious agendas are perceived to distort the curriculum.

The city academy scheme has provided faith groups with an additional way of involving themselves in schooling. Forty per cent of the academies proposed in early phases are sponsored by faith charities or evangelical individuals. This has generated controversies over religious agendas being pushed through the government's flagship schools. Two academies in the north-east – established by Reg Vardy – have attracted particular focus. It is alleged that, in these schools, creationism and intelligent design are taught in science lessons, rather than in RE, as alternatives to scientific theory.

Private schools

Like faith groups, the private sector has a relatively long history. Independent schools evolved in the 13th century, including the elite **public schools**. The fee-charging sector continued to grow into the 21st century and there are now 1,280 private schools, educating 7 per cent of children in England and Wales.

Though private schools are independent of government, politicians have attempted to share some of their benefits more widely. In 1980, for instance, the **assisted places scheme** was created and New Labour has experimented with similar voucher policies – and has threatened to remove the charitable status of schools which cannot demonstrate benefits to local communities.

Education

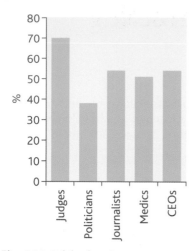

Fig. 4.14 *Whilst the private sector educates just 7 per cent of children, their pupils account for a disproportionate number of people in powerful and prestigious occupations*

■ **Key term**

City technology colleges: centres specialising in sciences, maths and technology – similar to the secondary technical schools of the tripartite system. To offset the costs of establishing schools, a major stumbling point which saw few secondary technicals established, businesses were invited to invest in the schools – in return, acting as governors.

✔ Some would argue that, free from red tape and political agendas, private schools can deliver efficient, quality education. They could also contend that it is a parent's right to pay for a better education for their children. In this context, the problem with the private sector is not its existence, but that not everyone is able to access it – and policies like voucher schemes aim to address this.

✘ Others are more critical, arguing that whilst private schools exist, meritocracy is impossible. There is certainly evidence to suggest that buying private schooling sets children on a privileged life path. In part, this is linked to the smaller class sizes and better resources available in the private sector. However, the social networks created in such institutions are equally important, leaving pupils with the 'insider' contacts to obtain good jobs and influential positions. For critics, voucher schemes are little more than a subsidy for the rich; the very poorest cannot afford the remaining fees.

■ Business and industry

Given education's links to the economy, it is predictable that employers have some involvement with schools. Indeed the idea is nothing new, and the tradition of apprenticeships provides historical context. More recently, governments have attempted to involve businesses directly in the provision of schooling – for instance, the Education Reform Act 1988 created **city technology colleges** (CTCs). New Labour has been enthusiastic about this form of partnership. Most notably, the city academy programme (targeting inner-city areas), and later the trust school programme (which is much broader) asked private businesses to invest 10 per cent of the costs of establishing schools, in exchange for input over their ethos and running – with remaining costs provided directly by government.

✔ The ideal of these programmes is to involve key stakeholders in education provision, whilst attracting additional funding to deprived areas. The schools are intended to have the independent ethos and resources to make them a 'half-way' between private and state schools. There is some evidence to support the view that public–private initiatives can be successful, suggesting that CTCs attain better results.

✘ Some of the criticisms surrounding policies such as city academies are empirical, with ambiguity in the data on their successes. Some have failed to produce expected results, whilst the successes elsewhere may be linked to selection or high exclusion rates. Other criticisms are ideological, with unease at giving businesses too much influence over schooling, worried that the broad and important functions of education might be reduced to producing 'good' workers – and hijacked by the political or religious agendas of managing directors.

■ Summary questions

8 Identify one historical way in which each of these key groups have been involved in education.

9 Give one way in which each has increased its involvement over the last 20 years.

10 Outline one positive of each group's involvement in education.

11 Identify one criticism levelled at each non-governmental organisation.

Education

Vocational education and training

Learning objectives:

- Examine the development of vocational education and training in England and Wales.

- Explore some of the debates surrounding vocational education and training.

Key terms

Youth Training Scheme: a controversial policy which withdrew social security payments from 16- and 17-year-olds in exchange for a guarantee of training in either businesses or colleges.

NVQ: a vocational qualification focused on a specific job, for instance, plumbing, accountancy.

GNVQ: intended to be a half-way measure between academic and vocational pathways – focused on a sector of work, rather than a specific job. Examples include health and social care, ICT and so on.

Key Skills: the core abilities of communication, numeracy, IT, team-work, independence and problem-solving. These were introduced under Curriculum 2000 in an attempt to better meet the needs of business and industry.

Parity of esteem: the idea that schools and types of courses should be different, but equal.

Summary questions

12 Identify four different ways in which vocational education and training have evolved over time.

13 Give two different types of vocational qualification.

14 Outline four separate debates surrounding vocational education and training.

How to ensure that education meets the needs of employers is a favourite debate of politicians. As such, vocational education forms an important theme in policy.

Historical context

Historically, vocational training occurred as apprenticeships; however, the emergence of state schools was linked to economic need. Industrialisation had left Britain in need of an education system capable of producing a skilled, literate and numerate workforce. The importance of vocational education was also emphasised in the design of the tripartite system.

While comprehensivisation shifted the focus of schooling to providing a fair chance for all, the 1980s saw a refocus on employers' need through a movement called New Vocationalism. This included the introduction of compulsory work experience and the establishment of the **Youth Training Scheme**. In 1993, the government introduced two new qualifications – the **NVQ** and **GNVQ** – aimed at formalising the existing patchwork of vocational qualifications.

Labour has continued to develop vocational education. For instance, they made **Key Skills** central to the post-16 curriculum, and rebranded the GNVQ as the AVCE and then the Applied A-level. The party also introduced the New Deal aimed at the young unemployed, and attempted to extend vocational pathways from the narrow 16–18 age bracket into schools and throughout life.

Debates over vocational education

Like any social policy, vocationalism has been surrounded by argument – and it is possible to identify four distinct themes. There has been a persistent problem of realising **parity of esteem** between pathways, despite efforts to 'rebrand' qualifications. Where academic courses enjoy prestige, vocational equivalents are seen as 'second rate'. Some schools have amplified the problem by using these courses to boost results – creating 'grade farms' which push through as many students as possible rather than providing quality education.

Social biases have also plagued vocational pathways, which contain a higher proportion of working-class and ethnic minority students. Academic pathways, in contrast, tend to have a disproportionate number of white, middle-class students.

There have also been tensions between vocational and liberal priorities. Whilst the former sees education as the focused preparation for a career, the latter argues that education should be producing rounded citizens, with grounding in a range of disciplines and subjects – pulling the purpose of education in two contradictory directions.

Finally, vocational policies can harbour political agendas. The most recurrent argument is that pushing young people into vocational programmes gives governments an easy way of creating 'low unemployment'. Critics have also argued that trainees provide cheap labour and weaken trade unions.

The post-compulsory sector

Key terms

Polytechnic: higher education institutions created from 1965 to expand provision. Initially focused on applied science and technology, they quickly broadened their subject range. In 1992, the polytechnics were granted the ability to gain university status, and many (though by no means all) are now known as 'metropolitan' universities.

Aim Higher: a programme run by universities and the DfES which aims to widen participation in higher education by raising awareness, aspirations and attainment amongst students of under-represented groups. Activities include mentoring, summer camps and careers/ applications advice.

Summary questions

15 Outline four education policies which have widened participation to the post-compulsory education.

16 Give an argument in favour of and an argument against the use of student loans.

17 Identify two problems with the pattern of increasing participation in higher education.

It is important to note that education does not end at the age of 16 but continues into further (sixth-form and CE colleges) and higher sectors.

Context and trends

Traditionally, post-compulsory education was the preserve of the elite; in 1900 only 1 per cent continued to university. With the expansion of state education, this proportion grew to 6.5 per cent by the 1960s. Since then, participation has increased dramatically, and 44 per cent now attend university. This explosion is linked to two policy trends: vocationalism created new pathways, whilst an expansion of institutions occurred with the creation of **polytechnics**.

New Labour committed to continuing this expansion, with a target of 50 per cent of under-30s in higher education by 2010. To realise this, they attempted to reduce drop-out rates at 16, with policies such as EMA – which eases the financial burden of continuing in education. They also attempted to work with universities to widen participation with bursaries and the **Aim Higher** programme. Grants have been replaced with loans to finance increasing numbers of students. In addition, Labour have attempted to make universities self-sustaining with the introduction of variable tuition fees – a move which also marketised admissions by allowing better universities to charge higher fees.

Despite the increase in post-compulsory participation, the sector is plagued by social biases: poorer students and those of some ethnicities remain under-represented. This is amplified in the most prestigious courses, where 'non-traditional' students are very much the minority.

There has also been debate over funding. For some, the move to loans is positive, financing expansion and ensuring that those who benefit from degrees pay for them. Critics express concern that debt burdens might discourage poorer students.

Research study: Callender and Jackson (2005)

These authors argue that the prospect of debt makes working-class students avoid university. Researchers gave a questionnaire to a stratified sample of prospective students – finding that poorer students were more 'debt averse', and that this had an impact on their decision to go to university, their choice of institution and course. In further research, Callender demonstrated that poorer students leave university with higher levels of debt, and are more likely to need to work to support themselves.

Finally, there has been direct criticism of widening participation. Some argue that it has 'dumbed down' universities to accommodate less able students. Others argue that the rapid increase of university study has devalued degrees, which are no longer a rare sign of excellence.

Chapter summary

_i_ Further resources

S. Gibbons and O. Silva, *Faith Schools: Better Schools or Better Pupils*, 2007, from http://cee.lse.ac.uk

D. Gillborn and D. Youdell, *Rationing Education: Policy, Practice, Reform, and Equity*, Open University Press, 2000

- The education system of England and Wales has developed significantly over the past 150 years.

- Key reforms included the 1870 Act (primary education), the 1944 Act (secondary education organised by ability), comprehensivisation (admission by location), the 1988 Act (marketisation and parental choice) and reforms enacted under New Labour.

- A number of debates have been sparked by these reforms.

- The most fundamental is over how children are assigned to schools (or admissions policy). Selection by religion, ability, location and parental choice have all been used – each with its own strengths and controversies.

- A further debate is over the extent of involvement of non-governmental agencies in education. In particular, the place of religion, private schools and businesses in education provision has been a controversial debate.

- Vocational education and training (i.e. education for work) has been an increasingly important area of policy. However, like all reforms it has raised a number of debates.

- The nature, extent and social make-up of the post-compulsory sector has also been an area of considerable contemporary argument.

Research methods in the context of education

Types of research methods

Learning objective:

- Examine some of the methods used by sociologists when studying education.

AQA Examiner's tip

The AQA AS examination includes questions about research methods in the context of education.

Key terms

Longitudinal surveys: surveys that are repeated at intervals over a period of time, to track changes that may be taking place.

Quantitative: research that concentrates on collecting statistical data.

Objective: this has two meanings. It can refer to 'facts' that exist independently of the observer, or it can refer to a researcher being free of bias.

Response rates: the percentage of the sample who return completed questionnaires.

Qualitative: research where the sociologist aims to understand the meaning of social action.

Participant: anyone who takes part in research. Some researchers use the term 'subject', but 'participant' is preferable because it suggests that the person is an equal in the process rather than an inferior.

Types of research methods

In order to properly understand the nature and limitations of the research referenced in this topic, it is fitting to end with a brief exploration of the types of methodology used in sociological research.

Surveys

A survey is a broad name for any type of research that seeks to study a large and representative sample, usually by asking questions. Surveys can use a range of different methods, including structured interviews or, most commonly, questionnaires. They are used to discover patterns and extents – of achievement, beliefs, actions and opinions – and can be cross-sectional or **longitudinal**. Because of the large amounts of information generated, these approaches tend to be **quantitative**: a more practical approach when dealing with large amounts of data in an **objective** way. Quantitative data has its limitations, however, and, most notably, surveys lack depth and detail of insight.

As such, these forms of method are used to demonstrate broad overviews of *what* is happening in education – whilst other methods are used to explain *why*.

Questionnaires

Many surveys are based on a questionnaire. As they can be administered and analysed with relative ease, questionnaires offer a way of gauging the extent of belief, action and opinion amongst teachers, parents and students. When sent by post, their anonymity is also useful, as it may lead to more honest responses. However, as with any method, questionnaires can have problems. They rely on reading and writing, and the less literate may therefore be omitted from data (a crucial error in the context of educational research). Furthermore, they suffer from low **response rates**, which might bias samples – and limit the depth of understanding gained.

Interviews

Like questionnaires, interviews are a 'question-asking' method of research: however, they tend to be face to face rather than paper-based. The amount of structure involved in an interview varies, from being entirely open-ended to having pre-set questions and answers. As a consequence, interviews can be used to generate either **qualitative** or quantitative data. Used properly, they are a powerful research tool, giving a means of understanding how people think. Furthermore, they are flexible and can take the research in unforeseen, but crucial, directions. However, researchers using the method must be careful – not least because what people say they do is not necessarily how they behave. In conducting interviews, researchers must also be careful not to lead **participants** to give particular answers – through leading questions, body language, tone of voice and so on.

Ethnographic methods

Where surveys tend to focus on broad, generalisable understandings, **ethnographic research** methods attempt to form a focused insight of a particular group or way of life. They have long been a favourite of interpretivist sociologists for their rich and detailed qualitative data. The depth of understanding produced can also make them far better than their quantitative counterparts in understanding the underlying reasons for people's behaviour. In general, however, this type of data suffers from common problems. Accusations of subjectivity blight qualitative studies as they rely heavily on interpretations made by researchers. Furthermore, the time taken to conduct this form of study limits the number of cases covered.

Research using ethnographic approaches tends, therefore, to give detailed insights into *why* particular **social phenomena** occur, seen from the standpoint of the 'actors' involved. However, such research lacks breadth and representativeness – and thus only limited generalisations can be drawn.

Observation

Ethnographic researchers have drawn heavily on observation in studying groups and interactions within schools. The approach has enabled them to directly observe behaviour within the school and has been important, for example, in understanding differential treatment by teachers. However, while this data is useful, participants tend not to act 'normally' when they know they are being observed. Furthermore, the researcher has to interpret the reasons behind behaviour – and observations are therefore often combined with interviews.

Participant observation

Some researchers have used **participant observation** to understand how it feels to be part of a student group. This can offer rich insiders' understandings of the focus of study, allowing the researcher to actually experience what if feels like to be a member of a particular group. Generally, however, this approach tends to be overt, due to the distinct ethical and practical problems of infiltrating groups in educational contexts and conducting covert research. Such an approach raises problems, however, as participants who are aware of the observer's presence may not act naturally. Furthermore, all observations require an outsider to 'make sense' of what they observe – intensifying issues of subjectivity. Sometimes, this is avoided by using interviews to test interpretations and theories.

Non-participant observation

Given the practical and ethical problems of conducting participant observation in schools, it is more common for sociologists interested in education to draw on non-participant forms of the method. This approach is far more ethical and practical – and brings with it the benefit of maintaining critical distance, thus improving **validity**. However, the researcher consequently sacrifices some of the insider closeness of participant observation.

Experiments

Experiments are rarely used in sociological research, but there are exceptions in the study of education (e.g. Rosenthal and Jacobson, 1968; Goddard-Spear, 1984). This is possibly because the school presents a 'sealed environment' in which variables can be manipulated far more easily than in other social contexts. Whilst this form of field experiment lacks the control, precision

Links

A more detailed exploration of survey-related methods can be found on p303.

Kirkland Rowell's study (p156) uses a large sample to ensure that findings are representative. As such, it is possible to more confidentially make generalisations from their findings.

For an example, see Kirkland Rowell's study (p156) and Callender and Jackson (p168).

Key terms

Ethnographic research: ethnographic means 'writing about a way of life'. Various methods can be used, but the most common one is participant observation.

Social phenomena: a social fact or situation that is observed to exist or happen.

Participant observation: observation where the researcher joins in the life of the group being studied.

Validity: actually supporting the intended point or claim.

Links

For examples of interviews used in educational research see Osler and Starkey (p134), Hargreaves *et al.* (p138 and p140), Hey (p140), Bernstein (p146), Labov (p149), Becker (p150), Sewell (p151), Myhill and Jones (p156) and Gewirtz *et al.* (p163).

See pp138–9 for more information on interpretivist approaches to education.

A more detailed exploration of ethnographic methods can be found on p238.

For an example of overt participant observation see Hey (p140).

Education

■ Key terms

Cause and effect: a term borrowed from research in the natural sciences field. Investigating cause and effect means trying to discover whether two seemingly linked factors are in fact a 'cause' and an 'effect', whether there might be other factors involved, or whether the link is coincidental.

Secondary data: data collected by others and used by the researcher.

Official statistics: statistical data that has been collected by the government or its agencies.

■ Links

For examples of observational research, see Hargreaves *et al.* (p138), Hey (p140) and Sewell (p151).

A more detailed exploration of secondary data can be found on p248.

Revisit pp139, 153 and 157 to see in context the use of official statistics in the sociology of education.

For examples of this type of research see Hey (p140).

and certainty offered by truly scientific laboratory experiments, they can begin to test claims about **cause and effect**. However, they also possess important limitations, not least that manipulating the school environment raises distinct ethical problems relating to deception and harm.

■ Secondary data

In studying education, researchers do not always generate their own data – drawing instead on the wealth of pre-existing sources, known as **secondary data**. Some of these sources are quantitative, and support the aims of survey-type research; others are qualitative, and give more ethnographic types of insight.

Official statistics

The **official statistics** published by the government are of crucial importance to educational researchers: particularly those relating to test and exam results, exclusions, and participation in further and higher education. Most importantly, it is this data that enables researchers to identify patterns of underachievement. As this data is collected centrally and regularly, it gives an overview of the attainment of the vast majority of students, and a sense of trends and changes over time.

Sociologists cannot, however, simply accept this data at 'face value'; there are many ways in which it can be distorted. Governments may, for instance, manipulate data to make themselves look good, while schools may 'work the system' to improve their position in league tables. Furthermore, the way results are recorded has changed over time – and this can make comparisons problematic.

Reports, books and personal documents

Finally, some sociologists have made use of a range of documents in studying education. The most obvious of these is analysis of exercise books and school reports. Some researchers have, however, taken a much more eclectic approach, making use of the vast array of 'incidental data' generated throughout the school (for instance, notes passed in class). The strength here is that such documents can offer a vivid and unusual insight into the social realities of teachers and students – in a way that even interviews cannot touch. Furthermore, as the documents occur naturally, there is little risk of them being distorted by the research process. However, it is often important to couple such data with more conventional research (such as interviews); otherwise subjectivity might be amplified by a lack of understanding of the context in which the documents were produced.

■ Summary questions

1. Give a strength and a limitation of the use of survey-type research in educational research.

2. Identify a strength and a weakness with postal questionnaires.

3. Outline one positive and one negative aspect of interviews.

4. Give two problems in using covert participant observation in educational research.

5. Give two problems in using overt non-participant observation in educational research.

6. Suggest two ways in which secondary sources might be used in educational research.

Chapter summary

 Further resources

www.statistics.gov.uk – The website of the National Office for Statistics, the government department responsible for collecting and publishing official statistics about the UK's society and economy.

www.ucas.ac.uk – UCAS is the central organisation that processes applications for full-time undergraduate courses at UK universities and colleges.

- Sociologists utilise a range of different research methods to study education.

- In using survey-type approaches, researchers aim to pinpoint extents and ranges of opinions, actions and beliefs.

- Both questionnaires and interviews interrogate what people think and do.

- Ethnographic approaches aim to achieve more focused insights into the experiences and processes surrounding particular groups in education.

- Here, methods such as participant and non-participant observation are crucial – though the latter is used more frequently in educational research.

- Sociologists also draw on secondary sources in studying education.

- Official statistics are used to establish patterns of achievement and under-achievement in schools.

- Personal documents – such as school reports – are used to support ethnographic research.

Education

AQA Examination-style questions

1A Read Item 1(a) below and answer parts (i) to (iv) that follow.

(a) According to some sociologists, many working-class children are disadvantaged by their early experiences. Studies of pre-school socialisation show important differences between social classes that contribute to differences in educational achievement. Some working-class parents have lower expectations of their children, place less emphasis on constant improvement and do not reward success systematically. Working-class homes, with fewer books and educational toys, may provide a less stimulating learning environment. Similarly, some working-class children are not taught to use the elaborated speech code used both by middle-class families and by the school.

The government considers these factors so important that it has sought to intervene. For example, Sure Start involves over 500 local programmes in deprived areas, working with disadvantaged families to promote young children's intellectual, linguistic and social development so that they are in a position to do well when they start school.

(i) Explain what is meant by the term self-fulfilling prophecy. *(2 marks)*

(ii) Suggest three functions that education may perform for individuals and/or society. *(6 marks)*

(iii) Outline some of the reasons for the educational under-achievement of boys. *(12 marks)*

(iv) Using material from Item 1A and elsewhere assess the view that working-class under-achievement in education is the result of home circumstances and family background. *(20 marks)*

B This question requires you to apply your knowledge and understanding of sociological research methods to the study of this particular issue in education.

Read Item 1(b) below and answer the question that follow.

(b) Investigating gender and subject choice

Sociologists have been interested in finding out how far there is a link between gender and the subjects pupils choose to study. For example, Stables and Wikely (1996) investigated the patterns of subject choice, looking to identify which subjects are more likely to be chosen by girls and which by boys.

Researchers have wanted to find out the reasons behind these patterns. They have researched the effect that peer group pressure might have on choice and to what extent teacher expectations channel boys and girls into different subjects. Others have investigated the reasons why some subjects are perceived as being masculine whilst others are seen as feminine.

Using material from Item 1B and elsewhere, assess the strengths and limitations of one of the following methods for the study of gender and subject choice:

(i) unstructured interviews

(ii) official statistics. *(20 marks)*

AQA specimen question

C This question permits you to draw examples from any areas of sociology with which you are familiar.

(i) Explain what is meant by the term 'closed question'. *(2 marks)*

(ii) Suggest two ethical factors that may arise in relation to participant observation. *(4 marks)*

(iii) Suggest two strengths of the use of quantitative methods in sociological research. *(4 marks)*

(iv) Examine the debate between positivist and interpretivist approaches to sociological research. *(20 marks)*

2A Read Item 2(a) and 2(b) below and answer parts (i) to (iv) that follow.

(a) Marxist sociologists believe that the primary role of education is simply to reproduce the existing class system. However, they disagree as to how this occurs. For example, Bowles and Gintis believe that it is the product of the hidden curriculum and the correspondence principle, namely that schooling in capitalist society mirrors the world of work. By contrast, Paul Willis believes that working-class pupils end up in working-class jobs because they actively reject the values of the school.

Another Marxist, Pierre Bourdieu, argued that reproduction occurs because the middle class possess cultural capital, which they are able to turn into educational success because schools are themselves middle-class institutions. Although Bourdieu can be described as a Marxist, there are similarities with Bernstein's ideas about the role of restricted and elaborated speech codes in producing unequal educational achievement.

(b) According to Tony Sewell (1998), one reason for the under-achievement of black boys is labelling by teachers who hold racist stereotypes of the 'black macho lad'. According to this stereotype, all black boys are anti-school and resentful of authority. Teachers see them as not equipped to learn and they leave school with few qualifications. However, Sewell found that only a small minority of black boys in fact belonged to such a 'rebel' subculture. Most either accepted the school's goals, or were opposed to the school but still wanted to achieve.

Sewell also argues that factors outside school play a part in under-achievement. These include the absence of fathers in some black families and the image of the ultra-tough ghetto superstar put forward as a role model by commercial youth culture.

(i) Explain what is meant by 'cultural capital' (Item 2A). *(2 marks)*

(ii) Suggest three criticisms that could be made of Marxist views of education (Item 2A). *(6 marks)*

(iii) Outline the different functions that the educational system may perform for individuals in society. *(12 marks)*

(iv) Using material from Item 1B and elsewhere, assess sociological explanations of ethnic differences in educational achievement. *(20 marks)*

AQA, 2006

B This question requires you to apply your knowledge and understanding of sociological research methods to the study of this particular issue in education.

Read Item 2(c) below and answer the questions that follow.

(c) Investigating material deprivation and educational achievement

Some sociologists are interested in the effect of material deprivation on educational achievement. For example, Callender and Jackson (2005) investigated whether poor students were less likely to go to university because of the prospect of getting into debt. Harker (2006) reviewed evidence commissioned by the housing charity Shelter to look at the links between housing and academic attainment. She found that poor housing had negative effects on many levels.

Adapted from Education Chapters 3 and 5 of this textbook

Using material from Item 2(c) and elsewhere, assess the strengths and limitations of one of the following methods for the study of educational achievement and material deprivation:

(i) Questionnaires

(ii) Interviews *(20 marks)*

C This question permits you to draw examples from any areas of sociology with which you are familiar.

(i) Explain what is meant by a 'pilot study'. *(2 marks)*

(ii) Suggest two factors that may influence a sociologist's 'choice of topic to be investigated'. *(4 marks)*

(iii) 'media reports' in their research. *(4 marks)*

(iv) Assess the usefulness of official statistics in sociological research. *(20 marks)*

AQA, 2006

Health

Introduction

Health is important to all of us. We would all like to have good physical and mental health, and are increasingly encouraged to look after our health by making the correct 'lifestyle choices'. The media constantly shows us what we should and should not be eating, how much we should exercise, the latest diet fad and why we should not smoke or drink.

Sociologists are interested in how health is not just about individual responsibility, but also how health and illness link to the wider social structure: in particular, areas such social class, gender, ethnicity and age. Certain groups experience higher levels of health and better treatment than others, and sociologists are concerned with finding out the reasons why, and if anything could or should be done to make the provision of health care fairer.

A number of important areas have emerged in the sociology of health:

- Sociologists are interested in competing definitions of health, illness and disability. Two main models are explored – the biomedical and the social models – which see health, illness and disability in very different ways.

- A relatively recent and growing area of interest is the sociology of the body. This concerns how the body has been viewed differently throughout history, and how and why body image has become so important today.

- Sociologists are concerned with how health and illness link to social class, gender, ethnicity and age. Key areas of concern are levels of health and illness within these groups, as well as access to health care services.

- Mental illness has been approached in a number of different ways by sociologists and psychologists, and there is much disagreement as to what constitutes mental illness and even whether it exists at all in the same way as a physical illness.

- The role of medicine and the health professions interests sociologists in terms of the power of doctors, doctor–patient relationships and the rise of alternative medicine.

Health awareness has never been so topical. The National Health Service (NHS) is always in the news, and is often portrayed in a critical way. Key questions are being asked about resources and funding, particularly with regard to an ageing population. Ethical questions are being asked and dilemmas faced about hot topics such as abortion, euthanasia, cloning, drug treatments and testing. Despite a free NHS, major inequalities remain. The sociology of health may not be able to provide all the answers to issues such as these and others, but it can certainly raise some very interesting questions.

Health

Health and illness

Learning objectives:

- Understand how difficult it is to define health and illness.

- Understand the medical model of health.

- Understand the social model of health.

Fig. 5.1 *Medical treatment, such as surgery or medication, is used to 'fix' the body where possible*

💡 Hint

It is a good idea to write out all of the key terms on small cards and to keep looking over them and learning them throughout the year.

Link

The medical model of health is explored in more detail on pp206–7.

AQA Examiner's tip

It is important to present as balanced an argument as possible. Words and phrases like 'however', 'on the other hand' and 'it could also be argued' should feature heavily in essay questions. There is never just one view of an issue in sociology.

💡 According to the World Health Organization, health is 'not merely the absence of disease and infirmity, but complete physical, mental and social well-being'. However, it is debatable whether any of us ever feel 'complete well-being', so by this rather broad definition, none of us is completely healthy. Other definitions of health tend to be narrower and may focus on lack of obvious illness or disease to indicate health. It is clear to sociologists that health and illness mean different things to different people, and that their meaning changes over time and place: they are, therefore, social constructs.

In the UK, for example, whether or not you feel in 'good health' will depend upon your own definition of health, which may be influenced by your class, gender, ethnicity or age. Some people will take the day off work because they are 'feeling ill', whilst others with a similar level of objectively measurable 'illness' (for example, a raised temperature) will go to work.

The medical model of health

The medical model (sometimes called the biomedical model) defines health in terms of the absence of disease, with ill-health arising from biological or physical causes. People feel ill, see their doctor and are treated with medicines such as antibiotics. Sometimes treatment will take place in a hospital with other medicines or surgery. The human body is seen as a machine that sometimes needs repairing. If a complete fix is not possible, then it is the job of medicine to prolong life and make the person as comfortable as possible.

The social model of health

The social model challenges the medical model by placing a stronger emphasis on the social causes of health and illness, which include poverty, unemployment, living conditions and the work environment. This model also looks at how health differs according to social class, gender, ethnicity and age.

The social model is also often critical of doctors, who are seen as having too much power in classifying someone as ill and then treating them with medicine, provided by powerful drug companies. Doctors do not usually consider alternative therapies, which may be better at dealing with the social causes of ill health.

However, it is possible to be too critical of the medical model of health. It is clear that medicine has contributed to improvements in health and that most doctors are 'on the side' of the patients. Also doctors themselves are increasingly aware of alternative therapies and may even recommend them.

Summary questions

1. What is meant by the term 'social construct'?
2. Why are health and illness social constructs?
3. What is the medical model of health?
4. What is the social model of health?

Disability

Learning objectives:

- Explore the history of disability.
- Understand the medical model of disability.
- Understand the social model of disability.

When thinking about disability, the image of someone in a wheelchair might come to mind, or an elderly person with a stick. They are disabled because they were born that way, or had an accident, or because they are old. Some people may even be embarrassed by them and would rather keep them at a distance, for example in a school for children with 'special needs' or a care home for the elderly.

This marginalisation of the disabled in society reflects the marginalisation of disability as a topic within sociology. It is only recently that the sociology of disability has emerged, and one of the reasons for the growing interest is the actions of the disabled themselves, who have become increasingly vocal about discrimination and prejudice in society in the same way that minority ethnic groups and women have done in the past.

The history of disability

Finkelstein (1980) argues that disability is the product of capitalist society. Before capitalism became established, people with disabilities were not segregated from the population or seen as a separate group with 'special needs'. They eked out a living by begging and doing agricultural work, and were looked after within their families. With the development of factories though, people with disabilities became more 'visible' and were seen as a social and medical problem that needed taking care of. In Victorian Britain this 'care' involved placing them into institutions alongside the mentally ill, old and poor. Conditions and care standards were very poor. By the mid-20th century, the focus had shifted to trying to 'cure' disability as much as possible, and people with disabilities had become a group separated from mainstream society and treated differently. Someone's disability now became their **master status** and they became 'less' of a person because it was difficult to 'see beyond' the disability.

> ### Key term
>
> **Master status:** if you are labelled as a criminal, prostitute or mental patient, this overrides any other status you have such as parent, neighbour or citizen.

Models of disability

There are two main models that have influenced modern thinking about disability: the medical model and the social model.

The medical model

In the medical model, people with disabilities are seen as the 'problem' that needs to be helped or cured. They need to adapt to society around them and fit in as best they can. There is no suggestion that society needs to change. This model reflects the World Health Organization definition of disability, and is the model most widely used by those in the caring professions.

The medical model promotes the view of people with disabilities as dependent and justifies their exclusion from society. In this model power rests with health care professionals rather than the people with disabilities. Medical diagnoses of disability are used to regulate and control access to welfare benefits, housing, education, employment and leisure. People with disabilities are disempowered in this model, which has led to it being increasingly rejected by people with disabilities themselves, in favour of the social model.

The social model

The social model has largely been developed by disabled people themselves. In this model disability is caused by the barriers that exist within society, which discriminates against those with disabilities. One of the most important writers in this area is the sociologist Tom Shakespeare (1998), who argues that disability should be seen as a social construct: a problem created by the attitudes of society and not by the physical state of the body. Shakespeare argues that disability is created by societies that do not take into account the needs of those who do not fit in with society's ideas of what is normal.

For Shakespeare, rather than using the term 'disability' or 'disabled', a better word to use is 'impairment'. This would refer to the loss of function of a part of the body. People only have disabilities if society treats them as second-class citizens and makes it harder for them to function normally. People who are short-sighted are not seen as 'disabled' as they can wear lenses or glasses, and in the same way public transport and buildings can be constructed to enable physically impaired people to operate alongside everyone else. For Shakespeare, having an impairment is to be different but not abnormal, and disability only exists because of the prejudice and discrimination that exists in society against people with impairments.

Clearly, the meaning of the word 'disabled' differs according to whether you are using the medical model or the social model. In a similar way, the term 'disabled person' can mean 'someone with physical or mental disabilities' (medical model) or someone 'disabled' by the prejudicial attitudes of society to their physical or mental impairments (social model).

The social model of disability focuses on the many barriers that still exist in areas such as education, the workplace, transport and housing. It also looks at the portrayal of the disabled in the media. Within this model much campaigning work is carried out, and this model of disability is increasingly changing the way disability is seen, at least in the developed world. It has also had a major impact on anti-discriminatory legislation such as the Disability Discrimination Act 2004. Under the terms of this Act, businesses, including offices and shops, have to make reasonable adjustments so they do not discriminate against disabled customers or employees.

Summary questions

5 What is meant by the 'marginalisation' of people with disabilities?

6 What does Finkelstein argue?

7 What does Shakespeare mean about disability being a social construct?

8 Suggest three 'reasonable adjustments' that a shop could make to avoid discriminating against people with disabilities.

Fig. 5.2 *The media portrayal of disability is slowly changing for the better*

Health

The sociology of the body

Learning objectives:

- Understand how perceptions of the body have changed throughout history.
- Consider the causes of eating disorders.
- Evaluate feminist perspectives on the body.

The 'sociology of the body' is a new area in sociology, and one where much work remains to be done. The focus is on how something as seemingly individual and 'given' as your own body is influenced by attitudes and pressures in the wider society. In the same way that health, illness and disability are social constructs, so is the body. Attitudes to the body have changed over time and between cultures, and the body is increasingly taking centre stage in society. All of us are increasingly judged on how we look, and whether or not we look after our bodies with the 'correct' diet and exercise programmes.

The sociology of the body has recently become more important for a number of reasons, including:

- Society is now far more concerned with the importance of having a healthy body, and people are more aware of how this is linked to diet, exercise, alcohol and smoking.
- Plastic surgery is increasingly available and affordable: if you have not got the body or face you want, why not improve it!
- Debates about reproduction (frozen embryos), abortion and euthanasia all focus on the body. The latter, for example, focuses on who has the right to end life – the individual, doctors or the state.
- Feminism has raised the profile of this area of sociology by focusing on the negative effects the mass media has on women in particular.

Body image

Central to the sociology of the body is the idea of body image, i.e. what should we look like. Increasingly this is not down to individual choice but rather down to what is acceptable in society. It is women who often face the greatest pressure to have the 'perfect body', but what this comprises has varied according to time and place.

The body throughout history

In the Western world today, people are expected to be slim. Diet programmes and exercise regimes generate millions of pounds and are endorsed by celebrities and organisations such as WeightWatchers, which exist to help people – particularly women – reach their perfect size. However, thinness has not always been seen as desirable – mainly because it was associated with lack of food and poverty, as it still is in many developing nations. A glance at paintings in an art gallery shows that women in the past were often far more 'rounded' than most women today. The idea of 'slimness' as the ideal female shape originated among the middle class in the late 19th century, and it has taken hold ever since.

Eating disorders

The current strong social focus on body image is thought to be linked with the increasing prevalence of eating disorders. Anorexia, the most commonly known disorder, is generally (although not always) a Western disease. In the developing world, when people starve to death, it is through lack of food. Contrastingly, people in the Western world with eating disorders starve to death despite there being plenty of food available.

Health

Anorexia is an illness influenced by social factors and pressures, in particular the media. Hollywood movie stars and popstars are, on the whole, extremely slim. It is no surprise that some 20 per cent of women in Britain experience eating disorders at some point in their lives as they try to emulate the rich and famous. Research shows that over 60 per cent of girls aged 13 have already begun to diet, showing an unhealthy interest in food and their bodies at a very young age. Most will not go on to develop eating disorders, but some will, and the numbers are increasing.

Bulimia, bingeing on food followed by self-induced vomiting, has also become increasingly common among young women. Anorexia and bulimia are often to be found in the same individual.

Causes of eating disorders

The causes are many, complex and multidimensional: each person will have been affected by a different range of factors, possibly including the following:

Social/cultural causes

Sociologists are obviously most concerned with this explanation, which focuses on the role of the mass media in constantly equating thinness with attractiveness. Much of the media present the ideal woman as ultra thin, and women respond by trying to copy that vision. Naomi Wolf, a radical feminist discussed below, calls this 'the beauty myth'.

Biological causes

Some studies have suggested that eating disorders are genetically based. Others have looked at the role of serotonin, a brain chemical, which may make the individual withdraw socially and have less desire for food.

Psychological/emotional causes

Some research has linked various personality traits, such as perfectionism, obsessiveness and low self-esteem, to eating disorders. Other links have been made to overprotective parents, traumatic life events and physical or sexual abuse.

However, it is not just Western girls who suffer from eating disorders.

Research has shown that eating disorders are not solely a Western problem. Bennet, Sharpe, Freeman *et al* (2004) investigated whether anorexic existed in a culture where it is not perceived as socially desirable to be thin. They screened 668 female secondary school students in Ghana for their body mass index (BMI) and found that 10 had low weight due to self-starvation. Their reasons for this included religious fasting and enjoying the self-control and denial of hunger.

The area of eating disorders and body image is a complex one, and to focus on blaming one factor alone, such as the media, may not be helpful. It should also be noted that 10 per cent of all those suffering from eating disorders are men, and the number is increasing as men, too, become increasingly concerned with appearance.

■ Feminist perspectives on the body

The key writer in this area is Naomi Wolf, who wrote a book called *The Beauty Myth: How Images of Beauty Are Used against Women* (1991). Wolf, a **radical feminist**, argues that as women have become more successful in all aspects of society, the 'myth' of female beauty is used to control them and 'put them in their place'.

■ Hint

The BBC News website is a particularly useful and up-to-date source of information for sociology students.

■ Key term

Radical feminism: a type of feminism that focuses on how men oppress and control women.

5.1 Health, illness and disability

Women are bombarded by the media with images of the 'perfect' woman. Society judges women, and women judge themselves, against this standard. Wolf calls this 'beauty pornography'. By this she means that the media portrayal of women is a deception, which causes women to spend too much time and money worrying about beauty: if you do not look as skinny as the fashion models, starve or exercise; if your breasts are too small, get implants; if your thighs are too fat, get a doctor to stick a vacuum cleaner under your skin and suck the fat out! Wolf says that women should be judged, and should judge themselves, in ways which focus on other qualities and values, not just ones to do with a socially constructed beauty myth.

The most dangerous aspect though for Wolf is in the realm of women's health. The beauty myth is responsible for the obsession with dieting and the resulting eating disorders that are doing such damage to women. For Wolf, it is no coincidence that incidents of anorexia and bulimia have increased as advertising and the media generally have become more influential in our lives.

AQA Examiner's tip

It is a good idea to get into the habit of using an internet search engine to find out more about the areas that interest you. Try typing 'Naomi Wolf' into a search engine and you will see a range of articles both supporting her ideas and challenging them.

Summary questions

9 What does the sociology of the body focus on?

10 Suggest two reasons why interest in this area has grown in recent years.

11 Suggest three possible causes of eating disorders.

Health

Chapter summary

Further resources

Tom Shakespeare, *Disability Rights and Wrongs*, Routledge, 2006

www. bcodp.otg.uk – The British Council of Disabled people (BCODP) is an umbrella organisation for groups controlled by disabled people.

www.disabledparentsnetwork.org.uk – A UK-based organisation of disabled people who are parents or who hope to be parents.

www.edauk.com – Information and help on all aspects of eating disorders from an eating disorder charity.

My Left Foot (1989) – A film adapted from the book about the Irish artist and author Christy Brown whose cerebral palsy kept him confined to a wheelchair.

Born on the Fourth of July (1989) – A film based on the true story of an American, Ron Kovic, paralysed in the Vietnam war.

Notting Hill (1999) – A film in which disability is a minor theme, but useful as the disabled character is not treated in a patronising way.

Inside I'm Dancing (2004) – A film about two young men with disabilities who fight the system to try and live independent lives.

Murderball (2005) – A film about the little-known sport of quadriplegic rugby (murderball) played by those with some form of physical impairment in all four limbs.

- Health and illness are difficult concepts to define.
- Sociologists argue that health, illness, disability and the body are social constructs.
- The medical model of health focuses on biological causes of ill-health.
- The social model of health focuses on social causes of ill-health.
- Attitudes to disability have changed over time.
- Some sociologists prefer the term impairment to disability.
- As more focus is placed on the body, eating disorders increase.

Key terms

Morbidity: a term that refers to statistics about illness. It is usually measured by the number of hospital admissions, time taken off work sick and self-reported illness from health surveys.

Mortality: a term that refers to statistics about death. The mortality rate is the number of deaths per thousand of the population per year.

In the UK, your chances of becoming sick (**morbidity**) and even of dying (**mortality**) are not random. They are directly linked to several factors, including social class, gender, ethnicity and age. On average, the higher your social class, the healthier you will be. Even your chance of surviving the first year of life is linked to social class. The infant mortality rate for a child born to the poorest parents is very much higher than that of a child born to professional parents.

Although falling, infant deaths are 50 per cent more common among those from manual backgrounds than among those from non-manual backgrounds.

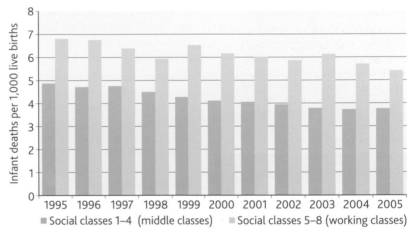

Fig. 5.3 *Infant mortality rates in the UK are significantly higher for the lower social classes*

Those of a higher social class are also less likely to die of conditions such as heart disease, strokes and lung cancer. They also live longer. The only exception to this trend is malignant melanoma (skin cancer caused by the sun), where holidays in sunnier climates are possibly the culprit.

The Black report

The first major study in the area, the Black report (1980) divided the population into five social classes and examined the health differences between each. The report showed that despite a free NHS for more than 30 years, a clear health gap existed between the working and middle classes. It also showed that in many ways the gap was worse in Britain than in many other European countries. It is strongly believed by some that the government tried to repress the findings of this report, producing few copies in the hope nobody would notice. A further study carried out 18 years later, the Acheson report (1998), again showed a clear health gap between the classes. Other smaller studies since then merely confirm these findings.

The Black report suggested four possible reasons for the differences in health between the social classes, and these headings are still used in most studies and reports on health and social class today.

Health

Hint

Any 'rate', such as the infant mortality rate, is always per thousand per year, whether it is referring to marriages, divorces or deaths.

Hint

It is important to avoid stereotyping in areas such as this. There may be different overall patterns of eating, smoking and exercising between the social classes, but not all working-class people eat fried food constantly, and not all middle-class people spend their spare time in a gym and eat healthily.

Link

Another reason the working class have poorer health – access to health care – is discussed on p191. This considers the argument that working-class people go to the doctor less often than the middle class, and even when they do see a doctor are likely to receive less time and attention.

Fig. 5.4 *Lifestyle changes, such as giving up smoking or drinking, can promote better health in individuals*

Summary questions

1. What is the name of the first major study in the area of social class and health?

2. What are meant by the terms morbidity and mortality?

3. What are the four reasons given for the differences in health between the social classes?

The artefact approach

The view that although it appears that people in the lowest social class (unskilled workers) have the poorest health, this is misleading. The lowest social class is such a small and declining group, that to compare it to other social classes is pointless. However, other reports have combined the bottom two social classes to create a larger working class, which can then be effectively compared to the middle class. The health gap is then clearly visible and even growing.

Theories of natural and social selection

This is the view that your social class does not influence your health; rather, your health influences what social class you end up in. In other words, if you are in the lowest social class it could be because ill-health prevents you from holding onto a middle-class job.

Behavioural/cultural explanations

This is the view that individual lifestyle is the greatest factor in health. If you are ill, it may well be linked to four key areas: smoking, drinking, diet or exercise.

All of the evidence suggests that the working class are more likely to smoke and drink heavily (especially men). They also eat less in the way of fruit and vegetables, and eat more food that is higher in fat, sugar and salt. They also exercise less. This approach tends to blame the working class for their higher rates of morbidity and mortality, and argues that the middle class simply have a healthier lifestyle.

However, there are many criticisms of this view. The Black report itself felt that material factors were more important than cultural ones. One further criticism is that although smoking, for example, is clearly a harmful activity, it seems to harm the working-class smoker more than the middle-class smoker! A study by Marmot *et al.* (1978) of civil servants showed that those who smoked in the lower grades were more likely to die of smoking-related illnesses than those who smoked in the higher grades, so it appears that other factors are at play here.

Another objection is that smoking and drinking heavily may well be caused by working-class employment conditions, which are more likely to lead to stress, anxiety and depression. In other words, it is no good telling someone to stop smoking or drinking if their poor conditions of work encourage them to take refuge in these habits.

Materialistic/structural factors

This is the view that the working class suffers worse health than the middle class because of lack of money, poor housing, dangerous or unhealthy working conditions, and living in run down and unhealthy areas. This is a different approach from the cultural one, which tends to blame people for being ill. The materialistic approach is in a way seeing the working class as victims of an unfair society: if they are ill, it is not their fault, rather it is the fault of other factors, such as:

■ Low income, which could lead to a poorer diet because fresh food can be more expensive than unhealthier processed food. Lack of money could also discourage the taking of exercise.

■ Poor housing, which could result in cold, damp living conditions, leading to a greater chance of contracting illnesses such as asthma, bronchitis and pneumonia.

■ Poor working conditions, which could lead to a greater likelihood of injury or even death in the workplace. Working-class work environments, like factories and building sites, are more dangerous than middle-class environments, like offices, banks and schools.

Gender

Learning objectives:

- Understand the reasons why women may suffer from more illness than men.

- Understand the reasons why women live longer than men.

Key term

Triple shift: a feminist concept that argues that many women today have three responsibilities. They have paid jobs, do the bulk of the housework and childcare, and deal with the emotional issues in the family.

Links

See p201 for more on gender and the link to mental illness.

This area links to the sociology of the family: the triple shift is a key concept within the area called the sociology of housework/domestic labour debate (p81). The triple shift is also mentioned on p201, in the context of gender and mental illness.

AQA Examiner's tip

In an exam question, you should not say things like 'All men die before women' because this is clearly not true. Words like 'on average' and 'most of the time' should be used instead.

Why do women suffer from more illness than men?

Women live longer than men. Average female life expectancy is 81 and average male life expectancy is just 76. Almost two-thirds of all deaths before the age of 65 are male. However, women are more likely to visit the doctor, go to hospital, have operations, and have days off sick from work. They also take more medication and are more likely to say that they suffer from a whole range of conditions, from headaches to depression. The question for sociologists is whether women really are sicker than men, or whether they are simply more likely to seek help.

Stress

Many feminists have argued that women suffer from the **triple shift**. This means that they are responsible for paid work, housework/childcare, and dealing with the emotional issues within the family. It is thought that the triple shift can cause women to suffer from emotional problems such as stress, depression and anxiety because they are doing too much without enough support from their partner. One often over looked pressure is the challenge of raising of young children. With increased geographical mobility, many mothers lack the support of the extended family and this, combined with the 24/7 demands of a young child, can lead to both physical and mental health problems.

Poverty

Women are more likely to experience poverty than men because of single parenthood, earning less money and having a worse pension. Poverty is linked to ill-health because it can lead to a lack of healthy food, living in a cold, damp house and lack of money for exercise.

Why do women live longer than men?

However, on average women still live longer than men. There are various reasons suggested for this, including the fact that they are more likely to seek medical help. Men tend to drink and smoke more, and exercise less – women are also far more aware of health issues and areas such as healthy eating. Men's lives tend to be more hazardous than women's and their occupations, such as construction work or factory work, can be more dangerous. Men also drive faster, play more dangerous sports, and take more risks generally, as well as working longer and more unsociable hours, and being more likely to do overtime and shift work. This can lead to stress and depression, which in turn can link to excess drinking and smoking.

Health

Summary questions

4 How many years, on average, do women live longer than men?

5 List three differences in health between men and women.

6 What two reasons are suggested for why women may suffer from more illness than men?

7 Give three reasons why women generally live longer than men.

Ethnicity

Fig. 5.5 *Some minority ethnic groups are more likely to live in run-down areas, which can be another factor in ill-health*

Summary questions

8 Who conducted the first major study in this area?

9 Name two differences in the health of minority ethnic groups compared to white people.

10 Give four reasons for the differences.

Health differences between ethnic groups

There is less information available on the link between health and ethnicity than for other areas and therefore findings need to be treated with caution. However, in 1997, one major study was conducted in this area by James Nazroo, which found a number of interesting things. Compared to the white majority ethnic group:

■ Those from Indian and Pakistani backgrounds suffer from more heart disease, with death rates around 40 per cent higher than the national average.

■ Deaths from strokes for those born in the Caribbean and India are about twice the national average.

■ Most minority ethnic groups have a higher rate of morbidity.

■ Most minority ethnic groups showed higher rates of stillbirths and infant mortality. About one in 100 pregnancies in the UK for African-Caribbean and Asian women end in a stillbirth, and mothers from the Caribbean and Pakistan experience infant mortality rates around double the national average.

■ People from African-Caribbean, Indian, Pakistani and Bangladeshi backgrounds are more likely to die from tuberculosis and liver cancer.

■ African-Caribbeans are more likely to be admitted to mental hospitals, and once admitted receive harsher forms of treatment than other groups.

Biological explanations: African-Caribbeans may genetically be more likely to experience higher blood pressure, which can lead to heart attacks and strokes. This group is also affected by sickle cell anemia: a potentially fatal blood disorder. However, biological explanations are only relevant in a minority of cases.

Cultural and behavioural explanations: Relatively high rates of heart disease among Asians have been blamed partly on the use of ghee, a less healthy form of cooking fat, and higher rates of diabetes on high carbohydrate foods, which encourage obesity. Greater rates of smoking and lower levels of exercise may also be an issue, but all of these areas are generally seen as less important than structural explanations.

Materialistic and structural explanations: As with social class, this view argues that heart problems among minority ethnic groups must be seen as a result of ill-health caused by low incomes and poor working conditions. The issue here is more an issue of social class than ethnicity: groups originally from Pakistan and Bangladesh are more likely to live in poorer houses whereas Indians and Chinese are more likely to be middle class, and generally suffer from fewer health problems than other Asian groups.

Racism and discrimination: This could lead to unemployment or excessive shift work, compulsory overtime and anti social working hours. This in turn could lead to physical or mental illnesses.

Age and region

Learning objectives:

- Consider how health and illness link to age.

- Consider how health and illness link to region.

- Explore how rates of health and illness in the UK compare with other countries.

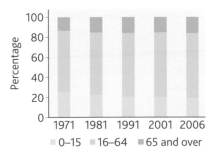

Fig. 5.6 *Sixteen per cent of the UK population are aged 65 or over and this is set to increase*

Link

On p192 concepts such as the postcode lottery and the inverse care law, which also link to this area, are explored.

Key term

Life expectancy: the average number of years a new-born baby can be expected to live.

Summary questions

11 How does the north/south divide link to health?

12 What is meant by the term 'life expectancy'?

13 Give three reasons for morbidity differences between a developed and a developing country.

Age and region

Sixteen per cent of the total population of the UK is now over 65, and the number of pensioners will rise by 6 million over the next 40 years and, as medical knowledge improves, more people will survive into old age. Expectations of health are increasing: people want not just an old age but a *healthy* old age, and this is often linked to social factors. On average, the healthiest older people in society are the white middle class, and the least healthy are poorer people, especially from minority ethnic backgrounds.

People living in the north of the country are less healthy, on average, than those in the south. Research by Shaw *et al.* (1999) into the lives of a million people in the healthiest parts of the country, compared with a million people in the unhealthiest areas, reached disturbing conclusions about the poor health areas:

- The infant mortality rate is twice as high.

- There are nearly three times as many people with long-term illnesses.

- There are over four times as many households with children living in poverty.

This so-called north/south divide is linked to such things as social class and ethnicity. The working class and minority ethnic groups are more likely to live in poorer city areas, and the white middle class in the suburbs and rural areas. However, these are not the only factors because poorer people living in the richer areas also tend to be healthier, which may be due to better air quality, more space to exercise and fewer environmental hazards.

International comparisons

It is clear that people in the developed world, on average, experience higher levels of health than those in the developing world. If life expectancy between countries is examined, the countries with the highest levels (more than 80 years) are in the developed world, and the countries with the lowest (less than 40 years) are in the developing world.

Reasons for the vastly differing morbidity and mortality rates include:

- Poverty, malnutrition, drought and famine.

- Lack of health care provision, such as doctors, nurses and hospitals.

- The health care system in many developing countries is based on the Western model of health care, when the emphasis should be on more basic, affordable and accessible health care.

- Communicable diseases such as typhoid are major killers, as are air-borne diseases, such as tuberculosis.

- Nine out of 10 people with HIV/AIDS are in the developing world.

Health

Chapter summary

- Morbidity refers to illness.

- Mortality refers to death.

- The Black report showed a clear difference in morbidity and mortality rates between the middle and working classes.

- Many reasons have been suggested for these health differences: some focus on lifestyle and others on the unfair structure of society.

- Morbidity rates are higher for women than men. This may be because women are sicker than men, or because women go to the doctor more than men.

- Despite higher morbidity rates, women live longer than men.

- There are clear health differences between ethnic groups. Explanations focus on biology, lifestyle, the structure of society and racism.

- Other areas of interest to sociologists include the links between health and age, health and region, and how health and health care provision in the UK compares to other parts of the world.

Health

Health care in contemporary society

Inequalities in the provision of health care

Learning objectives:

- Consider the geographical inequalities in the provision of health care in the UK.

- Explore the area of private health care.

In the UK, health care is largely free, and has been since the National Health Service (NHS) was established in 1945. However, in other countries, particularly in the US, health care is provided by private and occupational insurance schemes. The provision of health care in the UK is a hot political issue, largely due to the increase in cost of providing health care to an ageing and more demanding population.

Inequalities

There are various inequalities in the provision of heath care. For example, the medical profession has a great deal of power in determining which areas of health care receive funding. Some, such as surgery and high-technology medicine, are seen as more important than others like geriatrics.

Another factor is region: each is allocated money by the government, and supposedly more goes to the poorer regions. However, in reality, poorer regions generally receive less funding. Well-resourced and specialist teaching hospitals are usually located in the richer parts of the country, enabling them to attract the best-qualified staff, which in turn attracts further funding.

> **Hint**
>
> The NHS is an area that is always in the news, and you should keep your eyes open for documentaries and discussion programmes on this subject.

Fig. 5.7 *The quality and availability of NHS services depends greatly on the region where you live*

Health

Inverse care law: the concept, developed by Dr Tudor Hart in 1971, that those in society who have the greatest health care needs (often the poorest) receive less health care than those who have lower health care needs (often the richest in society).

■ Link

There is more information about the inverse care law on p193.

■ Postcode lottery

Differences in access to NHS treatment has given rise to the term 'postcode lottery'. In other words, where you live determines the quality and availability of NHS services, and this can affect both doctors' surgeries and hospitals. Services affected include availability of drugs for cancer and Alzheimer's disease, access to NHS cancer-screening programmes, and NHS waiting times. The discrepancies can be huge: for example, well-off areas like Kingston and Richmond in Surrey have 50 per cent more GPs than deprived Barnsley in Yorkshire: this is called the **inverse care law**.

■ Private health care

There is much evidence that serious inequalities exist within the NHS system. An area that is growing in importance is that of private health care providers such as BUPA. Private health care is paid for directly or via private health insurance and is seen as unfair for various reasons, including:

- Private health care and health insurance are linked to social class and wealth. Should the ability to pay enable you to receive faster and possibly more effective treatment than someone using the NHS?

- The private health sector takes doctors away from the NHS. Even those who remain may work privately for some of the time, which limits the number of hours they can work for the NHS.

Summary questions

1. What is meant by the term 'postcode lottery'?

2. Give two examples of how the postcode lottery could affect someone's health.

3. Give two criticisms of private health care.

Health

Social class

Learning objectives:

- Evaluate how access to health care can depend on social class.

- Understand the inverse care law.

Previously we have seen that the working class is, on average, less healthy than the middle class. Despite this working-class people are actually less likely to attend doctors' surgeries to receive treatment. They are also less likely to take part in preventative health treatments, such as screening programmes for cancer.

On the other hand, they are more likely to use accident and emergency services. This is probably because conditions that could have been treated by the GP have worsened, and also because working-class men in particular will have more accidents at work that require treatment.

The argument that the working class needs more health care than the middle class, but actually receives less treatment, and less effective treatment, is an aspect of the inverse care law.

This law works as follows:

- Doctors are less likely to set up practices in poorer areas. This means that there are fewer doctors in poorer areas, more patients per doctor and hence longer waiting times.

- Middle-class people are given more time by the GP than working-class people, partly because middle-class people ask more questions, and are more confident and assertive. They are also more likely to have further treatment.

- Doctors find it easier to interact with middle-class patients as they have similar levels of cultural capital. Middle-class patients are simply more 'at home' and comfortable with the doctor than working-class patients are.

- Middle-class people are more likely and more able to take time off work to attend appointments than working-class people. Middle-class jobs are often more flexible in terms of hours, and no pay will be lost for taking time off.

- Transport can be an issue. The poor are less likely to own a car than the middle class, and are far more likely to have to rely on public transport. This makes visiting the doctor that much more difficult and may lead to some people putting off seeing the doctor, making the condition even worse.

- The middle class are more likely to fight against inadequate medical services and campaign against hospital closures.

- Although the NHS is largely free, access to private health care is clearly linked to social class. The upper and middle classes are more likely to be able to afford private medical insurance and be offered schemes such as BUPA as part of their employment packages.

Link

The concept of cultural capital is a key one within the sociology of education, where it is used as one of the reasons why middle-class children do better than working-class children at school. See p136 for further information.

AQA Examiner's tip

This is another area where it is easy to stereotype the social classes, so caution should be exercised. Overall patterns and trends do exist, but not every middle-class person can take time off when they want and jump into their car, and not all working-class people struggle to talk to the doctor.

Summary questions

4. What is meant by the inverse care law?

5. Give two reasons why the working class is more likely to use accident and emergency services.

6. Suggest three reasons why the inverse care law exists.

Health

Gender

Learning objective:

- Explore the reasons why women are more likely to go and see the doctor than men.

Link

There is more on the subject of socialisation on p59.

Fig. 5.8 *Women are often the ones responsible for taking the children to the doctor*

Health

Why do women go to the doctor more often than men?

Some sociologists argue that women are genuinely sicker than men; others argue that women only *appear* to be sicker than men because they are more likely to seek medical help. It is also possible that both of these arguments are true. Indeed, research indicates that between the ages of 15 and 64 women are 50 per cent more likely to go to the doctor than men for several reasons.

The process of socialisation that women go through means that they are brought up to be more emotionally expressive than men. From an early age, girls spend more time with their parents, teachers and friends communicating and expressing their emotions. As such, visiting the doctor and talking about illnesses is easier for women than it is for men. Men spend less time talking about their emotions and feelings, and so are more likely to seek help only when the symptoms and/or pain become too much to bear, or because of pressure from their partners. One argument is that women go to the doctor for prescribed drugs and use natural health remedies, while men opt for non-prescribed drugs like alcohol and cigarettes.

Women tend to be more aware of health issues generally, through magazines and television programmes aimed at them which often focus on things like diet, exercise, contraception and family health. They tend to be more 'in tune' with health issues and are more likely to recognise and deal with symptoms when they arise.

Women are more likely to be looking after young children, and may go to the doctor on their children's behalf, giving them more of an opportunity to discuss their own problems. They are generally the ones who deal with children when they are ill, and often take on the emotional role in the family as part of the triple shift, dealing with their own health, their partner's and the children's.

Working part time, or looking after a pre-school child, can give women more time to go to the doctor. Men are more likely to work longer hours and will struggle to see the doctor as most surgeries are only open during normal working hours.

Doctors may also be more likely to diagnose women as being ill than men because of stereotypical/sexist views. They may see women as more vulnerable and weak, and therefore more in need of medical help. They may be less inclined to suggest treatment for men, particularly as men may be less willing to talk about general symptoms of ill-health.

Summary questions

7 What is meant by the term socialisation?

8 How does socialisation link to gender and health?

9 Give two other reasons why women see the doctor more than men.

Ethnicity

Learning objective:

- Evaluate the reasons why some ethnic minority groups use health care services less than others.

Key terms

Ante-natal clinics: clinics for women to attend prior to giving birth.

Post-natal clinics: clinics for women to attend after having given birth.

Previously it was shown that ethnic minorities, on average, experience worse health than white people in the UK. One of the reasons for this could be that ethnic minorities do not make full use of the health services that are available. A number of reasons have been put forward to explain this:

- Asian women, particularly Bangladeshis and Pakistanis, are less likely to visit **ante-** and **post-natal clinics**. This could be because of poorer language skills amongst some Asian women, made worse because of the lack of translation services in the NHS. It could also be because of cultural and religious issues which prevent them from associating with men (both health professionals and the partners of other pregnant women).

- Poor language skills will clearly be an issue when visiting the doctor. This could lead to the doctor not understanding symptoms and therefore suggesting unsuitable treatments. It could also mean than the doctor spends less time with Asian patients in the same way that doctors spend less time with working-class patients. However, it is important not to stereotype here and assume that all Asians have poor language skills, as so do many white people.

- Asian women often prefer to see female doctors because of cultural and religious reasons, but the number of female doctors tends to be lowest in the areas where most Asians live. This obviously presents Asian women with a dilemma, and makes it less likely that they will receive medical treatment when necessary. Asian women may not get to see a doctor at all, or will experience longer waiting times.

- Asian women, particularly Pakistanis and Bangladeshis, are less likely to use preventative health care such as screening programmes for breast and cervical cancer. Again, issues of modesty are at play, linked to culture and religion. Some commentators have argued that Asian women should be offered separate and alternative health care programmes to white people, but this is a controversial issue and one that is difficult to resolve. This links to wider ideas about integration and the importance of ethnic identity.

- Poverty is another issue. Ethnic minorities contain some of the lowest income families in Britain, and so the factors that limit working-class use of health services, like transport difficulties and inability to take time off work, apply equally to them.

Summary questions

10 Why do Asian women often prefer to visit female doctors?

11 Why are Asian women less likely to visit ante- and post-natal clinics?

12 Why might poverty be an issue?

Health

Age

Although older people are the age group most in need of health services, they tend to underuse them relative to their needs. They may consider that they are 'causing a fuss' and wasting the doctor's time if they overuse the services provided. Older people may also put up with a lot more pain and discomfort than younger people, or may feel it is 'just old age'.

■ NHS funding

People are now living longer and this has many implications. The NHS is paid for out of the tax system, which depends on people working and paying their taxes. Older people will have retired or only work part time, and hence pay less tax. Some commentators have argued that the NHS will one day struggle to provide adequate health care for everyone, and that treatment and medicines will have to be rationed. Health authorities are increasingly making choices about who to provide treatment for, raising questions about whether one group 'deserves' a better level of service than others and who should be responsible for making these life-and-death decisions over resources.

■ Institutional ageism

The charity Age Concern published a report in 1999 which accused the NHS of institutional ageism. It argued that the elderly were denied the best treatments because of their age and highlighted a number of key areas:

■ Women over the age of 65 are not invited for routine breast screenings, even though almost two-thirds of deaths from the disease occur in this group.

■ A fifth of all heart units operate an age-related admissions policy, even though two-thirds of those treated for heart attacks were over 65.

■ Many clinical trials investigating cancer excluded the elderly, despite a third of cancers occurring in the over 75s.

■ Specialist rehabilitation services for patients with brain injuries in several areas focus on returning people to work, and so in effect have an age restriction of no older than 65 years.

Age Concern has also highlighted the number of elderly patients who have found 'not for resuscitation' on their medical notes. The charity feels that elderly patients are being discriminated against in a bid to avoid bed-blocking and because of a lack of resources. They also claim that elderly patients are denied treatment for a range of conditions from high blood pressure to cancer, and that doctors fail to offer them the best advice.

Summary questions

13 What is the financial implication of an ageing population?

14 Suggest two reasons why older people may underuse the NHS.

15 Name three areas in which ageism may take place in the NHS.

Health

Chapter summary

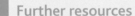

Further resources

Tudor Hart, 'The Inverse Care Law',
Lancet, 1971

www.ageconcern.org.uk – Age
Concern is a charity that campaigns
for the elderly in the UK.

- Despite health care in the UK being largely free since 1945, there are still serious inequalities in the provision of health.

- These inequalities are linked to region, social class, gender, ethnicity and age.

- The 'inverse care law' refers to those with the most health care needs, such as the working class, receiving the worst levels of health care, and vice versa.

- Women are far more likely to see the doctor than men. This may be because they suffer greater levels of sickness, or because of factors like socialisation.

- Minority ethnic groups, especially women, use health care services less than the white majority. Possible explanations for this tend to focus on language, religion, culture and poverty.

- The NHS has been accused of ageism in its provision of services. An ageing population also raises important questions over where limited resources should be focused.

Health

The sociological study of mental illness

The biomedical/psychiatric approach

Learning objectives:

- Understand how difficult it is to define mental illness and why that is so.

- Explore the history of mental illness.

- Consider how the biomedical/psychiatric model of mental illness has become the dominant one.

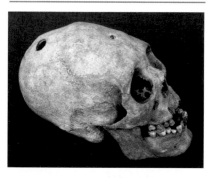

Fig. 5.9 *In prehistoric times, mentally ill people were sometimes thought to be possessed. Drilling holes in the skull was thought to release spirits causing possession*

Key term

Psychoanalytic approach: a branch of psychology which seeks to liberate patients from unconscious thoughts and fears that inhibit their freedom.

Summary questions

1 Why is 'mental illness' a social construct?

2 How have the mentally ill been treated throughout history?

3 According to the medical/psychiatric model, which two factors cause mental illness?

💡 Defining mental illness

A common-sense definition of a mentally ill person might be someone who acts in a way that is different or 'abnormal'. However, ideas about 'normal' and 'abnormal' behaviour vary according to society, and also over time, so some sociologists would argue that mental illness is a social construct. For example, when the suffragettes campaigned for the right to vote in the early 20th century, they were seen by many in society as acting abnormally and even as being mentally ill.

A brief history

Throughout history those who do not 'act normally' have been treated with suspicion and often rejected. In prehistoric times mental illness was thought to be caused by evil spirits, and one rather drastic solution was to drill a hole in the skull to release the spirit! In the Middle Ages, those who acted irrationally were often thought to be possessed and/or labelled as witches.

Over time, however, views on mental illness changed, and asylums were built to keep the mentally ill apart from wider society. Conditions in the asylums were initially very poor, but near the turn of the 19th century, psychologists and social reformers began to campaign for more humane treatment, and gradually the medical/psychiatric view of mental illness, described in the next section, grew to be the accepted one.

The medical/psychiatric model

In the Western world the dominant approach to mental illness is the medical/psychiatric model. This takes the view that people who exhibit signs of 'abnormal' behaviour are suffering from a real illness and need to be treated by a qualified medical practitioner. Mental illness, according to this perspective, is caused by two main factors:

1 Disturbing experiences which have normally occurred in childhood and need to be treated by a **psychoanalytic approach**.

2 A chemical/hormonal imbalance in the brain which can be treated by medication, for example anti depressants.

In the UK, both approaches are used to treat mental illness, but the use of medication is most common. Over 3.5 million people are taking anti depressants at any one time, and women are twice as likely to take them as men. More than 31 million prescriptions for anti depressant drugs such as Prozac were issued in 2006. However, is it possible all these people are taking medication for an illness that does not even exist?

The labelling perspective

Learning objectives:

- Understand how the labelling perspective on mental illness differs from the traditional medical/psychiatric model.

- Explore the ways in which the labelling perspective has been criticised.

Labelling theory

In the 1960s a controversial challenge to the medical/psychiatric model of mental illness arose – *labelling theory*. Labelling theory sees mental illness as a social construct rather than an illness and, in this context, it is about the power of certain groups in society (i.e. doctors and psychiatrists) to label other less powerful groups in a negative way (i.e. as mentally ill), and then treat them differently because of it (i.e. with medication, therapy or even long-term residential care).

The concept of mental illness

Two important writers in this area are Thomas Szasz (1974) and Thomas Scheff (1968). They argue that people go through stages in their lives when they feel unhappy, lonely and miserable, but to label this as 'clinical depression' and treat it as an illness is wrong. In the UK, doctors prescribe anti depressant drugs to an increasing number of people, but according to writers like these, they are treating a condition which does not exist. Likewise, more children are being 'diagnosed' with things like attention deficit hyperactivity disorder (ADHD), which according to labelling theorists is not real either.

Critics argue that bad behaviour in children is often normal and that children are being misdiagnosed and over-medicalised.

The effects of labelling

Once a person is labelled as mentally ill, other people are likely to treat them differently. All that they say and do can be seen as a symptom of their mental illness. If they try and protest, they will be seen as aggressive; if they do not respond, then they are too passive. Sociologist Erving Goffman (1968) said that doctors, social workers and psychiatrists will engage in **spurious interaction** with those labelled mentally ill.

Admittance to an institution

In the past, but less so today, patients labelled as mentally ill could be admitted to a mental hospital or an asylum. Once the labelling process has reached this stage, it is increasingly difficult to convince people that you are not ill. Rosenhan's famous experiment illustrates even specialists' inability to distinguish between the sane and the insane once admitted to an institution.

Research study: Rosenhan's study (1973)

Rosenhan asked eight researchers to admit themselves to various American psychiatric hospitals by pretending that they were hearing voices. Once admitted they behaved perfectly normally, but were all treated as if they were mentally ill and diagnosed as schizophrenics. Whatever they did in the institution, even simple things like writing notes, were seen as a sign that they were mentally ill. These pseudo (pretend) patients remained in hospital for between seven and 52

Links

The concept of labelling is also used extensively in the sociology of education (see p138) and in crime and deviance, which is covered in A2. Labelling is often linked to social class and ethnicity.

ADHD can be linked to the sociology of education. Are some children labelled as naughty suffering from a real illness that needs treatment?

AQA Examiner's tip

It is important not to present psychiatrists as the 'baddies' in this debate and the labelling theorists as the 'goodies'. There are arguments for and against both perspectives!

Key term

Spurious interaction: when you do not really listen to another person because you do not believe what they are saying.

Health

days. Although they were not detected by the staff, many of the other (real) patients suspected that they were not ill! In a second study, staff at another hospital who knew of the first study, were informed that during the next three months one or more pseudo patients would attempt to be admitted. Out of 193 patients, 41 were considered by the staff to be impostors. Actually, no pseudo patients were used at all, and all patients suspected as impostors were genuine patients.

■ Link

See p213 for more about how Rosenhan can be criticised on ethical grounds.

■ Criticism

The obvious and very important criticism of this perspective is that mental illness is not just a social construct but a very real condition that affects an increasing number of people. Mental illness may be more difficult to diagnose and treat than a physical condition like a broken leg but it is no less real or serious. The many thousands of psychiatrists that exist would be quick to refute the labelling approach as naïve or even dangerous.

As the next section illustrates, some sociologists also disagree with labelling theory and argue that mental illness is real and caused by social factors such as poverty and lack of power. In addition, the work of people like Rosenhan is seen to be dated, as institutional care for the mentally ill has become increasingly replaced by a focus on 'care in the community', meaning that patients are treated at home or in day centres. Rosenhan can also be criticised on ethical grounds, and also on the small sample he has based his findings on.

Summary questions

4   How do labelling theorists view mental illness?

5   Who has the power to label?

6   What is meant by the term 'spurious interaction'?

7   What does Rosenhan's experiment illustrate?

8   How has labelling theory been criticised?

Mental illness according to social factors

Learning objectives:

- Consider how some sociologists argue that mental illness is a real condition and not just a label.

- Understand how rates of mental illness vary according to gender, ethnicity, social class and age.

Link

The triple shift is a key concept in the sociology of the family (p100) and health (see p223). Feminists argue that the family is often a place where women are exploited and experience patriarchy.

An alternative sociological approach to labelling theory is to accept that there *is* such a thing as mental illness, but to look at the *social* causes of mental illness rather than the biological or psychological causes. So, for example, if women suffer from depression more than men, this could be linked to social factors like stress caused by doing the bulk of housework, childcare and emotional work in a family: the triple shift.

Fig. 5.10 *The triple shift refers to the stress involved in doing the bulk of the housework, childcare and emotional work in a family*

Gender

Women are more likely than men to be diagnosed as having a mental illness. They are six times more likely than men to suffer from depression and anxiety. For other types of mental illness, though, the rates are similar. Some sociologists have argued that the higher rate of depression is because women are more likely to seek help, and that men 'suffer in silence'. Feminists, though, argue that women really are more likely to get depression and anxiety because of the pressures they face in their role as women.

Research study: Brown and Harris (1978, 1989)

Brown and Harris look at both social class and gender. They argue that working-class women are more likely to suffer from depression than middle-class women. This is because working-class women will have experienced more negative events in their lives such as poverty, ill-health and divorce. If women also have 'vulnerability' factors, such as three or more children at home or unemployment, depression can occur. However, Brown and Harris do not argue that all working-class women will become depressed: they may have

Health

201

'protective factors' on their side, for example a supportive partner, which will usually overcome other problems and prevent the women becoming depressed. Brown and Harris are arguing that mental illness is a real condition and not just a label. They differ from the traditional psychological approach, though, in that they are more concerned with the social causes and not the medical causes.

■ Ethnicity

A major study in this area by Nazroo (1997) shows that African-Caribbeans in the UK are more likely to suffer from depression than other groups, with African-Caribbean men particularly affected. Rates for other forms of mental illness are similar to the rest of the population. Reasons for the higher levels of depression could be the higher rates of male African-Caribbean unemployment in the UK, which in turn can be linked to male African-Caribbean underachievement at school. This, combined with experiencing prejudice and discrimination in society generally, goes some way to explaining the higher depression rates. However, it is also the case that African-Caribbeans are much more likely than white people to come into contact with psychiatrists through the police, courts or prisons. African-Caribbeans are also more likely to be involuntarily detained under the Mental Health Act 1983. It would seem that labelling theory can again be applied here. It may be the case that higher rates of treatment for African-Caribbeans may reflect stereotypical attitudes amongst psychiatrists rather than any actual higher levels of illness.

■ Social class

Mental illness is not distributed randomly across the social classes. The poorer a person is, the more likely they are to be diagnosed as having a mental illness. One argument is that they are poor because of the mental illness. In other words, they cannot hold down a job because of stress or depression, which leads to them getting the sack, becoming unemployed and hence being poorer. On the other hand, it could be argued that it is the stress of being poor that *causes* the mental illness.

■ Age

Older people are more likely to get Alzheimer's disease and dementia, which are very much real medical conditions. However, sociologists would argue that the elderly often get labelled as mentally ill even when they are healthy and that their families and doctors often engage in spurious interaction with them. It may also be the case that being put into residential care, which may lack mental stimulation, would cause many people to lose hope and become more confused and reliant on others, thus confirming the label of being mentally ill. Research shows that the brain needs to be exercised just as the body does – if it is not, it slows down. It has also been argued that one of the most effective ways to keep the brain healthy is by interaction with others, especially family and friends. Some elderly people are effectively abandoned in care homes, so it is no surprise that mental problems occur.

■ Link

The higher rate of African-Caribbean depression can be linked to higher unemployment rates, which can in turn be linked to African-Caribbean underachievement in education (see p143). African-Caribbean boys, on average, do less well in term of qualifications gained than other ethnic groups.

Fig. 5.11 *Many elderly people are put into residential care, which may not be a stimulating enough environment for them*

Summary questions

9 How does the triple shift link to mental illness?

10 What causes mental illness, according to Brown and Harris?

11 Give two reasons why African-Caribbeans are more likely to suffer from depression than other ethnic groups.

Health

Chapter summary

 **Further resources**

www.sane.org.uk – Sane is a leading mental health charity.

One Flew over the Cuckoo's Nest (1975) – A well-known film starring Jack Nicholson, who alters the dynamics of a mental hospital.

A Beautiful Mind (2001) – A film based on the true story of a mathematical genius and his diagnosis as a schizophrenic.

Girl, Interrupted (1999) – A film about a troubled teenager whose suicide attempt lands her in a mental hospital.

- The medical/psychiatric approach to mental illness is that it is caused by biological and psychological factors.

- Definitions of mental illness vary according to time and location.

- Some sociologists and psychiatrists argue that mental illness is a social construct, and focus on the labelling of someone as mentally ill.

- Other sociologists argue that mental illness is a real condition, but caused by social factors and not biological or psychological factors. These sociologists look at the link between mental illness, class, gender, ethnicity and age.

- Working-class women may suffer from more mental illness than middle-class women because of more negative events in their lives.

- African-Caribbeans may suffer more from depression than other groups because of educational underachievement, unemployment and racism. This may then be reinforced by negative labelling by authorities, such as the police, doctors and psychiatrists.

- Older people may experience being labelled as mentally ill more than other groups, and family, friends and health care professionals may engage in spurious interaction with them.

Medicine and the health professions

The history of disease

Learning objectives:

- Explore the history of disease.

- Understand the role of medicine in tackling disease.

The main killer diseases in the Western world today are cancers, heart disease and strokes, but in the 19th century, they were tuberculosis, pneumonia, bronchitis and influenza (flu), typhoid and cholera. Before this, the plague – spread by the fleas carried by black rats – killed many, including up to half of the population of Europe in the 14th century.

Today people live longer and healthier lives. Few people die of flu, tuberculosis or pneumonia in the Western world now. Many associate this with the development of medicine, but some sociologists have challenged this view.

■ Medicine and the decline of infectious disease

Few people die of the diseases of the past because of the pioneering work of medical scientists, such as Alexander Fleming, who discovered antibiotics, and Edward Jenner, who invented the first smallpox vaccine. This approach to medicine has been called a 'march of progress' view, which sees medical science advancing at a steady pace, with new discoveries being made continually. According to this view, people are healthier today because of more effective drugs and immunisation.

However, sociologists have challenged this view. McKeown (1979) argued that the role of medicine in reducing morbidity and mortality rates in the 19th and 20th centuries has been exaggerated. He contended that people became healthier and lived longer because of a number of social and economic developments – such as better sewage disposal and improved food hygiene – rather than medical ones.

Among the key areas which improved people's health were the following:

Public hygiene

Without efficient sewage disposal, infectious diseases like cholera and typhoid spread easily. In the UK, sewer systems were built after 1850 and these, combined with cleaner piped water, made a huge difference to public health.

Better diet

The high death rates of the past were partly due to hunger and malnutrition, which made people prone to infection. As living standards improved, people could afford a better diet. This, combined with improvements in food hygiene and the sterilisation and bottling of milk, led to improvements in health.

Declining family size

From around the 1870s, the birth rate began to fall. This led to smaller families, which enabled a better diet and health care for children. Women's health also improved as they spent less time child-bearing, and were less likely to die giving birth.

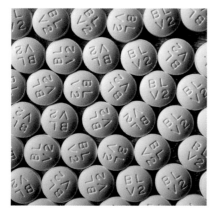

Fig. 5.12 *The discovery of antibiotics was one of the most significant discoveries of the 20th century*

■ Link

Declining family size is also covered on p48.

Housing legislation

Laws were passed in 1890 that enabled local authorities to purchase and then demolish slum housing, rehousing inhabitants in better accommodation. This reduced overcrowding which helped to stop the spread of infectious disease.

Summary questions

1. What is the 'march of progress' view of medicine?
2. What were the main killers in the past?
3. What are the main killers today?
4. What does McKeown argue has caused infectious diseases to decline?

Health

The medical model of health

Key terms

Homeopath: a practitioner of homeopathy, a system of treating illness by prescribing minute doses of a drug that in large quantities would cause the symptoms of the disease in a healthy person.

Aetiology: the branch of medicine that deals with the causes or origins of disease.

Preventative medicine: a term that refers to any aspect of health care that seeks to prevent people becoming ill in the first place or in detecting disease early, as with breast screening programmes.

Link

This medical model is also discussed on p178.

A brief history

From the Middle Ages to the late 18th century, medical care was only available to wealthy people who often had their own doctor. Medical knowledge and care was limited, and sometimes did more harm than good. 'Blood letting', which allowed an excess of blood to be released to cure the patient, was a popular treatment for many diseases. From the beginning of the 19th century, medical treatment improved as scientific discoveries were made. Medicine became a profession and the General Medical Council (GMC) was set up to keep a register of suitably qualified practitioners. The GMC could exclude those who did not practise conventional medicine, such as **homeopaths**, and the biomedical model of health became established.

The rise of the medical model

The biomedical model of health has the following key features:

- A focus on treating the symptoms of a disease rather than finding its root causes, which may be things like poor housing, overcrowding, poverty or work-related stress.

- A belief that any disease is caused by a virus or bacteria – known as **aetiology**. The disease, once identified scientifically, can then be targeted by the correct combination of drugs and treatment.

- A belief that medicine, as practised by GPs and hospitals, is the best way to keep people healthy.

- A belief that medical science is progressing, and that more cures and better treatments will be found, given time and funding.

Criticism

The biomedical model of health has become increasingly criticised and challenged recently. Arguments put forward include:

- The root causes are as important as the symptoms of a disease, and need to be tackled if a patient is to remain healthy. Modern medicine just puts a sticking plaster over the wounds caused by difficult social conditions.

- More money should be spent on preventing people becoming sick in the first place – this is called **preventative medicine**. The biomedical approach should only be considered alongside alternative medicine, which should be offered to all patients.

- Modern medicine is not the answer to all our medical problems and seems ineffective against new diseases such as vCJD (caught from infected meat where the cattle had BSE – otherwise known as mad cow disease). There is still no cure for AIDS or even the common cold.

- It is changes such as better public health, hygiene and diet that have a greater effect on our health than scientific discoveries.

Iatrogenesis

One of the most important critics of the biomedical model was Ivan Illich (1975), who argued that the biomedical model causes as much ill-health as it cures! Illich called this **iatrogenesis** – the belief that medical intervention, in the form of surgery and drugs, can actually do more harm than good. Some of the dangers of modern medicines are as follows:

- Some have serious side-effects.
- Some are addictive.
- Widespread use of antibiotics lead to people and viruses becoming resistant.
- Many hospital patients contract MRSA, a dangerous antibiotic-resistant infection that kills over 1,500 people per year in the UK. This is on the increase in UK hospitals.

Illich argued that it is the pressures of modern life that cause most illness. People need to take control of their own lives and not rely on health care professionals to look after them.

The rise of alternative medicine

The biomedical model has also faced other challenges, not least that of alternative medicine. This is a general term used to describe those forms of treatment which are not generally recognised by the medical profession. Alternative medicine has grown in popularity recently, with Britons spending over a billion pounds a year on treatments: a figure which is swiftly increasing. Alternative therapies exist for all manner of complaints, from circulation and digestive problems to depression and stress. Some of the most popular include **acupuncture**, **aromatherapy** and **reiki**.

The move away from doctors and conventional medicine is all part of what has been called a 'flight from deference'. This means that people today are less trusting of and less **deferential** towards all authority figures, including doctors, compared to the past.

Additionally, the internet has given people instant access to information about alternative medicines, which are seen as less likely to cause addiction and dangerous side effects. The use of alternative medicine is seen as a more holistic approach to health, i.e. tackling not just the symptoms but the possible mental and emotional causes as well.

Criticism

The main criticism levelled at alternative medicine is that many of the treatments have not been tested in the rigorous way that conventional medicines have. It has also been argued that relying on alternative medicine could be dangerous in the case of serious diseases like cancer, where conventional treatments are more effective.

Key terms

Iatrogenesis: the idea that medical intervention makes people sicker.

Acupuncture: an ancient Chinese art based on the theory that energy in the body can be stimulated by inserting fine needles into the body at specific points.

Aromatherapy: the use of essential oils in treatments to improve physical and emotional well-being.

Reiki: a technique developed in Japan in which the practitioner channels spiritual energy to promote the body's own capacity to heal itself.

Deferential: a term that means expressing trust and respect to those seen as superior.

Hint

MRSA is very topical at the moment, and it would be worth keeping an eye open for up-to-date information on this and other related areas.

Summary questions

5 What is meant by the term 'iatrogenesis'?

6 Give two characteristics of the biomedical model of health.

7 Name three criticisms of the biomedical model of health.

8 Give four reasons why alternative medicine has become more popular.

Health

The nature of the sick role

Learning objectives:

■ Understand what is meant by the sick role.

■ Explore how the idea of the sick role has been criticised.

The concept of the sick role was developed by Talcot Parsons (1975). Parsons was a functionalist, and one of the key concerns of functionalism is how society maintains itself. One thing that keeps society going is people working, earning money, supporting their families and being good citizens. If people cannot work because of illness, society needs to manage this process, hence the sick role. We cannot have too many people sick, or sick for too long. According to Parsons, the sick role implies two rights and two obligations.

Rights:

1 The sick person does not have to go to work, tidy the house, look after children etc. and is excused from normal obligations.

2 The sick person is not to blame for their illness, and needs to be cared for.

Obligations:

1 The sick person is expected to get better as soon as possible. They must not prolong their illness to avoid going to work or school.

2 The sick person is expected to seek medical help if necessary, and to take whatever medicine/treatment is provided.

If these rights and obligations are fulfilled, the process of being sick can be managed successfully by society, so society itself stays healthy. Problems only arise if it becomes socially acceptable to be off sick when you could in fact work. This is why in the UK the long-term sick are often labelled as skivers: from a functionalist point of view, this **stigmatisation** is vital to ensure people take as little time off as possible.

■ Criticism

Not everyone who becomes sick adopts a sick role. Some go to work when they are ill, perhaps because they cannot afford to take time off. In addition, the decision to go to a doctor is linked to class, gender, age and ethnicity.

Parsons argued that individuals are not blamed for their illness. However, this is not always the case. AIDS sufferers, for example, are often blamed for getting ill. Likewise, people suffering from mental illness are also often stigmatised.

Not everyone seeks conventional medical help when they are ill. People today will increasingly challenge the authority of the doctor, get other opinions, self-diagnose and self-treat, sometimes using alternative therapies.

It is important to remember, however, that Parsons developed the concept of the sick role decades ago, and cannot be blamed for failing to foresee some future developments which have taken place.

The sick role only works when the illness is temporary and curable. For people with a long-term illness or a disability, it may be more important for them to behave as 'normally' as possible and not to appear sick.

■ Key term

Stigmatisation: the process of labelling a group as deviant and then treating them negatively.

AQA Examiner's tip

There is a tendency in sociology to criticise functionalist ideas simply because they are old-fashioned. Just because something was written a while ago does not automatically make it wrong! All theories are open to criticism, but criticise them in a more sociological and sophisticated way than by just saying that they are dated.

Summary questions

9 Who developed the idea of a sick role?

10 Why does society need a sick role?

11 What is meant by the term 'stigmatisation'?

12 Give two criticisms of the idea of a sick role.

Health

Different sociological perspectives of health

Learning objective:

■ Consider the differences and similarities in the ways that feminists, Marxists and postmodernists view health.

Key terms

Postmodernism: the belief that society is no longer governed by history or progress.

Postmodern age: according to most postmodernists the history of the world can be divided into three stages: pre-modern (before about 1760), modern (about 1760–1980) and postmodern (about 1980 onwards).

Grand narrative: also known as metanarrative, this is a postmodernist concept that refers to any area of knowledge that claims to offer complete explanations. Medicine, religion and most sociological theories can all be seen as examples of this.

AQA Examiner's tip

Try to include some theory in every essay question, even if it does not directly ask you to. This does npt apply just to health but to all areas of sociology.

Summary questions

13 What do feminists mean by 'the medicalisation of childbirth'?

14 Give two Marxist views on health.

15 Why do postmodernists argue that the biomedical model of health is a grand narrative?

💡 Feminism

Whilst feminists are interested with many issues concerning women and health, there are other key areas that concern them.

The medicalisation of childbirth

Pregnancy and childbirth have come to be seen as 'medical problems' rather than as a natural process. Male doctors see pregnancy and childbirth in terms of a medical procedure to be controlled and regulated, hence the emphasis on hospital rather than home births.

Status of nurses

Most nurses and midwives are women, and they have lower pay and status than the mainly male doctors and surgeons.

Contraception

Contraception is mainly aimed at women. Although the contraceptive pill provides sexual freedom, it also has potentially harmful side-effects.

Capitalism and women's health

Marxist feminists have made the link between capitalism and women's health. Women's health is big business, and a huge profit can be made from things like weight-loss and anti-ageing products. Also, maintaining women's health is important to ensure both that they give birth to the next generation of workers and that they provide their husbands with the sexual and emotional fulfilment necessary for them to keep working!

Marxism

Further to the Marxist feminist views discussed above, Marxists have made other observations on the subject, including:

■ The main purpose of health care in the West is to ensure a supply of workers for the factories and offices controlled by the capitalists.

■ The pharmaceutical industry is big business. Doctors must keep giving out medication and are targeted by pharmaceutical companies to use their products.

■ Tobacco and alcohol are legal and make vast profits for capitalists. They are allowed to exist because of the pressure manufacturers put on the government and the huge tax revenue they generate.

■ Doctors are agents of social control. They (indirectly) work for the capitalists as their job is to get people back to work as quickly as possible.

Postmodernism

Postmodernists are academics and philosophers who stress the choices and freedoms we all have in this **postmodern age**. However, the dominance of the biomedical model of health restricts our choice and it is only recently that alternative forms of medicine have become acceptable. Postmodernists welcome alternative medicinal treatments as they allow us to take control of our bodies and many see the biomedical model as just another **grand narrative** that seeks to control us.

Chapter summary

- According to some sociologists, the role of medicine in the decline of infectious disease has been overstated.

- Social and economic developments, such as improvements in public hygiene and diet, greatly reduced morbidity and mortality rates in the 19th and 20th centuries.

- The biomedical model of health has become the accepted model for most people today, despite increased criticisms.

- Iatrogenesis is the view that the biomedical model of health actually makes people ill.

- Alternative medicine is becoming more popular today, despite the lack of scientific evidence into its effectiveness.

- Talcott Parsons developed the concept of the sick role which comprises two rights and two obligations of people who are sick.

- Feminists, Marxists and postmodernists all have strong views on health and health care.

Research methods in the context of health

Types of research methods

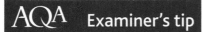

Learning objective:

- Examine some of the methods used by sociologists when studying health.

 It is essential, when considering sociological evidence about health, to understand how the evidence was collected and to make judgements about its reliability, validity and representativeness.

Surveys

Questionnaires

The social survey method, with a postal questionnaire on mental health issues (using mainly closed questions), was used by the sociologist Nazroo in his 1997 book *Ethnicity and Mental Health*.

Advantages:

- The sample of 8,000 is large and therefore more likely to be representative of the population.
- The method is reliable: it can be repeated by other sociologists at a later date.
- The research should be objective, provided that the questions were carefully worded, clear and unambiguous, and did not 'lead' the respondents.

Disadvantages:

- There is an issue about the validity: did those filling in the questionnaire always tell the truth? Did they all understand the questions? For example, Nazroo refers to the difficulties of translating the term 'depression' into South Asian languages.

Interviews

A semi-structured interview is like a guided conversation, where the researcher ensures that the discussion is focused on the topic of the research but does not ask many pre-set questions. It is sometimes called an informal interview and is open ended and free flowing.

This method was used by the radical feminist Anne Oakley for her 1979 book *From Here to Maternity*, about the experience of becoming a first-time mother. She interviewed over 100 women before and after they gave birth. The interviews were in-depth, detailed and involved open questions. Oakley was interested in the mothers' views on hospital births, how they felt having a child would change their lives and what support they were receiving from their partners. When the women asked Oakley about her experiences as a wife and mother, Oakley responded as honestly as she could.

Advantages:

- Oakley argues that unstructured interviews are particularly useful when interviewing women because they are seen as non-hierarchical and non-exploitative and they give women a chance to speak openly and at length.
- Oakley gained the trust of the women, so they spoke honestly about their experiences; the evidence is likely to be valid.

AQA Examiner's tip

The AQA AS examination includes questions about research methods in the context of health.

Link

A more detailed exploration of survey-related methods can be found on p232.

Health

Disadvantages:

■ As Oakley recognises, this was a small and possibly unrepresentative sample, and all the women were white.

■ The research took many months to complete.

■ Oakley recognised that she became friendly with the women, and that her own experiences may have influenced her research and the interviewees' responses. She was not objective or detached.

■ She found that some of the mothers asked her for advice which she did not feel qualified to give.

■ The research is not reliable as it cannot be repeated on the same group of women.

Longitudinal surveys

There is a mass of data about health and illness in two of the major longitudinal studies, the National Child Development Study (NCDS) that started in 1958 and the British Cohort Study (BCS) that started in 1970. The NCDS started as a study into stillbirths and infant deaths among the babies born in a particular week but has widened to cover the physical, educational, social and economic development of those being studied. The BCS, like the NCDS, started with a strictly medical focus at birth, but now covers physical and educational development at the age of five; physical, educational and social development at the ages of 10 and 16, and economic development; and other wider factors at 26, 29 and 34 years.

■ Ethnographic methods

Observation

Participant observation involves joining a group of people and taking part in their everyday lives. The researcher tries to see and experience the world as they do. Overt participant observation is when those being studied are aware of the researcher's role. Covert participant observation is when the researcher's true role and identity is kept secret.

A good example of overt participant observation is Whittaker (1996). The broad aim of the study was to identify the social and cultural context of general practice. This piece of research employed a variety of methods (long-term participant observation, in-depth interviews, health diaries and focus group discussions, combined with analysis of official statistics), using the strength of one to balance the weaknesses of another.

The covert participant observation method was used by the psychologist Goffman in his 1968 study of an American asylum. Goffman took on the role of assistant athletic director. However, the patients and most of the hospital staff were unaware of his true role, which was to see how patients responded to being placed in a **total institution**.

Advantages:

■ Goffman was able to observe behaviour in its natural setting so validity was high.

■ He should have been able to develop some **verstehen** with the patients and staff, seeing for himself how the patients dealt with life in the institution, and the range of responses and attitudes they developed.

Disadvantages:

■ Ethical issues are raised: Goffman did not have the informed consent and was not being honest to either the patients or the staff.

Link

A more detailed exploration of ethnographic methods can be found on p238.

Key terms

Total institution: a term used to describe an institution such as a psychiatric hospital or prison where the aim is for the behaviour of the inmates to be totally controlled.

Verstehen: a word meaning empathy. This means attempting to see the world through someone else's eyes, or to try and 'stand in their shoes' for a while.

Health

- The method is time-consuming.
- Goffman's research may not be representative as he investigated only one institution.

Experiments

There are two main types of experiment: the laboratory experiment takes place in the artificial environment of a laboratory and is often used by psychologists; the field experiment takes place in a natural setting – a hospital or an asylum for example.

The experimental method was famously used by the psychiatrist Rosenhan in his 1973 experiment in American psychiatric hospitals.

Advantages:

- This was a field experiment and so was therefore less artificial and more realistic than a laboratory experiment.
- Validity was high as the other patients and medical staff would have behaved normally, though at least one patient seems to have 'seen through' one of the researchers.

Disadvantages:

- There are serious ethical issues. Rosenhan's researchers did not have the informed consent of the other patients or the medical staff.
- The researchers could have been harmed by receiving unnecessary medical treatment and drugs, or caused indirect harm by distracting medical staff from the real patients.
- Only eight volunteers were used in just 12 mental hospitals, so the research may not be representative.
- Experiments can be time-consuming. Some of Rosenhan's pseudo-patients stayed in the mental hospitals for almost two months.

Secondary data

Official statistics

Official statistics are produced by national and local government bodies. There is a vast amount of information (quantitative data) available concerning every aspect of physical and mental health, health care and a myriad of related issues such as obesity, smoking, health and safety at work, and dental health.

Two important government reports on health are the Black report (1980) and the Acheson report (1998). These reports were based on a wide range of official statistics but also drew on data from previous social surveys. Both studies showed clear health differences between the working and middle classes.

McKeown (1979) used official statistics in his research on the impact of advances in medical treatments, such as the development of antibiotics and the introduction of vaccination programmes. By analysing the statistics of morbidity and mortality in relation to the timing of these developments, he was able to show that they were less important than wider social and environmental developments, such as better diets, cleaner water and proper waste disposal.

Advantages:

- Using existing data is cheaper than having to conduct your own research.

Links

A more detailed exploration of the use of experiments can be found on p245.

See p199 for further information on this study.

Links

A more detailed exploration of secondary data can be found on p248.

See p185 for further information on this study.

Health

■ Most official statistics are easy to obtain.

■ This can be seen as objective as the sociologist is not having any contact with the people the statistics are based on.

■ This is reliable as other sociologists can use the same sources to check the findings.

Disadvantages:

■ The categories used in government reports, such as social class and ethnicity, may not be used consistently, which makes comparisons difficult.

■ Official statistics are government statistics, and therefore may be biased.

Mass media

The mass media often feature information about health issues, such as healthy eating, dieting, the NHS, new drugs and cosmetic surgery.

The mass media can be used either as a source of information or as the subject of research. When used as a source of information, the following can be considered.

Advantages:

■ As the data already exists, there is no cost to the sociologist.

■ There is a large and easily accessible pool of information available.

■ Using the mass media is reliable as other sociologists can check your sources.

Disadvantages:

■ The most important problem is that of bias. Newspapers, especially, tend to reflect a political viewpoint, so stories about NHS failings, for example, need to be treated with caution.

Content analysis

When the mass media are the subject of the research, then the method of content analysis can be used. This involves the systematic study of the content of documents, such as magazines or advertisements. Sociologists may look for how different social classes or ethnic groups are portrayed. Feminists, in particular, would argue that this method is useful in studying areas such as body image. Naomi Wolf, in her 1991 book *The Beauty Myth*, has pointed out that magazines are full of images of slim and beautiful women.

Advantages:

■ There is little financial cost involved.

■ It is a reliable method.

■ There are no major ethical issues.

Disadvantages:

■ Interpretation of text and images will depend on the views and values of the sociologist and cannot therefore be objective.

■ There is little room for empathy.

Summary questions

1 Which research method does Anne Oakley favour?

2 What is meant by the term 'verstehen'?

3 Name two ethical problems raised by Rosenhan's research.

4 What did the official government reports by Black and Acheson reveal?

5 Name two problems associated with the use of official statistics.

6 How can the mass media be used by sociological researchers?

Health

Chapter summary

 Further resources

www.statistics.gov.uk – To see some of the official statistics on health, go to the National Statistics website and search on 'health'.

- Sociologists have used a wide range of research methods to study the sociology of health.

- These include social surveys (including longitudinal surveys), experiments, and overt and covert participant observation.

- Sources of secondary data include official statistics and the mass media.

- All of these methods have both strengths and weaknesses.

- Factors that should be considered when evaluating sociological research include the validity, reliability, representativeness of the data, and the time, cost and ethics of the research.

1A Read Item 1(a) below and answer the questions that follow.

(a)   Working-class people, on average, die younger and suffer more illness and disability than middle-class people. According to the materialist explanation, these inequalities are the result of factors such as income, employment and unemployment, housing and other aspects of the social and physical environment. Working-class people are more likely to live in poor-quality accommodation in more polluted environments; they earn lower incomes and are more likely to be out of work. These poverty-related factors damage their health.

This is sometimes also referred to as the structural explanation of health inequality, since it sees the unequal structure of society as the underlying cause.

However, it has been claimed that in countries such as Britain, material poverty is no longer the major reason for class inequalities in health. For example, some sociologists see cultural or behavioural factors as more important.

(i)   Explain what is meant by the term 'mortality rate'.   *(2 marks)*

(ii)   Identify three reasons why women on average live longer than men.   *(6 marks)*

(iii) Outline some of the reasons why some ethnic groups experience worse health than others.   *(12 marks)*

(iv) Using material from Item 2(c) and elsewhere, assess the materialist explanation of class inequalities in health.   *(20 marks)*

B This question requires you to apply your knowledge and understanding of sociological research methods to the study of this particular issue in health.

Read Item 1(b) below and answer the questions that follow.

(b)   Investigating interaction between doctors and patients in psychiatric wards

Some sociologists have been interested in investigating the attitudes of medical staff and how these may affect the way they treat patients. For example, Rosenhan (1973) explored the way nursing staff accepted that the patients they looked after were 'mentally ill', even when their behaviour was quite 'normal'.

Sociologists are also interested in the way patients respond. For example, Quirk and Lelliott (2001) were interested in the responses of patients during face-to-face interaction between medical staff. A lot of research has focused on how labels, meanings, attitudes and values are negotiated through interaction in psychiatric wards.

Using material from Item 1(b) and elsewhere, assess the strengths and limitations of one of the following methods for the study of interaction between doctors and patients in psychiatric wards:

(i)   participant observation

(ii)   questionnaires.   *(20 marks)*

AQA specimen question

C This question permits you to draw examples from any areas of sociology with which you are familiar.

(i)   Explain what is meant by the term 'interview schedule'.   *(2 marks)*

(ii)   Suggest two factors that may influence a sociologist's choice of research method.   *(4 marks)*

(iii) Suggest two limitations of the use of laboratory experiments in sociological research.   *(4 marks)*

(iv) Examine the ethical considerations sociologists may face when carrying out research.   *(20 marks)*

2A Read Item 2(a) and 2(b) and answer parts (i) to (iv) which follow.

(a)   In Western societies today, the bio-medical model of illness dominates the business of treating and curing the sick. There has been widespread public acceptance of the effectiveness of this approach to health care.

However, critics argue that modern medical treatment often results in iatrogenesis, and that many of medicine's claims to success are false. For example, many infectious diseases that were major killers in the past, such as tuberculosis, were not suddenly 'conquered' by medical advances, but steadily declined as housing and diet improved. Similarly, even if bio-medicine were effective in curing disease, this would still leave the working class at greater risk of falling ill in the first place – and, once ill, less likely to enjoy the same access to adequate health care as the middle class.

(b)   Life expectancy and death rates show that women generally live longer than men and that, in all age groups, death rates are higher for men than women. However, women consistently report higher rates of illness and lower rates of general well-being. This is especially true where they have young children. According to Nettleton (1995), in households with a child aged under one year, 39 per cent of women but only 20 per cent of men report 'always feeling tired'.

Women also have more consultations with doctors and more admissions to hospital.

However, when conditions associated with reproduction are excluded, the difference in admissions disappears among men and women aged 15–44 while, for other age groups, admission rates are actually higher for males.

(i)   Explain what is meant by the term 'biomedical model of illness'. *(2 marks)*

(ii)   Suggest three factors, apart from those referred to in Item 2(a), that may account for class differences in the risk of falling ill. *(6 marks)*

(iii) Outline the reasons why different social groups appear to have different rates of mental illness. *(12 marks)*

(iv)   Using material from Item 2(b) and elsewhere, assess sociological explanations of the patterns of women's physical illness and access to health care. *(20 marks)*

AQA, 2006

B This question requires you to apply your knowledge and understanding of sociological research methods to the study of this particular issue in health.

Read Item 2(c) below and answer the questions that follow.

(c)   Investigating health and social class

A lot of sociological research has been conducted into the links between health and social class. While working-class people are, for example, more likely to smoke and drink heavily than middle-class people, there are a number of factors which may contribute to this. A study by Marmot (1978) of civil servants showed that those in the lower grades who smoked were more likely to die of smoking-related illnesses than those who smoked in the higher grade.

Adapted from Health Chapter 1 of this textbook

Using material from Item 2(c) and elsewhere, assess the strengths and limitations of one of the following methods for the study of health and social class:

(i)   statistics

(ii)   non-participant observation. *(20 marks)*

C This question permits you to draw examples from any areas of sociology with which you are familiar.

(i)   Explain what is meant by the term 'sampling frame'. *(2 marks)*

(ii)   Suggest two problems that the researchers may have faced in using the 'doorstep survey'. *(4 marks)*

(iii) Suggest two reasons 'why some sociologists find official statistics useful' in their research. *(4 marks)*

(iv)   Examine the problems that sociologists may encounter when using postal questionnaires in their research. *(20 marks)*

AQA, 2006

Introduction

Sociological methods

Key terms

Empirical: relating to observation or experiment rather than theory.

Natural sciences: these include chemistry, biology and physics.

Positivist: the belief that knowledge must be based on observation or experiment.

Interpretivist: an approach in sociology that focuses on the meaning that social phenomena have for the people involved.

Value free: uninfluenced by the personal values of the researcher.

AQA Examiner's tip

It is a mistake to suggest that all sociologists, or sociological methods, are either 'positivist' or 'interpretivist'. It is not that simple. For many years, researchers have recognised that different approaches suit different subject matter, and that most social phenomena are best studied using a combination of methods.

Sociologists are inquisitive: they are curious about the social world around them, how it works, and how one social context or way of life compares with another. They want to know, understand and explain about society and social institutions, about organisations, and about how people interact with each other, and sometimes their findings will help to guide social policy and make the world a better place.

Good sociology is based on good **empirical** evidence that has been collected using reliable research techniques. Just as in good research in the **natural sciences**, the evidence and the conclusions drawn from it are published so that others can judge whether the evidence supports the conclusions.

Three forms of research are undertaken by sociologists:

■ **Descriptive research.** This aims only to describe what is being studied, to gather information and to increase our knowledge of the social world, asking questions like 'How do the exam results of boys compare with those of girls?' or 'How do doctors and nurses interact with patients in hospital wards?'

■ **Explanatory research.** This starts with description but goes on to look for the causes of social phenomena, such as 'Why do boys do less well than girls in exams?' or 'Why do some ethnic minorities suffer worse health than others?' It looks for the causes of problems, social and/or sociological.

■ **Action research.** The researcher is actively involved in planning and introducing some change of policy and practice in a particular setting (e.g. a school, a hospital) and then in studying the impact of the change as it happens in order to evaluate its effects.

Sociologists study people and social phenomena: the appropriateness of research methods chosen depends on how social phenomena are viewed. If considered similar to natural phenomena, the research methods of the natural scientists can be borrowed; however, if considered different from natural phenomena, other different research methods should be used. This is the basis of the debate between **positivist** and **interpretivist** approaches to sociology.

■ **Positivist approach.** This argues that social phenomena are as real and objective as natural phenomena, and that sociologists should study only what they can objectively see, measure and count. It further argues that sociologists should use methods that produce quantitative data, aim to avoid personal involvement and produce **value-free** evidence.

■ **Interpretivist approach.** This argues that social phenomena are different from natural phenomena, and that people are active, conscious beings who act with intention and purpose. For example, a family is not just a group of people with a biological relationship but a group of people who perceive themselves as a family and act accordingly. Social researchers need methods that enable them to investigate these shared understandings, generating qualitative data.

Choosing what to research

Learning objective:

Learning objective:

- Understand how sociologists choose what to research.

💡 Selecting a topic

The first step in doing research is to decide what to study. The sociologist's choice will be influenced by:

- **The interests and values of the researcher** Obviously, any researcher will want to study topics they find interesting, but the question of 'values' raises some questions. If a researcher thinks a topic is important enough to research, perhaps because it raises moral or political questions, they may have strong feelings about it, so there must be a risk that these feelings will affect how they perceive the situation and conduct their research. For example, many sociologists are interested in social inequality in all its forms (e.g. class, gender and sexism, ethnicity and racism). Some critics say that this makes sociology politically biased.

- **Current debates in the academic world** Sociologists, like anyone else, will be drawn to study topics that are creating interest and controversy among their colleagues.

- **Topics that are of general interest at the time** These are often to do with what the media, powerful people or everyday public opinion regard as 'social problems'.

Areas in which sociological research can be useful

Sociological problems

A sociological problem is any aspect of social life that sociology can help to explain. Sociologists are just as interested in 'normal' behaviour as they are in deviant or abnormal behaviour. Kate Fox, for example, says she is:

> fascinated by the minutiae of normal, typical everyday life and particularly fascinated by the good, honest, decent behaviour of the vast majority of people.

Social Science Teacher, 2007

Indeed, this is a major focus of 'Watching the English' (Fox, 2005), which includes experiments about how people behave when someone bumps into them, or when someone 'queue jumps'.

Social problems

A social problem is any aspect of social life that causes private unhappiness or public friction or disorder, and that politicians and/or the media think 'something should be done about', e.g. juvenile crime, poorly performing schools, poverty or marital breakdown. While social problems are therefore sociological problems, not all sociological problems are social problems.

Social policy

If the government takes an interest in a social problem, then some form of **social policy** will be put in place. A social policy is any action by government that has a direct effect on the welfare of the citizens of a country, usually by providing income or services such as education or a health service. Specific policies include such things as tagging young offenders, creating particular kinds of school, or providing income to poor families. Obviously, social policies are linked to the political beliefs of the government of the day; they are not neutral.

Sociological research can provide government with the information and data they need to develop such policies, and some is intended to draw attention to something that the sociologist thinks should be seen as a social problem that 'something should be done about' (for example, the effect of racism in the criminal justice system). Some sociologists are directly involved in developing government policy, but this takes them a step beyond their role as a sociologist; only some sociologists choose to take this route.

Overall, however, it is important to remember that sociologists are not only interested in deviant or problematic behaviour. For example, it is just as difficult to explain how many marriages last a lifetime as it is to explain why some end in divorce.

■ Considering the practical issues

The sociologist's choice of research topic, and of research method, will also be influenced by practical issues.

■ **Time and resources needed** First-time researchers often underestimate how long it takes to collect data, analyse it and write the report. A lone researcher, perhaps studying part time for a qualification, will only be able to do a small-scale study, for example a case study. Large-scale studies, using any method or combination of methods, need a team of professional researchers and can take years to complete.

■ **Access to the subject matter** Some areas of social life are more accessible to researchers than others. For example, it is harder to get permission to study what happens in a doctor's consulting room than to study what is going on in a school classroom. It is also worth remembering that rich and powerful people can deny an access researcher more easily than poor and powerless people can. This is one reason why we know more about the lives of poor and powerless people than about the lives of the rich and powerful.

■ **Whether funding is available** Large-scale research projects are expensive: salaries, equipment, living expenses, travel, computer resources, secretarial help and a thousand other items have to be paid for. Individuals and organisations can bid for funds from sources such as the government-funded Economic and Social Research Council, or from charitable trusts, but there is stiff competition for this money. Many researchers have very limited resources.

It can be helpful to remember that a researcher's choice of topic and research methods is affected by Practical, Ethical and Theoretical issues (PETs). These are interrelated, as shown in Figure 6.2.

Sociological researchers today use whatever technique or combination of techniques is appropriate to the subject of the research rather than being committed to quantitative versus qualitative data or positivist versus interpretivist perspectives.

Fig. 6.1 *Social policies, such as tagging young offenders, are linked to the political beliefs of the government of the day*

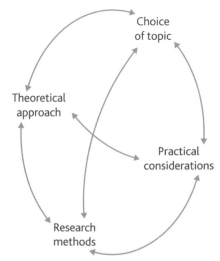

Fig. 6.2 *When designing their research, sociologists must consider practical, ethical and theoretical issues*

Sociological methods

221

Link

Further information about secondary data can be found in the Secondary data chapter, which starts on p248.

Link

There is more on sociological experiments on p245.

Reading around and formulating a hypothesis or research question

The next step in any research project is to read what others have already published on the subject. This saves repeating the same work, and may provide some secondary data. It will also give the researcher some ideas about how to approach their own project.

Hypotheses

It is all very well to be interested in a topic, but research must be focused on a specific issue. If the researcher already has a hunch about something, or wants to test an idea, they can formulate a hypothesis. This is simply a statement that can be tested. It is a prediction of what the research will find.

For example: 'Students who study AS-level Sociology watch the TV news more often than students who do not study AS Sociology' is a hypothesis. It can be tested by collecting evidence about the TV news-watching habits of the two categories of student. This will confirm or reject the hypothesis, or suggest what further research is needed.

In natural science, hypotheses are tested by experiments.

Research questions

Researchers doing descriptive research do not usually start with a hypothesis. They will have a general question that has prompted the research but they do not make predictions. However, they may develop a hypothesis as they learn more about what they are studying.

Summary questions

1 What is the difference between a social problem and a sociological problem?

2 What is 'social policy'?

3 What are some of the practical issues for researchers?

Choosing how to research

Learning objective:

- Understand how sociologists plan and design a research project.

Key term

Primary data: data collected by the researcher.

Link

A more in-depth look at surveys can be found on p232 and there is further detail about observation on p238.

Deciding what kind of data to use

First, there is the choice of whether to base the research on **primary data** (i.e. data collected by the researcher), or on secondary data (i.e. data that is already available). In either case, the data will have to be analysed and interpreted by the researcher.

Primary data

The most common methods of collecting primary data are:

- **By survey** Usually involving questionnaires (perhaps sent by post) and/or interviews, this generates mainly quantitative data.
- **By observation** This may be participant (where the researcher joins in the life of the group being studied) or non-participant (where the researcher remains detached from the group); this generates mainly qualitative data.

Figure 6.3 shows how the methods vary according to how many people can be studied and how closely the researcher is involved with the people being researched. It also shows how the methods produce more or less quantitative or qualitative data, and are therefore more or less appropriate to a positivist or interpretivist approach.

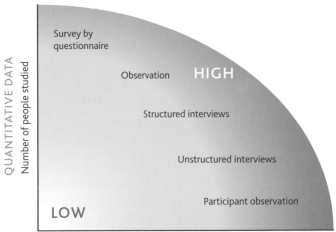

Fig. 6.3 *An overview of how various research methods compare with each other*

Link

Further information about secondary data can be found in the Secondary data chapter, which starts on p248.

Secondary data

Secondary data refers to data that is already available to sociologists. This includes:

- Official statistics collected by government agencies (quantitative).
- Reports in newspapers, TV and radio (mostly qualitative).
- Historical documents (quantitative and qualitative)
- Personal letters and diaries (qualitative).
- Research done by private or business organisations.

Sociological methods

223

Triangulation: the use of multiple methods in research as a means of producing more reliable data than a single method would produce.

Multiple methods: another term for triangulation.

Fig. 6.4 *There is a mass of evidence already available to sociologists*

AQA Examiner's tip

In the exam, do not suggest that triangulation is a method. It is a way of designing a piece of research.

■ Hint

When you are reading research, you should always check on how the researchers have operationalised their concepts.

Summary questions

4 Give an example of primary data.

5 Give two examples of secondary data.

6 What does 'to operationalise a concept' mean?

■ Preparing the research design

The research design sets out how the researcher will collect evidence, and what methods and techniques will be used. Some research designs may use only one method of data collection (for example, a survey using a written questionnaire). Many research designs use more than one method, perhaps combining observation with interviews, together with a study of documents or history, to look at the subject matter from several angles and gain a more complete picture. This is sometimes called **triangulation** (or **multiple methods**) and again illustrates how sociologists should not be pigeon-holed into positivist and interpretivist categories.

■ Operationalising concepts

All researchers have to 'operationalise' concepts. This means defining the phenomenon being studied so that it can be identified, and perhaps counted or measured, in a way that is clearly understood and that can be used consistently. This may be straightforward. For example, if we want to study changes over time in the age at which women give birth to their first baby, it is easy to agree on what is meant by 'age', 'women', 'give birth' and 'baby', and to express these in objective, quantitative terms. However, what if we want to study changes in health and illness over time? We have to decide what we mean by 'healthy' – that is, we have to operationalise the concept 'healthy'. Do we mean a state where the individual says they feel well, or a state where a doctor can find nothing wrong, or a physical condition where the individual can lead the sort of life they want to lead? And should we include mental health as well as physical health in our definition?

Clearly, how we define and operationalise 'health' will affect how many healthy people we find and, to make comparisons over time, we must always use the same definition.

■ Postmodernist criticism of sociological research

In recent years, postmodernist sociologists have questioned the whole basis on which all types of research are carried out, including research in the natural sciences. They argue that the 'truth' cannot be found because it does not exist as an objective reality. This would mean that what was true for a middle-class white male in England in 1995, might not be true for a black upper-class American woman in 2008.

It is not that either one is wrong, but that 'truth' is relative to social position, time and place. We each have our own interpretation of reality, and all interpretations are equally valid. All knowledge is selective and relative: none is 'better' than any other. It follows that any sociological researcher's account of 'reality' must also be relative and is therefore no more valuable as an account of the 'truth' than anyone else's.

The problem with this argument is that it leaves us with no way of judging whether the findings of any piece of social research are more valid or more reliable than any other. It must also mean that the postmodernist view is also 'just another' version of reality.

Gomm (2004) dismisses the postmodernist position by stating that, as a theory that denies the existence of truth, it cannot make a helpful contribution to research methods.

Chapter summary

Further resources

www.esrc.ac.uk – The Economic and Social Research Council 'aim[s] to provide high quality research on issues of importance to business, the public sector and government [including] economic competitiveness, the effectiveness of public services and policy, and our quality of life.'

- Sociologists choose what to research on the basis of their interests and values, current debates in the academic world, and topics of interest to the media, politics and public opinion.

- Sociologists study not only social problems but also the ordinary and everyday.

- The choice of research topic is also influenced by practical issues such as time, resources, access and funding.

- Research projects go through a series of stages, starting with identifying a hypothesis or research question.

- Researchers use both primary and secondary data and many research designs involve a combination of research methods.

- It is essential to operationalise research concepts.

- Postmodernists argue that 'truth' and 'reality' do not exist in any objective sense.

Sociological methods

How can sociological research be evaluated?

Evaluation criteria

Learning objective:

■ Understand the meaning and the importance of reliability, validity and representativeness.

💡 Good sociology is based on good evidence. It is not just a matter of opinion. That is easy to say, but it prompts the question: 'What is the difference between good evidence and poor evidence?'

There are three main questions to be asked about any piece of sociological research:

■ Is the method of data collection **reliable**?

■ Is the data valid?

■ Are the people or the social setting representative?

Fig. 6.5 *When evaluating sociological research, its reliability, validity and representativeness need to be considered*

Key term

Reliability: a reliable method gives the same result when the research is repeated.

Hint

The difference between an opinion and a judgement is that a judgement is backed up by good evidence. Sociologists should make judgements.

■ Reliability

To say that a method of collecting data is 'reliable' is to mean that anybody else using this method (or the same person using it on another occasion) would produce the same findings. Take a simple example from the natural world. If one person measures the acreage of a farm on one day, using surveying equipment that is in good condition, and another person measures it again a week later, using another set of equipment that is in equally good condition, the only reason why their results might differ would be that one of them had made a mistake in using the equipment or in doing the calculations. They have operationalised the concept of area by using 'acre' and have used this as the unit of measurement. The method is reliable.

A survey using a well-designed questionnaire is reliable. The same results should be gained, regardless of who is asking the questions. By contrast, research that involves a researcher working alone and relying on their own interpretation of what they see, like much participant observation research, must be suspect as to its reliability.

■ Validity

For data to be regarded as valid, it must be a 'true' picture of what is being studied. Or, to put it another way, is it really evidence of what it claims to be evidence of?

For example, suppose we wanted to investigate racist attitudes in the medical profession. If we designed a questionnaire that asked doctors about their attitude to ethnic minorities, we would certainly get some data that could be expressed statistically. But would this data be a measure of doctors' attitudes to ethnic minorities, or a measure of what they will say when they are asked about their attitudes?

A questionnaire may be well designed and produce reliable data but, if the data is invalid, it is of no use to the researcher. The data is a product of the research method rather than an account of what is being studied. Questionnaire-based research may be in danger of collecting data about how people will answer questions rather than about what they actually believe or how they actually behave.

The strength of participant observation is that, when done well, it produces valid data that reflects the reality of a situation, unaffected by the research method that is used. In this example, the researcher might get a more valid picture of doctors' attitudes to ethnic minorities by joining the staff of a hospital.

■ Representativeness

This is about how far the individual, group or situation being studied is typical of the rest of the population. If those being studied are typical, then we can claim that what is true of them is also true of the population.

Researchers who conduct quantitative surveys have various ways of selecting a sample and there are sophisticated tools to assess how far a sample is representative of the whole population. However, very small-scale research must always be questionable as to its representativeness.

■ Getting the balance right

In practice, good sociological research often involves a trade-off between reliability, validity and representativeness. This is done by collecting data in several different ways. Thus Barker (1984), in her study of the Moonies, used written questionnaires and face-to-face interviews, joined a group of Moonies (at their invitation) in their everyday life and for religious meetings and ceremonies, and read all she could about their beliefs. She also compared the attitudes of the Moonies she worked with to the attitudes of a group of non-Moonies.

AQA **Examiner's tip**

You will often be asked about reliability and validity in sociology exams. Make sure you know which is which and what the difference is.

■ Link

There is more detailed discussion of the different ways of selecting a sample on p232.

Summary questions

1 What is 'reliability'?

2 What is 'validity'?

3 What is 'representativeness'?

Sociological methods

Sociology and values

Learning objectives:

- Understand the problems posed by bias and objectivity.
- Appreciate the ethical issues of sociological research.

💡 Bias and objectivity

Science should be objective – that is, its methods and its findings should not be influenced by the personal interests or bias of the researcher. It is supposed to discover facts and be value free. There are major debates about the supposed objectivity of natural science but the problem of value freedom is even greater in sociology. The more that sociologists study topics that they feel strongly about, and the closer they get to the people they are studying, the greater the risk of bias creeping into their research.

Everyone has values – beliefs about what is morally right or morally wrong, but is it possible to keep these values out of the research process? Similarly, many sociologists hope that their work will influence social policy in areas such as education, crime or social welfare. It could be argued that this will lead to bias but, if it does, then it could be argued that the work of a natural scientist hoping to find a cure for disease is also biased.

Sociologists have argued for years about whether sociology:

- is value free
- can be value free
- should be value free.

Values and bias can enter into sociological research at every stage of the research process, including decisions on:

- what to research
- who pays for the research
- what research methods to use
- which questions to ask and which to leave out
- who, what, where and how to observe
- what secondary data to study
- what data or information to record (from questioning, observation or reading documents)
- how to interpret data and observations, and the conclusions reached
- what to include in the research report
- whether the report is published.

Most sociologists today would agree that sociology cannot be completely value free but there is disagreement about how to respond to this.

Some would argue that, while values will inevitably affect what topics a sociologist chooses to study (for example, a sociologist who feels strongly about domestic violence will be interested in studying it), the research methods should be as objective and value free as possible. Personal bias and opinions should not affect the questions that are asked, the observations that are made or the explanations that are offered.

Others would argue that some degree of bias and value is inevitable and that value freedom is a myth. The important thing is for the researcher to be open and honest about their values, so that the reader can take this into account when assessing the work.

Yet others would argue that sociologists should take a committed approach to their work, using it to defend the interests of the poor and the powerless and to challenge the authority and power of dominant groups. Feminists, for example, argue that sociology should challenge patriarchy. Marxists argue that sociology should reveal how the ruling classes maintain their power.

Some, including postmodernists, would argue that there are no facts or objective truths anyway and that there is no way of deciding whether one 'account' is any better (more accurate, more objective) than another.

Sociological research is always at risk of being biased and lacking objectivity. Research reports must therefore give a full account of how the research was done, and the data collected must be available for other sociologists to check, along with the conclusions. Bias is not necessarily a bad thing; what is wrong is to claim to present 'objective facts' when in practice the work has been influenced by personal values or opinions.

In theory at least, natural science is unbiased. Supposedly, natural scientists take an objective approach to their work and do not allow their personal feelings or values to affect their work. It is value free, in contrast to sociology – which is accused of being biased. In practice, there is considerable argument about whether natural science really is, or should be, value free.

Fig. 6.6 *Some argue that sociologists should use their work to defend the interests of the powerless*

Ethics in sociological research

Ethics is the study of what is morally right or wrong. There are ethical issues in social research just as there are in the natural sciences.

The main ethical principles of social research are that:

- No one should suffer any harm as a result of the research.
- Researchers should be honest and open about what they are doing.
- Participants' rights to privacy and confidentiality should be protected.
- No laws should be broken.

Harm

Obviously, sociological research should not risk physical harm to participants. This is seldom a problem. However, there may be a risk of harming someone:

- emotionally (for example, by asking insensitive questions)
- socially (for example, by damaging their reputation, or exposing them to ridicule or punishment).

Ethical research is designed to avoid these risks. In a very few cases, sociological research may put the researcher at risk of physical harm: for example, when studying criminal activity. This is rare and is not, in any case, an ethical problem in the sense that it is the researcher's decision as to whether to take the risk; they are not exposing anyone else to danger.

Honesty and openness

Ethical researchers seek the informed consent of participants, ensuring that they have agreed to take part in the research and that they know:

- that the research is going on
- who is doing it
- why it is being done
- how the results will be used.

AQA Examiner's tip

In the exam, do not just say that a piece of research is biased. Always explain why you think this. Was the sample biased? Or the questions? Or the conclusions drawn by the researcher? Or what?

It is not always a straightforward matter to gain informed consent. In some contexts, it may not be possible to inform everyone involved in the research, or they may not understand what is going on. For example, very young children or people with learning disabilities may not be able fully to understand what the researcher is doing.

Privacy and confidentiality

All research participants have a right to their privacy. They have a right to know what the research is about and to refuse to take part in it or to answer particular questions. If they do take part, they must be sure that whatever they say cannot be traced back to them as individuals, i.e. it is confidential.

Ethical researchers are careful to disguise the identity of individual participants when they write up their research. This is easy in the context of a survey, where individuals may be anonymous in the first place and where individual responses are merged into totals. It is more difficult when a small group of people has been studied through participant observation, and where particular characters are described or quoted. Simply changing the name of a location or an individual may not be enough to preserve their anonymity.

A good recent example of this occurred in June 2007 when the journal *Health and Place* published Francine Watkins' account of life in the village of 'Stonycroft', which included unflattering descriptions of some of the residents. It did not take long for the press to decide that this was in fact Little Milton in Oxfordshire, prompting a flurry of denials from the residents.

Legality

Perhaps obviously, researchers should not become involved in illegal activity. This can sometimes be a problem for a researcher studying criminal behaviour, who may be asked to help with or take part in the activity.

🔍 Evaluating research reports

You should always evaluate (in other words, weigh up the strengths and weaknesses) of research reports and evidence. It may help to ask the following questions:

- What were the aims of the research?
- Why was the topic chosen?
- What were the theoretical and practical issues? How might these have affected the methods or the findings?
- Who paid for the research to be done? How might this have affected the choice of topic, the methods or the findings?
- What research methods were used?
- Why were they chosen? Were they appropriate to the topic?
- What are the key concepts? How are they operationalised?
- Are the methods reliable?
- Is the data valid?
- How was the sample or group selected? How far is it representative of the wider population?
- What ethical problems are raised by the research? Were they properly dealt with?

Summary questions

4 Why is objectivity important in sociological research?

5 What are the main ethical issues in sociological research?

Chapter summary

Further resources

www.britsoc.co.uk – The British Sociological Association's 'Statement of ethical practice' can be found on their website. This provides awareness of and guidance on ethical issues that may arise in the research process.

- Good evidence is reliable, valid and representative.

- Some methods produce more reliable evidence, some produce more valid evidence, and some produce more representative evidence. It is helpful to balance these by using more than one method in a single piece of research.

- Ideally, science is objective and value free. However, there are major debates about whether sociology is, can be, or should be value free.

- There are serious ethical issues in sociological research, particularly when collecting primary data from respondents.

- All research should be carefully evaluated.

6.3 Social surveys

Carrying out a social survey

Learning objectives:

- Know and understand the process of carrying out a social survey.

- Understand the importance and types of sampling.

Key terms

Population: all the people, or other units, who are relevant to the research.

Interview schedule: the list of questions used by the interviewer.

Pilot: a small-scale trial of a questionnaire/interview schedule, carried out to check that the questions 'work' as they are expected to.

Sampling frame: the list of people, or other unit, from which a sample is drawn.

The survey method is widely used in sociology because it can obtain large amounts of data in the form of statistics (this is 'quantitative' data) from a large number of people over a wide area in a relatively short space of time. A survey is sometimes used on its own as the complete research design and sometimes in association with other methods, as part of a larger design.

Survey research is about asking questions. The researcher has to decide who to ask, what questions to ask and how to ask the questions (e.g. by post, by email or face to face).

The steps required in order to carry out a survey are as follows:

- Formulate the research question or hypothesis.
- Identify the **population**.
- Draft the questionnaire/**interview schedule**.
- **Pilot** the questionnaire/interview schedule.
- Finalise the questionnaire/interview schedule.
- Select the sample.
- Collect the data.
- Process/analyse the data.
- Write the report.

Who should be included in the survey?

After formulating the research question or hypothesis, the first task is to identify the population, which may be made up of individuals, or schools, or hospital wards, or whatever other social unit is being studied. Since many populations are very large, surveys are usually carried out on a sample (i.e. a small proportion). So, the next step is to select a sample, which should be representative of the population – what is true of the sample should be true of the population as a whole.

There are various different ways of doing this, and researchers should choose the method that best suits the form of research they are going to conduct.

Random sampling

In random sampling, every member of the population has an equal chance of being included in the sample. For this, a **sampling frame** (i.e. a list of the population) is needed.

Once the sampling frame is known, the sample can be 'random' (for example, chosen by taking names out of a hat, or using random numbers generated by a computer), or 'quasi-random' (for example, chosen by taking every tenth name from the list). Statistical checks can then be made that the sample is representative of the population.

Stratified random sampling

If the researcher has a sampling frame that shows the main characteristics of the population, it is possible to ensure that the sample includes the right proportions in each category. For example, if the researcher knows that, of 1,000 pupils in a school, 55 per cent (550) are boys and 45 per cent (450) are girls, the sample should contain the same boy to girl ratio. So, if the sample were to be, say, a tenth of the population (100 students), then it should consist of 55 per cent boys and 45 per cent girls – 55 boys and 45 girls.

Quota sampling

In this case, rather than identifying individuals in a sample and then contacting them, the researcher establishes how many participants are needed in each category and goes looking for them. For example, if a researcher wants to interview 50 men aged 40–55 who have mortgages and live in Hertfordshire, he or she can go to where such people are likely to be found and ask one after another if they are willing to be interviewed until the quota is filled. It does not require a sampling frame and is not truly representative. This method is often used in market research.

Snowball sampling

Here the researcher interviews an individual and then asks them to suggest who else might be interviewed. The sample can grow as large as the researcher wants. It will not be representative in the statistical sense.

Convenience sampling

A convenience sample is simply one that it is easy for the researcher to contact. For example, a researcher wanting to study how people felt about their treatment in NHS A&E departments would simply get permission to approach people at one or two A&E departments reasonably close by. The findings would be interesting but could not be considered representative of all A&E departments in the NHS. On the other hand, this would be a very good way to pilot a questionnaire.

💡 Asking questions

The next stage of the process is to think about the questions to be asked and how to ask them. These can take the form of either a questionnaire or an interview.

Questionnaires

These are simply lists of questions written down in advance and asked in a fixed order. They can be administered face to face, by telephone, or by post or email (when the respondent will write the answers).

Questions may be:

- **Closed** The range of possible answers is fixed.
  For example: Did you vote at the last general election? Yes/No

- **Open-ended** The respondent can answer however they like.
  For example: Why did you vote at the last general election?

- **Multiple-choice** There are a number of options the respondent can choose from when answering.
  For example: Did you abstain from voting because:
  a   you did not think it would make any difference
  b   you thought none of the candidates were worth voting for
  c   you forgot
  d   you were away from home
  e   other reason?

■ **Scaled** There are a number of options based on a scale ranging from one possible answer to its opposite.
For example: How do you rate Gordon Brown's performance as Prime Minister?
Excellent – Good – Satisfactory – Unsatisfactory – Poor

Closed, multiple-choice or scaled questions can produce quantitative data, but limit the answers the respondent can give, so they may be less valid. Open-ended questions enable the respondent to express themselves but produce data that is difficult to express quantitatively.

Interviews

Interviews can be structured or unstructured. In a structured interview, the researcher reads out a list of questions (the interview schedule) and writes down or records the respondent's answers. An unstructured interview is more like a guided conversation, where the talk is informal but the researcher asks questions to ensure that the participant keeps to the subject of the research. Many sociological interviews are halfway between: a mix of structured and unstructured, or semi-structured.

Responses from structured interviews can be expressed quantitatively; responses from unstructured interviews produce qualitative data that have to be analysed and written up by the researcher, though it may be possible to convert some into statistical terms.

Fig. 6.7 *Interviews are a useful research method for gathering sociological data*

Piloting

Before going ahead with full-scale research, a pilot study should always be carried out. This provides the opportunity to test questionnaires and interview schedules on a small group of people from the research population, in order to check that the questions asked are clear and unambiguous, that they do not upset or lead the participants, and that they will produce the kind of data that is wanted. If necessary, the draft questionnaire or interview schedule can then be revised in the light of any problems encountered before the main research takes place.

Summary questions

1. What is the purpose of sampling?

2. What is the difference between closed and open questions?

3. Why is it important to pilot a questionnaire or interview schedule?

Advantages and disadvantages

Table 6.1 summarises the advantages and disadvantages of questionnaires and interviews (both structured and unstructured). It is important to remember that, despite the various difficulties encountered in using the survey research method, when conducted properly, a survey can produce reliable data that is representative of a large number of people.

	Questionnaires (by post, telephone or email)	Structured interviews (face to face or by telephone)	Unstructured interviews (face to face or by telephone)
Potential advantages	• Can reach large sample • Personal influence of researcher is slight • Produces quantitative, reliable and representative data	Similar to questionnaires, but: • Higher response rates • Can 'probe' the participant's responses by asking follow-up questions • Can assess truthfulness of participant	• Can create rapport with participant • Can follow up responses in depth • Produces valid qualitative data
Potential disadvantages	• Response rates may be low • Answers may be incomplete • Data may not be valid or even truthful • Cannot be sure who completed the questionnaire • Limits possible answers the participant can give	• 'Interview effect', e.g. participant may wish to impress or please the interviewer • 'Interviewer effect' age/gender, etc. of interviewer may influence participant's answers • Time-consuming, so fewer participants and less representative • Limits possible answers participant can give	• Personal bias of interviewer • Data may be less reliable • Time-consuming

Table 6.1. *Advantages and disadvantages of ways of asking questions in social surveys*

Response rates

However carefully a sample is identified, if not enough people agree to take part in the research the results will be unrepresentative. Postal questionnaires tend to have low response rates. A sample that starts out as representative will become less so if the response rate is low.

Time and cost

It is not always the case that surveys are cheaper than other methods of research, or that they can be done more quickly. A large-scale survey can be very expensive and data-processing can take a long time. However, it is broadly true to say that, for the same cost and in the same time, more data can be collected by social survey than by ethnographic research.

Fig. 6.8 *Postal questionnaires can have low response rates, meaning that the sample studied can become unrepresentative*

■ Validity

Overall, the main problem with surveys, using any type of question, is that they are contrived situations and must therefore lack validity, as discussed in the previous chapter. The participant always knows that they are involved in social research, so we can never be sure that the answers they give to questions are frank, true or accurate. This is not to say that they are deliberately lying; they may genuinely believe the answers they give. Observing participants in a real-life situation may, however, suggest a different picture.

■ Showing change over time

Most surveys provide a snapshot of the social context that is being studied. They cannot provide a description of change over time. Longitudinal surveys, which take place over a long period of time, are a way of addressing this problem.

Some are panel surveys, where the same group of people is interviewed at intervals over a period of years. Examples include two of the British birth cohort studies, the 1958 National Child Development Study (NCDS), and the 1970 British Cohort Study (BCS). These studies have followed up all babies born in a single week in the year the study began from birth to adulthood, with new data about many aspects of cohort members' lives being collected at regular intervals. For example, the most recent BCS survey, done in 2004, has revealed how poor standards of numeracy and literacy at age 21 affect every aspect of the lives of adults, but particularly of women.

The main problems of panel surveys, in addition to the problems of all surveys, are the cost of maintaining them (for nearly 50 years in some cases), keeping in touch with the sample and the question of whether being a member of the sample affects how people think or behave.

In other longitudinal surveys, the same questions (or very similar questions) are repeated at intervals but with different groups of respondents: prime examples of these include the British Social Attitudes Survey, the British Crime Survey and the Census.

Summary questions

4 Why are response rates important?

5 Why might a survey be considered not to produce valid evidence?

6 What is the main advantage of a longitudinal survey?

Chapter summary

Further resources

http://qb.soc.surrey.ac.uk – The Centre for Applied Social Studies (CASS) has a bank of survey questionnaires where you can study all the different types of questions.

www.iser.essex.ac.uk/ulsc – To find out more about longitudinal surveys, including the British Household Panel Survey, visit the United Kingdom Longitudinal Studies Centre website.

www.cls.ioe.ac.uk – Further information about longitudinal studies can be found at the Centre for Longitudinal Studies website.

www.homeoffice.gov.uk/rds/bcs1.html – For the British Crime Survey, see the Home Office website.

www.statistics.gov.uk/census/ – Census statistics can be found on the National Statistics website.

- The survey method is widely used in sociology because it can obtain large amounts of data in the form of statistics (quantitative data) from a large number of people over a wide area in a relatively short space of time.

- The researcher must identify a population and then select a sample, using one of a range of possible sampling techniques.

- Questions can be asked using a questionnaire or in an interview.

- Questionnaires and interview schedules should be piloted.

- Like all research methods, social surveys have advantages and disadvantages, but there is always a doubt about their validity.

- Surveys take a 'snapshot', but longitudinal surveys make it possible to study change over a period of time.

Sociological methods

Participant observation

Learning objectives:

■ Understand what is meant by 'ethnographic research'.

■ Understand the principles of participant observation.

'Ethnographic' means simply 'writing about a way of life'. Various methods are used in this kind of research but the most well known is participant observation. As the name suggests, this is a research method in which the researcher takes part in the life of the people or group that is being researched, while at the same time observing and taking notes about what is going on. The researcher collects mainly qualitative data.

■ Origins

The origins of this method lie in the work of the early **anthropologists** such as Malinowski, Evans-Pritchard and Radcliffe-Brown, who did most of their research in the first part of the 20th century. Malinowski, for example, studied the people of the Trobriand Islands. He believed that the only way to get a valid picture of their way of life was to study them at first hand by living among them and learning their language, taking notes and recording his observations on a day-to-day basis.

The method of participant observation took a while to be adopted by sociologists who, in the 1920s and 1930s, were still mainly concerned with studying the structure of societies from a **macro** perspective rather than looking at the intricacies of everyday life from a **micro** perspective. The Chicago School of researchers in America in the 1930s was the exception to this. The leader of this group, Robert Park, encouraged his colleagues to take part in all aspects of the life of the city and to 'go get the seats of your pants dirty in real research'. This approach was continued in the 1950s and 1960s by Howard Becker, who spent several years studying medical students as well as a variety of deviant groups, and Erving Goffman, who is best known for his research in 'total institutions', particularly mental hospitals.

Key terms

Anthropology: originally the study of the culture of small pre-industrial societies, its methods are now used in many contexts.

Macro: large scale.

Micro: small scale.

Link

There is more information on community studies on p242.

■ What is involved

In a participant observation study, the researcher joins the group or social situation that is being studied. The aim is to understand what is happening from the point of view of those involved, to 'get inside their heads' and to understand the meaning that they give to their situation. The research is naturalistic: it is done in the natural setting and is not based on the artificial situation created by an interview or questionnaire. The research may take many months or even years. It is used particularly by researchers who are interested in the sociology of deviance but has also been used in a variety of community studies carried out in Britain and in the US.

Level of participation

How far the researcher participates in the research varies from one project to another, and at different stages of the same piece of research. The researcher may be:

- **A complete participant** The researcher conceals the fact that they are doing research and this is known as **covert observation**. It is rare since almost all researchers also interview the people they are studying, usually in an unstructured way.

  An example is the work of the investigative journalist Fran Abrams, who took on three different jobs that paid the minimum wage in order to research how it was possible to survive on such low pay (Abrams, 2002).

- **A participant observer** The researcher is actively involved with the group but known to be researching. This is **overt observation**. An example of this is Thornton's research into raves and dance clubs in the 1990s (Thornton, 1995). She went to dance clubs but also interviewed the clubbers, so there was no secret about her research.

- **A non-participant observer** The researcher is a detached and unobtrusive onlooker. This may be either covert (for example, using a two-way mirror to observe behaviour) or overt (for example, a researcher might sit in a classroom watching what is going on and making notes).

  This is necessary when the researcher is very different from those being researched because of, for example, their age or sex. Paul Connolly used this method, together with interviews, when researching racism and gender identities in a multi-ethnic inner-city primary school (Connolly, 1998).

Covert research goes against the principle of informed consent, discussed previously in this topic, and so may be considered unethical. A researcher might argue that the research would be impossible if the group members knew they were being studied (for example, if they are involved in criminal activity), but this may simply mean that some sorts of sociological research should not be undertaken.

Overt research is more ethical but runs the risk of affecting the behaviour of the people who are being studied.

Key terms

Covert observation: observational research where the researcher conceals the fact that they are doing research.'

Overt observation: observational research where the researcher is open about the fact that they are doing research.

Fig. 6.9 *It is important that the participant observer is as inconspicuous as possible*

Sociological methods

■ The stages of participant observation

Choosing the topic and group

The reasons for choosing a topic will be much the same as those listed in the section on social surveys. However, participant observation is particularly appropriate for studying deviant groups such as street gangs who would be unlikely to respond to a questionnaire. There are also several studies of occupational groups (for example, police officers, factory workers), many of whose activities are invisible to the general public.

Joining the group

Occasionally, the researcher is already a member of the group being studied (for example, Holdaway's 1983 study about the police). The researcher may be invited to do the research (for example, Barker and her work on the Moonies, 1984). If the group has a formal membership, the researcher can join it (for example, Festinger *et al.*'s work on religious sects, 1956). Very often, the researcher has to find a way of joining the group they want to study. This is usually done by befriending an individual who then introduces the researcher to the group. This individual typically becomes the researcher's **key informant** (for example, Doc in Whyte's study of 1955).

Taking part in the life of the group

In the early stages, the researcher will tend to keep quiet, listening to and observing what is being said and done and gaining the trust of the group until their presence is taken for granted. From the start, the researcher will take notes and keep a field diary, as inconspicuously as possible. After a while (sometimes a long while), ideas will begin to crystallise in the researcher's mind and it will be possible to start asking questions, particularly of the key informant. How far this is possible will depend largely on whether the group members know that the research is being done, i.e. whether the research is overt or covert. Towards the end of the research, there may be an opportunity to conduct unstructured interviews.

The researcher must strike a balance between getting involved with the group and remaining an observer. If the researcher gets too involved – 'goes native' – they will lose the detached perspective (objectivity) that a researcher must have.

Leaving the group

Eventually, the researcher must leave the group and begin writing up and analysing the notes and other material they have collected. Leaving the group may raise ethical questions. Will friends feel let down? Has the group come to depend on the researcher for advice or help? Has the researcher simply been using the group for their own ends?

Writing the report

The research report should describe the group's behaviour, suggest reasons (hypotheses) for this behaviour and, crucially, show how the evidence supports these suggestions. The researcher will have developed some tentative hypotheses about the group throughout the research, but the report must show how far the evidence supports these hypotheses.

Key term

Key informant: an individual who is the main link between the researcher and the group being researched and provides much of the information about the group.

Summary questions

1 Why is participant observation considered 'naturalistic'?

2 What is the difference between overt and covert observation?

3 Why is participant observation often used to study deviant groups?

4 What is meant by 'going native'?

Advantages and disadvantages

Learning objectives:

- Be aware of the strengths, weaknesses and ethics of participant observation.

- Be aware of other methods of ethnographic research.

Advantages

- Participants behave as they normally do, so evidence is valid.
- It takes the viewpoint of the participants rather than the researcher, i.e. it does not impose the researcher's framework on the participants, as a questionnaire does.
- It can dig deep into social interaction.
- The researcher is open to new insights (questions are not fixed in advance).

Disadvantages

- It studies small groups, so may not be representative.
- It cannot be checked or repeated, so may not be reliable.
- It is time-consuming in relation to the amount of data collected.
- The researcher's presence may change the behaviour of the group.
- The researcher may be biased, or even 'go native'.

If the research is covert, further potential disadvantages can occur:

- It raises serious ethical issues, particularly in relation to informed consent.
- The researcher may be 'at risk' if their identity is revealed.
- The researcher may not be able to ask the questions they would like to ask, as this would risk giving away the fact that they are doing research.

Ethics

We have already considered the ethics of overt or covert observation and the question of informed consent. However, participant observation raises particular problems in relation to the other ethical principles outlined previously.

These include the following questions:

- How can the researcher protect the confidentiality and anonymity of the people who have been researched? Simply changing names and locations may not be enough.
- If the group or individuals can be identified, is there a risk of any harm to them, whether of ridicule or, more seriously, of arrest or reprisals?
- Is there any risk to the researcher if certain information is published? Is this a good reason for not publishing it?
- Are there any circumstances when a researcher should breach confidentiality (e.g. where a serious crime is being planned)?

Link

Refer back to the section on 'Ethics in sociological research' (p229) for a reminder of the ethical principles that need to be considered in sociological research.

Sociological methods

241

Key term

Case study: the study of a single example of a phenomenon.

■ Other methods of ethnographic research

Case studies

A **case study** is an in-depth study of a single example of whatever it is that the sociologist wants to investigate. It may be an individual, a group, an event, or an institution or organisation. A range of research methods are possible but participant observation, often with some form of interview, is often used.

Case studies do not claim to be representative but can often throw vivid light on some aspect of social life that then prompts further and more extensive research.

Life histories

A life history is a type of case study in which the aim is to describe and interpret a person's life because it is in some way remarkable, or because it is typical of some marginalised or 'invisible' social group. Life histories are usually gained through unstructured interviewing and may be reported in the person's own words. Letters and documents may also be used. Focusing on an individual can highlight what is critical in the experience of a particular social group in a way that no amount of surveys or participant observation can do.

Community studies

A number of studies of whole communities, such as a village or a small town, have been conducted using ethnographic methods (e.g. participant observation) together with a range of other sources of data (surveys, public documents, census data, other secondary sources). This is a good example of the importance of using multiple research methods in combination rather than relying on just one.

Link

For more on the various sources of secondary data, see pp248 and 250.

Summary questions

5 What are some of the ethical issues with participant observation?

6 What is a case study?

7 What is a community study?

Fig. 6.10 *Community studies are a good example of where multiple research methods might be used*

Chapter summary

Further resources

www.britsoc.org.uk – The British Sociological Association has produced ethical guidelines which can be found on their website.

- Ethnographic research studies the whole way of life of a group of people.

- The most common method is participant observation, where the researcher joins a group and observes how they act and behave. It is often combined with interviewing.

- The extent of the researcher's participation varies from one study to another.

- The researcher may work overtly or covertly.

- This kind of research is naturalistic. It is considered to be valid because it aims to present the views of those being studied rather than imposing the researcher's ideas or questions on them.

- However, there is a risk of the researcher affecting how the group behaves, and of being or becoming biased. Also, the situation or group being studied cannot be assumed to be representative.

- There is the usual range of ethical issues, particularly if the research is covert.

Learning objective:

- Understand the principles of cause and effect.

Fig. 6.11 *Historically there has been a debate over whether sociology is a science similar to the natural sciences, e.g. chemistry*

💡 Similarities

Sociologists accept that there is good sociology and bad sociology, but would claim that good sociology is superior to common sense. As we have already seen, good sociology is based on good evidence that results from good research and draws logical conclusions based on that evidence. That is what makes sociology a social science rather than just common sense or journalism.

The question of whether sociology is a science like the natural sciences was more important in the 19th and 20th centuries than it is now. At that time, it was thought that natural science could be objective and unbiased, discovering the 'facts' about causes and effects in the world, and that it would be possible to develop a 'science of society' by, as far as possible, copying the positivist research methods used by natural scientists. Today, not only is this view held by very few, if any, sociologists but there is also a debate about whether this is a correct view of how natural scientists do their research.

Cause and effect

The question of cause and effect is crucial to good science, of any kind. It is important not to assume that, just because two things seem to vary in line with each other, one is the cause of the other. If factors A and B occur together, and B changes when A changes, these factors are correlated, but it does not follow that A causes B. There may be no causal link between them, that is, it is just coincidence; it may be that B causes A; it may be that a third factor, C, is influencing them both.

For example, a researcher might find that young people who watch violent films (factor A) are violent towards other young people (factor B). It could be that:

- There is no causal link between watching violent films and violent behaviour.
- Watching violent films causes violent behaviour.
- Violent behaviour causes young people to watch violent films.
- A third factor (e.g. violence in the home) causes both the film-watching and the violent behaviour.

The purpose of explanatory research, in any of the sciences, is to determine which of these possibilities is right.

Summary questions

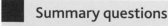

1. What does 'correlation' mean?
2. What is the difference between sociology and common sense?

Experiments

Learning objective:

- Be aware of the role and the limitations of experiments in sociology.

Key terms

Control group: the group that is not subject to an independent variable.

Experimental group: the group that is subject to the independent variable.

Dependent variable: the variable that changes as a result of the independent variable.

Independent variable: the variable that is controlled by the experimenter.

Laboratory experiments

In the natural sciences, the classic research method is the laboratory experiment. Typically, this involves setting up a **control group** and an **experimental group**, treating these groups in different ways, and then comparing the results.

Let us imagine a psychology experiment to test the hypothesis 'Having classical music playing in the background is a more helpful aid to students' exam revision than pop music'. The scientist might:

- Start by identifying the other variables that could affect the revision process, e.g. the age and sex of the students, the light, the temperature, the volume of the music, and what is being learned.
- Set up two groups (the control group and the experimental group), which are matched for variables such as age and sex – in other words, the scientist 'controls' these variables.
- Give the members of each group the same learning task in the same circumstances but with one variable changed for the experimental group (e.g. playing pop music, whereas the control group is listening to classical music).
- Measure how much each group has learned.

If there was a difference in how much each group had learned (the **dependent variable**), the scientist might conclude, after many other experiments and changes to the variables, that the type of music (the **independent variable**) affects learning.

Laboratory experiments are widely used by psychologists, but they have serious limitations in sociology due to the following reasons:

1 The laboratory is an artificial situation: it hugely simplifies any social interaction so what happens may have little relevance to the 'real world' (a validity problem).

2 Experiments can only be on a small scale and for a short time.

3 If the subjects (participants) in an experiment know that it is being done, they may not act as they usually do (a validity problem).

4 If the subjects are misled about the nature of the experiment, they cannot give informed consent (an ethical problem).

5 It is not possible for a researcher to control all the variables that might affect the subjects' behaviour (e.g. their mood, their state of health, their feelings about the whole experience).

Field experiments

Although sociologists make little use of laboratory experiments, there are several well-known examples of field experiments, where the researcher sets up a situation to observe in the 'real world'. Often-quoted examples include Rosenthal and Jacobson's experiment about the effect of teachers' expectations on pupils' performance or Rosenhan's experiment with pseudo-patients.

Link

Further information on Rosenthal and Jacobson's experiment about the effect of teachers' expectations on pupils' performance can be found on p139 and more details about Rosenhan's experiment with pseudo-patients can be found on p200.

Fig. 6.12 *A famous field experiment involving factory workers found that output improved as the participants responded positively to being researched*

Perhaps the best-known example of a field experiment is Elton Mayo's study that first identified the 'Hawthorne Effect'. In the late 1920s, Mayo and his colleagues set up a series of experiments in the Hawthorne plant of General Electric Company to identify which environmental variables affected the output of a team of workers. They varied the light, the humidity, the heat, the hours of work and other factors. The problem was that they found that output improved whatever they did, including making working conditions worse. They concluded that the key was that the employees were responding to the fact that they were being researched; they were pleased to be the centre of attention, they had formed a strong group loyalty, and they wanted to please the researchers. The key independent variable was the fact that the experiment was taking place, not any of the variables that Mayo was controlling. The research participants were human beings, not inanimate objects with no will of their own.

While it is true that field experiments may reduce some of the problems of laboratory experiments in sociology, they are still subject to the following problems:

1   The researcher has even less chance of controlling all the possible variables.
2   There may be issues about participants giving informed consent.

However, if due attention is given to minimising the ethical issues, field experiments can give important insights into social behaviour.

■ Making comparisons

Experiments may be of limited use in sociology, but the basic principle of comparing one situation with another to try to identify causes lies behind most explanatory research in sociology, as in any social or natural science. For example, many attempts to explain why working-class children do less well than middle-class children in education have compared the variables in their home backgrounds. Before-and-after comparisons can study the effects of a change of policy or new legislation. Comparing rates of disease between different social groups can reveal the cause of the disease: indeed, this is how the link between smoking and lung cancer was established.

Summary questions

3   What is a 'control group'?

4   Why do sociologists not use laboratory experiments?

5   What is a 'field experiment'?

Chapter summary

Further resources

The original accounts of Rosenhan's experiment 'on being sane in insane places' (1973) and Rosenthal and Jacobson's 'Teachers' expectancies: determinants of pupils' IQ gains' (1966) can easily be found on the internet.

- Good sociology is based on good evidence that results from good research and draws logical conclusions based on that evidence.

- When looking for causes, it is important not to assume that a correlation between two phenomena means there is a causal relationship.

- Natural scientists make extensive use of the laboratory experiment, where they can control all the variables.

- Sociologists do not use laboratory experiments but can sometimes set up field experiments. While these can be helpful, they have their limitations.

- All explanations, in any context and in any form of science, are based on comparing one thing with another.

Sociological methods

Official statistics

Learning objectives:

- Know about the range of types and sources of secondary data.
- Know how sociologists can make use of secondary data.

Secondary data are those which are available to the sociologist because they already exist. A huge amount of secondary data exist, both quantitative and qualitative, about the present, the recent past and the more distant past.

Official statistics sources

An important form of secondary data is official statistics, which are the statistics produced and published by the government and its agencies. These are collected in three main ways.

Government surveys

The best-known government survey is the Census of Population, which is carried out every 10 years. By law, every household in the UK has to complete a census form. The main questions (e.g. how many people there are in the household, their age, sex, relationships, occupation) are much the same for every Census. Other questions (e.g. about housing, ethnic origin, travel-to-work details) may vary from one Census to the next.

Registration

By law, all births, marriages and deaths, and certain illnesses, must be registered when they occur. The resulting data is published at least annually and provides a record over time.

Record-keeping

All government agencies, and many private organisations, are required to provide certain information to government at regular intervals. For example:

- Schools have to keep records of their pupils and their achievements for the league tables.
- Doctors and hospitals have to keep records of how many patients they have treated and for what conditions.
- Employers have to keep records of how many employees they have and to make returns to Her Majesty's Revenue and Customs about, for example, income tax and VAT.

The government publishes hundreds of booklets and leaflets containing official statistics. Of these, the most comprehensive and easily understood is the annual 'Social Trends' survey, which contains statistics drawn from every area of public life. The 2007 edition of 'Social Trends' (no. 37) lists 32 major surveys that are regularly carried out by the government.

How can sociologists use official statistics?

The advantages of official statistics are that:

- they are readily available, in terms of both time and cost
- they cover a wide range of subjects in considerable detail
- they cover large populations, so are usually representative
- they are generally reliable
- they enable comparisons to be made over time.

However, disadvantages include that:

- the classifications used may omit information that the sociologist is looking for
- the data may not be valid
- the data may be incomplete
- the data may have been 'massaged' for political purposes.

Some official statistics need to be treated with caution, since it may be in the interests of the people who supplied the data not to be entirely truthful (for example, data about income and wealth that is supplied to HM Revenue and Customs).

Some official statistics (for example, the number of babies born in a year) can be taken at face value as valid, reliable and as accurate as can reasonably be expected. Sociologists can use these with reasonable confidence.

However, the official statistics that are of particular interest to sociologists are those produced through a social process which is sometimes called 'the construction of official statistics'. Crime statistics, for example, are not the result of a simple process of counting 'facts' in the world, but of a complex process of observation and decision-making by members of the public, victims, the police and the courts. The same applies to official statistics of health, which are compiled from the records of doctors and hospitals.

The point is not whether the statistics are right or wrong, but that a crime is a different sort of 'fact' from the fact of a birth, or a three-bedroom house, or the number of 11-year-olds in the population.

Summary questions

1. Name three sources of secondary data.

2. Give an example of secondary data that can be assumed to be both valid and reliable.

3. Identify (a) two advantages, and (b) two disadvantages of official statistics.

Sociological methods

Other types and sources of secondary data

Learning objectives:

- Know about the range of types and sources of secondary data.

- Know how sociologists can make use of secondary data.

Earlier research

Some sociologists revisit the data collected by earlier sociologists, either to add to what they have collected themselves or to check, and perhaps question, the conclusions drawn by the earlier research.

A good recent example is *Education and the Middle Class*: in this study, Sally Power *et al.* (2003) deliberately set out to mirror Jackson and Marsden's classic study *Education and the Working Class* (1962), drawing on work done by a range of other sociologists in the previous 40 years.

Documents

There are two kinds of documents that sociologists can use: personal and public. Which they choose (or whether they choose both) will depend on the nature of their research.

Personal documents

Personal documents include such things as letters and diaries. These are likely to be used by sociologists who take an interpretative or qualitative approach and want to understand more about the experience and world views of people in the past. Such documents have not usually been produced with research in mind, though some researchers ask participants to keep diaries while the research is in progress.

Published biographies and autobiographies may also be considered to be in this category though they are, of course, intended for publication so may be less spontaneous or truthful than letters or diaries.

Public documents

These include school records, parish records, social work records, court records, hospital records, reports of government enquiries and a host of other resources.

Fig. 6.13 *When evaluating documents, it is necessary to consider their authenticity, credibility, representativeness and meaning*

Sociological methods

Evaluating documents

Scott (1990) suggests four criteria for evaluating documentary evidence.

1 **Authenticity** Was the document really written by the author? Is it genuine?

2 **Credibility** Is it free of error distortion? Was the author present at the event described? Was it fresh in their memory? Why was the document produced, when, for whom and in what context?

3 **Representativeness** Is the document typical of its kind? Is it complete? Is the author typical of the people of their group or their time?

4 **Meaning** Are there any hidden meanings in addition to the 'surface' meaning? To check this, we need to look at the context in which the document was produced.

Mass media

Films, television programmes, TV news, newspapers and even novels are rich sources of evidence for the sociologist. It is important to remember that these accounts of events have been created by an author or journalist, rather than being factual objective descriptions of events. This is not the same as saying that they are biased (though they may be) but it means that the account is an interpretation from a particular perspective. The TV news, for example, is 'created' by reporters, camera operators, editors and newsreaders, in the sense that they choose what to report and how to report it.

Content analysis

Most documentary data is qualitative, but it is possible to convert this into quantitative data using content analysis. Using this technique, the researcher classifies the content of the document into categories (e.g. in a newspaper, this could be 'political news', 'economic news', 'sports news', 'advertisements' and so on) and then counts how much of the content falls into each category. This makes it possible to make quantitative comparisons between documents. For example, Jagger (2001) used this technique to analyse lonely hearts adverts in newspapers.

The internet

The internet has made available to sociologists a vast range of data and research that was previously very hard to access. Researchers can tap into extensive amounts of data based on large representative samples. The power of the computer then makes it possible to analyse and re-analyse this data in ways and in a depth of detail that was previously impossible. This has led to a revival of interest in quantitative research which fell somewhat out of favour in the later part of the 20th century.

There can be no doubt that the internet is a wonderful source of secondary data of all kinds, but it is also full of nonsense, bias and error. It is often hard to find exactly the information that you need and it is not always easy to assess whether it is accurate or trustworthy. Anyone can post information on the internet which, while making it the most democratic medium of mass communication the world has ever seen, also means that there is no control over the quality of the content, unlike for books and journals.

AQA Examiner's tip

Make sure that you are clear about the difference between primary and secondary data.

AQA Examiner's tip

Try to give some approximate statistics in your answers, rather than just saying 'most' or 'a few'.

Summary questions

4 What are the main types of document that a sociological researcher might use?

5 How might documents be evaluated?

6 What is 'content analysis'?

7 What are the main advantages and disadvantages of the internet as a source of information?

Sociological methods

Chapter summary

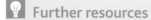

Further resources

www.statistics.gov.uk – For details about the Census, look at the official website.

http://neighbourhood.statistics.gov. uk – This website will provide you with some detailed data about your own area.

www.statistics.gov.uk – The printed version of Social Trends is quite expensive but it is available on the website of the Office of National Statistics, the agency responsible for managing the flood of official statistics.

www.censusatschool.ntu.ac.uk – CensusAtSchool is a free website designed to help students develop their data-handling and statistical skills by using data from all over the world that is real and relevant to them.

www.data-archive.ac.uk – The UK Data Archive website contains the largest amount of digital data in the social sciences and humanities in the UK.

www.essex.ac.uk – Further sociology data can be found on the ESDS Qualidata website.

www.vts.rdn.ac.uk – The Virtual Training Suite website has an excellent tutorial to help sociologists learn how to evaluate any 'evidence' that they find on the internet.

www.atss.org.uk – The Association for the Teaching of Social Sciences (ATSS) website has links to a wide range of other sites that are useful for sociology students.

www.intute.ac.uk – Intute is a free online service offering social sciences resources for research and education.

- Secondary data are data that are available to the sociologist because they already exist.

- An important form of secondary data is official statistics, which are the statistics produced and published by the government and its agencies.

- Official statistics have many advantages for sociologists but also many disadvantages.

- Some official statistics are both valid and reliable, but many are 'socially constructed'. Sociologists are interested in the process of how official statistics are constructed.

- Other sources of secondary data include earlier research, documents and the mass media.

- Documents can be evaluated in terms of their authenticity, credibility, representativeness and meaning.

- The technique of content analysis can be used to study the mass media and other kinds of document.

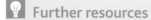

Sociological methods

6.7 Research methods

A summary

Most sociologists would claim that what makes sociology superior to common sense or journalism is that it aims to draw reasoned and rigorous conclusions from reliable, valid and representative evidence about its subject matter – people, social facts, social institutions and social processes. Furthermore, the evidence, how it was collected and the conclusions drawn from it are all made available for others to check and scrutinise, so that if there are mistakes or the evidence does not support the conclusions, this will be pointed out.

Whether they are interested in describing the social world or in trying to explain it (or both), sociologists use a variety of methods for obtaining evidence. In the past, particularly in the 1960s and 1970s, there were lively disagreements about theoretical perspectives in sociology and, hence, the merits of different methods. Today, it is generally agreed that it is sensible to use a variety of research methods, and sometimes a combination, according to the topic that is being studied.

However, this does not mean that a researcher can choose whatever methods they take a fancy to. It is important to take a systematic approach, to consider some of the issues that underlie the research process, and to understand why some methods, or combinations of methods, are more suitable in particular situations than others.

What is being studied?

This is the question that underlies the debate between positivist and interpretivist approaches. The positivist approach takes the view that the only valid and reliable evidence is what we can observe, count and measure. Researchers should not speculate about processes that they cannot observe – for example, we cannot observe people's motives for behaving in a particular way. Positivism is a perfectly sound way of approaching most research in the natural sciences, where we can assume that the things being studied (e.g. plants, minerals, chemicals) are not self-consciously aware of their actions and do not choose to behave as they do. It is possible to observe them, to make comparisons between one situation and another (perhaps in a laboratory experiment) and to uncover the 'laws of nature'.

The interpretivist approach argues that the subject matter of sociology – people – is fundamentally different from the subject matter of the natural sciences, because people are self-consciously aware of what is happening in a social situation, give meaning to it and can make choices about how to act. Social facts and social phenomena exist because the people involved share an understanding of them and give them a similar meaning. So, to explain an event in the social world, whether it is two people interacting in the street or a major social change, we have to take account of how the people involved make sense of it and how this influences their actions. We can do this by observing them, taking part in their lives and asking questions.

■ How do sociologists conduct research?

Most researchers would accept that it is sensible to use the research methods that are best suited to the subject matter, without being too preoccupied with disputes about positivism and interpretivism. Using a combination of methods can help to balance the weaknesses of one method with the strengths of another. Sociologists do not fall into one of two camps labelled 'positivist' and 'interpretivist'.

A number of factors, including personal interests and current debates in the subject, will influence what a sociologist chooses to study and what methods to use. In addition to the theoretical debates outlined above, these include practical factors and ethical factors.

Practical issues include:

■ time (how much time has the sociologist got to complete the research?)
■ money (can the sociologist get any financial support?)
■ labour-power (is the sociologist working alone or in a team?)
■ access (can the sociologist get access to the people or situation to be studied?).

Ethical issues include ensuring that:

■ the people being studied have given their informed consent to the work
■ no harm will come to them
■ respondents' privacy, anonymity and confidentiality are safeguarded.

Having taken all these factors into account, the researcher will produce a research design. This may involve a single research method, such as a survey or participant observation, or a combination of methods, and may make use of both primary data (collected by the researcher) and secondary data (already available because recorded by someone else).

Essentially, a researcher has three ways of collecting evidence:

■ asking questions
■ observing
■ reading information that others have already recorded.

Each of these can be used to collect either quantitative data (in the form of numbers) or qualitative data (usually in the form of words, often quoted directly from the people being studied).

Whichever method is used, the researcher will have to operationalise the key concepts they are using. They will have to define these abstract concepts in such a way that valid, reliable and unambiguous empirical observations can be made about them.

■ Quantitative data

A researcher who wants to obtain primary quantitative data about how people live their lives, or their attitudes or beliefs, will usually carry out a survey on a representative sample of the population being studied. The questions may be in the form of a questionnaire, possibly delivered through the post or by email, or a structured interview, where the researcher asks the questions face to face or over the telephone and notes the responses. The data collected should be reliable but may not be entirely valid.

Laboratory experiments, though they produce primary quantitative data, are seldom used in sociological research because of problems of validity, ethics and scale.

When the research is based on documents, or on the mass media, the technique of content analysis may be used. For example, a researcher studying the lives of people in the past might analyse the content of old letters and diaries in quantitative terms; similarly, a study of the content of the mass media might analyse how much time or space is spent on each topic in the news media.

A large amount of quantitative secondary data is available to sociologists from the official statistics that are published by the government and its agencies. Some of these (for example, the number of marriages that take place in a year) can be treated as reliable matters of fact. Others, such as crime or health statistics, are the outcome of social processes that can be studied in their own right.

Qualitative data

Sociologists who want to collect primary qualitative data, usually in an ethnographic study of the way of life of a group of people, will often use observation, which may be either participant or non-participant and either covert or overt. This should produce valid data but its reliability may be suspect and such studies are usually of small groups, which means that their representativeness may be questioned.

Many sociologists also use unstructured interviews, where the researcher has a relatively informal conversation with the research participant but asks a lot of questions and ensures that the discussion focuses on the topic that is being researched. The reliability of this method is often called into question.

Qualitative secondary data takes the form of letters, diaries and other personal documents, as well as film, video and TV. These can be analysed in terms of their meanings, symbols and use of language but also, as we have seen, in a way that produces quantitative data.

Evaluating research and research data

Some of the important questions that need to be asked about any piece of sociological research are as follows:

- Is the group or situation studied representative of any larger group or population?
- Is the data reliable? Would another researcher using the same methods, asking the same questions or making the same observations have come up with the same results?
- Is the data valid? Is it a true picture of what is being studied or has it been distorted by the research method used?
- Is the research objective? Does the research report claim to be free of bias? Does the researcher acknowledge how their values may have affected the outcome?
- Is the research ethically correct?
- Is there enough information in the research report for you to be able to answer these questions properly?

Further resources

A. Bryman, *Social Research Methods* (2nd edn), Oxford University Press, 2004

R. Gomm, *Social Research Methodology: A Critical Introduction*, Palgrave Macmillan, 2004

P. McNeill and S. Chapman, *Research Methods* (3rd edn), Routledge, 2005

K. Trobe, *Revising AS Sociological Methods*, Lindisfarne Press, 2001

M. Walsh, *Research Made Real*, Nelson Thornes, 2001

Sociological methods

References

N. Abercrombie, *Sociology*, Polity Press, 2004

F. Abrams, *Below the Breadline: Life on the Minimum Wage*, Profile Books, 2002

The Acheson report, *Independent Inquiry into Inequalities in Health*, HMSO, 1998

T.W. Adorno, *The Culture Industry*, Routledge, 1991

B. Anderson, *Imagined Communities*, Verso, 1983

F. Ansley, 1972, cited in J. Bernard, *The Future of Marriage*, Penguin, 1976

P. Aries, *Centuries of Childhood*, Penguin, 1962

M. Arnot, M.E. David and G. Weiner, *Closing the Gender Gap: Post-war Education and Social Change*, Polity Press; Blackwell, 1999

A.B. Atkinson and F. Bourguignon, 'The Comparison of Multi-dimensioned Distribution of Economic Status', *The Review of Economic Studies* 49, 183–201, 1982

A.B. Atkinson and J. Micklewright, 'Unemployment Compensation and Labor Market Transitions: A Critical Review', *Journal of Economic Literature* 29(4) 1679–727, 1989

O. Banks, *The Sociology of Education*, Batsford, 1971

E. Barker, *The Making of a Moonie: Brainwashing or Choice?* Blackwell, 1984

R. Barker, *Leisure Studies*, Collins, 2006

B. Barry, 'Social Exclusion, Social Isolation and the Distribution of Income', in J. Hills, J. Le Grand and D. Piachaud (eds.), *Understanding Social Exclusion*, Oxford University Press, 2002

A. Barnard and T. Burgess, *Sociology Explained*, Cambridge University Press, 1996

BBC, Citizenship Lessons 'Inadequate', http://news.bbc.co.uk/1/hi/help/3681938.stm

G.S. Becker, *Economics of Discrimination*, University of Chicago Press, 1971

G.S. Becker, *Human Capital: A Theoretical and Empirical Analysis with Special Reference to Education*, University of Chicago Press, 1993

H.S. Becker, *Outsiders*, Free Press, 1963

H.S. Becker, 'Social-class Variations in the Teacher–Pupil Relationship', in B. Cosin (ed.), *School and Society: A Sociological Reader*, Routledge & Kegan Paul, 1971

M. Benston, 'The Political Economy of Women's Liberation' in N. Glazer-Malbin (ed.), *Women in a Man-made World*, Rand-McNally, 1972

P. Berger, *Invitation to Sociology: A Humanistic Perspective*, Doubleday, 1963

B. Bernstein, 'Social Class and Linguistic Development: A Theory of Social Learning', in A.H. Halsey, J. Floud and C.A. Anderson (eds.), *Education, Economy and Society*, Free Press, 1961

B.B. Bernstein, *Class, Codes and Control*, Routledge & Kegan Paul, 1971

S. Best, J. Griffiths and T. Hope, *Active Sociology*, Pearson Education, 2000

T. Bilton, K. Bannet, P. Jones, D. Skinner, M. Stanworth and A. Webster, *Introductory Sociology*, Macmillan, 1996

The Black report, *Report of a Research Working Group*, DHSS, 1980

J.G. Blumler, 'The New Television Marketplace: Imperatives, Implications, Issues', in J. Curran and M. Gurevitch (eds), *Mass Media and Society*, Edward Arnold, 1991

J. Boaler and M. Staples, *Creating Mathematical Futures through an Equitable Teaching Approach: The Case of Railside School*, 2005, from www.stanford.edu/~joboaler/equitable.pdf

E. Bott, *Family and Social Network*, Tavistock, 1957

M.G. Boulton, *On Being a Mother*, Tavistock, 1983

P. Bourdieu and J.-C. Passeron, 'Cultural Reproduction and Social Reproduction', in R.K. Brown (ed.), *Knowledge, Education and Cultural Change*, Tavistock, 1973

P. Bourdieu and J.-C. Passerson, *Reproduction in Education, Society and Culture*, Sage, 1977

S. Bowles and H. Gintis, *Schooling in Capitalist America: Educational Reform and the Contradictions of Economic Life*, Routledge & Kegan Paul, 1976

H. Bradley, *Fractured Identities: Changing Patterns of Inequality*, Polity Press, 1997

A. Brah, 'Difference, Diversity and Differentiation', in J. Donald and A. Rattansi (eds), *'Race', Culture and Difference*, Sage Publications in association with the Open University, 1992

G. Brown and T. Harris, *The Social Origins of Depression*, Tavistock, 1978

G. Brown and T. Harris, *Life Events and Illness*, Guildford Press, 1989

K. Browne, *Introducing Sociology for AS Level*, Polity Press, 2002

A. Bryman, *Social Research Methods* (2nd edn), Oxford University Press, 2004

C. Callender and J. Jackson, 'Does the Fear of Debt Deter Students from Higher Education?' *Journal of Social Policy*, 34(4), 509–40, 2005

E.E. Cashmore, 'Rewriting the Script', *New Society*, December 1985

S. Chapman, *Revise AS Sociology*, Letts Educational, 2000

R. Chester, 'The Rise of the Neo-conventional Family', *New Society*, 9 May 1985

A.V. Cicourel, *The Social Organization of Juvenile Justice*, Heinemann, 1976

J. Clarke, S. Hall, T. Jefferson and B. Roberts, 'Subcultures, Cultures and Class', in S. Hall and T. Jefferson (eds), *Resistance through Rituals: Youth Subcultures in Post-war Britain*, Hutchinson, 1976

A.K. Cohen, *Delinquent Boys*, Free Press, 1955

M. Cole, *Bowles and Gintis Revisited: Correspondence and Contradiction in Educational Theory*, Falmer Press, 1988

T. Cole, *Whose Welfare?* Tavistock Press, 1986

P. Connolly, *Racism, Gender Identity and Young Children*, Routledge, 1998

C.H. Coolen, *Human Nature and the Social Order*, Shocken, 1964

D. Cooper, *The Death of the Family*, Penguin, 1972

Crown, National Statistics Online, 2007, from www.statistics.gov.uk

L. Culley, *Gender Differences and Computing in Secondary Schools*, Department of Education, Loughborough University of Technology, 1986

K. Davis and W. Moore, 'Some Principles of Stratification', in R. Bendix and S. Lipset (eds), *Class, Status and Power* (2nd edn), Routledge & Kegan Paul, 1967

R. Dobash and R. Dobash, *Violence against Wives*, Open Books, 1980

G. Driver and R. Ballard, 'Comparing Performance in Multi-racial School: South Asian Pupils at 16-plus', *New Community*, VII, 143–53, 1979

P. Dunleavy, *Developments in British Politics*, Macmillan, 1993

G. Dunne, 'A Passion for Sameness', in E.B. Silva and C. Smart (eds), *The New Family*, Sage, 1999

E. Durkheim, *The Division of Labour in Society*, The Free Press, 1947

S. Edgell, *Middle Class Couples*, Allen and Unwin, 1980

F. Engels, *The Origin of the Family, Private Property and the State*, Lawrence and Wishart, 1972

E. Ferri and K. Smith, *Parenting in the 1990s*, Family Policy Studies Centre, 1996

L. Festinger, H.W. Riecken and S. Schachter, *When Prophecy Fails*, Harper & Row, 1956

F. Field, *Losing Out: The Emergence of Britain's Underclass*, Blackwell, 1989

J. Finch and J. Mason, *Negotiating Family Responsibilities*, Routledge, 1983

V. Finkelstein, *Attitudes and Disabled People: Issues for Discussion*, World Rehabilitation Fund, 1980

M. Foucault, *Mental Illness and Psychology* (trans. A.M. Sheridan-Smith), Harper & Row, 1976

K. Fox, *Watching the English: The Hidden Rules of English Behaviour*, Hodder & Stoughton, 2005

B. Francis, J. Osgood, J. Dalgety and L. Archer, 'Gender Equality in Work Experience Placements for Young People', *Occupational Segregation Working Papers*, 2007, from www.eoc.org.uk/PDF/wp27.pdf

P. Freire, A.M.A.J. Freire and D. Macedo, *The Paulo Freire Reader*, Continuum, 1998

M. Fuller, 'Black Girls in a Comprehensive School', in M. Hammersley and P. Woods (eds), *Life in School: The Sociology of Pupil Culture*, Open University Press, 1982

J. Gershunny, 'The Domestic Labour Revolution', in M. Anderson, F. Bechhofer and J. Gershunny (eds) The Social and Political Economy of the Household, Oxford University Press, 1994

J. Gershunny and H. Laurie, 'Couples, Work and Money', in R. Berthoud and J. Gershunny (eds) *Seven Years in the Lives of British Families*, Policy Press, 2000

S. Gewirtz, S. Ball and R. Bowe, *Markets, Choice, and Equity in Education*, Open University Press, 1995

J.G. Ghevarughese, 'Foundations of Eurocentrism in Mathematics', *Race and Class*, 28(13), 1987

S. Gibbons and S. Machin, *Paying for Primary Schools: Supply Constraints Popularity or Congestion*, 2006, from http://cee.lse.ac.uk/cee%20dps/ceedp42.pdf

S. Gibbons and O. Silva, *Faith Schools: Better Schools or Better Pupils*, 2006, from http://cee.lse.ac.uk/cee%20dps/ceedp72.pdf

A. Giddens, *Sociology* (5th edn), Polity Press, 2001

D. Gillborn, *'Race', Ethnicity and Education: Teaching and Learning in Multi-ethnic Schools*, Unwin Hyman, 1990

D. Gillborn and D. Youdell, *Rationing Education: Policy, Practice, Reform, and Equity*, Open University Press, 2000

H. Glennerster and M. Evans, 'Beveridge and His Assumptive Worlds: The Incompatibilities of a Flawed Design', in J. Hills, J. Ditch and H. Glennerster (eds), *Beveridge and Social Security: An International Retrospective*, Clarendon Press, 1994

H. Glennerster, J. Hills, D. Piachaud and J. Webb, *One Hundred Years of Poverty and Policy*, Joseph Rowntree Foundation, 2004

M. Goddard-Spear, 'The Biasing Influence of Pupils' Sex in a Science Marking Exercise', *Research in Science and Technological Education*, 2(1), 55–60, 1984

E. Goffman, *The Presentation of Self in Everyday Life*, University of Edinburgh Social Sciences Research Centre, 1959

E. Goffman, *Stigma: Notes on the Management of Spoiled Identity*, Prentice-Hall, 1963

E. Goffman, *Notes on the Management of Spoiled Identity*, Penguin, 1968a

E. Goffman, *Asylums: Essays on the Social Situation of Mental Patients and Other Inmates*, Penguin, 1968b

P. Golding and G. Murdock, 'Culture, Communications and Political Economy', in J. Curran and M. Gurevitch (eds), *Mass Media and Society*, Edward Arnold, 1991

R. Gomm, *Social Research Methodology: A Critical Introduction*, Palgrave Macmillan, 2004

D. Gordon and C. Pantazis (eds), *Breadline Britain in the 1990s*, Ashgate, 1997

D. Gordon, A. Adelman, K. Ashworth, J. Bradshaw, J. Levitas, R. Middleton *et al.*, *Poverty and Social Exclusion in Britain*, Joseph Rowntree Foundation, 2000

O. Gough, 'The Impact of the Gender Pay Gap on Post Retirement Earnings', *Critical Social Policy*, 21(3), 311–34, 2001

P. Gregg, S. Harkness and S. Machin, *Child Development and Family Income*, York Publishing Services in association with the Joseph Rowntree Foundation, 1999

S. Hall, 'Our Mongrel Selves', *New Statesman and Society*, 19 June 1992

S. Hall, C. Critcher, T. Jefferson, and B. Roberts, *Policing the Crisis*, Macmillan, 1978, 1979

S. Hall and T. Jefferson (eds), *Resistance through Rituals: Youth Subcultures in Post-war Britain*, Hutchinson, 1976

S. Hamilton, *Equality in Education: Work Experience Placements*, SCRE, 2003.

L. Hancock, 'The Care Crunch', *Critical Social Policy*, 22(1), 119–40, 2002

M. Haralambos and M. Holborn, *Sociology, Themes and Perspectives*, Harper Collins, 2000

I. Hardill, A.E. Green, A.C. Dudleston and D.W. Owen, 'Who Decides What? Decision Making in Dual-Career Households', *Work, Employment and Society*, 11(2), 313–26, 1997

D. Hargreaves, *Social Relations in a Secondary School*, Routledge & Kegan Paul, 1973

D.H. Hargreaves, S. Hester and F.J. Mellor, *Deviance in Classrooms*, Routledge & Kegan Paul, 1975

L. Harker, *Chance of a Lifetime: The Impact of Bad Housing on Children's Lives*, 2006, from http://england.shelter.org.uk/files/seealsodocs/23199/Lifechancereport%2Epdf

F. Heindensohn, *Women and Crime*, Macmillan, 1985

V. Hey, *The Company She Keeps: An Ethnography of Girl's Friendship*, Open University Press, 1997

J. Hills (ed.), *New Inequalities: The Changing Distribution of Income and Wealth in the UK*, Cambridge University Press, 1996

S. Holdaway, *Inside the British Police: A Force at Work*, Basil Blackwell, 1983

M. Howard, A. Garnham, G. Finnister and J. Veit-Wilson, *Poverty: The Facts*, Child Poverty Action Group, 2001

C. Howarth, P. Kenway, G. Palmer, and R. Miorelli, *Monitoring Poverty and Social Exclusion*, Joseph Rowntree Foundation, 1999

J. Hutton, 'Ending Child Poverty and Transforming Life Chances', Speech to the Fabian Society, 10 May 2006

W. Hutton, *The State We're In*, Cape, 1995

H. Hyman, 'The Value Systems of Different Classes', in R. Bendix and S. Lipset (eds), *Class, Status and Power*, Routledge & Kegan Paul, 1967

I. Illich, *Medical Nemesis*, Calder and Boyars, 1975

B. Jackson and D. Marsden, *Education and the Working Class*, Routledge, 1962

E. Jagger, 'Marketing Molly and Melville', *Sociology* 35(1), 2001

M. Jones and E. Jones, *Mass Media*, Macmillan, 1999

R. Jowell (ed.), *The British Social Attitudes Surveys*, Ashgate, 1984, 1991, 1997

Man-Yee Kan, 'Gender Asymmetry in the Division of Domestic Labour', paper presented to the British Household Panel Survey, Institute for Social and Economic Research, 6 July 2001

S. Kane and M. Kirby, *Wealth, Poverty and Welfare*, Blackwell, 2003

N.G. Keddie, *Tinker, Tailor: The Myth of Cultural Deprivation*, Penguin Education, 1973

A. Kelly, *Final Report of the GIST Project*, GIST, 1984

A. Kelly, *Science for Girls*, Open University Press, 1987

W. Keys and C. Fernandes, *What Do Students Think about School? Research into the Factors Associated with Positive and Negative Attitudes towards Education*, National Foundation for Educational Research, 1993

C. Kirkwood, *Leaving Abusive Partners*, Sage, 1993

W. Labov, *Sociolinguistic Patterns*, University of Pennsylvania Press, 1973

R.D. Laing and A. Esterson, *Sanity, Madness and the Family*, Penguin, 1964

J.F. Lane, *Pierre Bourdieu: A Critical Introduction*, Pluto Press, 2000

G. Lauder, 'Taking Care with Welfare', *Sociology Review*, September 2003

T. Lawson, M. Jones and R. Moores, *Advanced Sociology through Diagrams*, Oxford University Press, 2000

E.R. Leach, *Runaway World*, BBC, 1967

O. Lewis, 'The Culture of Poverty', in G. Gmelch (ed.), *Urban Life: Readings in Urban Anthropology*, St Martins Press, 1966

M. Mac an Ghaill, *Young, Gifted and Black: Student-teacher Relations in the Schooling of Black Youth*, Open University Press, 1988

M. Mac an Ghaill, *The Making of Men: Masculinities, Sexualities and Schooling*, Open University Press, 1994

T. McKeown, *The Role of Medicine*, Blackwell, 1979

S. McLanahan and K. Booth, 'Mother Only Families', in A. Booth (ed.), *Contemporary Families*, National Council on Family Relations, 1991

M. McLuhan, *Understanding Media*, First Sphere Books, 1964

P. McNeill and S. Chapman, *Research Methods* (3rd edn), Routledge, 2005

K. Mann, *The Making of an English Underclass*, Open University Press, 1992

M. Marcus and A. Ducklin, *Success in Sociology*, John Murray, 1998

G. Marks and D. Houston, 'The Determinants of Young Women's Intentions about Education, Career

Development and Family Life', *Journal of Education and Work*, 15, 321–36, 2002

M.G. Marmot, G.A. Rose, M.J. Shipley and P.J.S. Hamilton, 'Employment Grade and Coronary Heart Disease in British Civil Servants', *Journal of Epidemiology and Community Health*, 32, 1978

D. Marsland, *Welfare or Welfare State*, Macmillan, 1996

D. Marsland and R. Segalman, *Cradle to Grave: Comparative Perspectives on the State of the Welfare*, Macmillan 1989

D. Mason, *Race and Ethnicity in Modern Britain*, Oxford University Press, 2000

J. Millar and K. Gardiner, *Low Pay, Household Resources and Poverty*, Joseph Rowntree Foundation, 2004

J. Milne, 'Hopes for Girls Fly Higher', *Times Educational Supplement*, 4 May 2007, from www.tes.co.uk/search/story/?story_id=2379179

H. Mirza, *Young, Female and Black*, Routledge, 1992

T. Modood, 'Culture and Identity', in T. Modood, R. Berthoud, J. Lakey, J. Nazroo, P. Smith, S. Virdee and S. Beishon, *Ethnic Minorities in Britain: Diversity and Disadvantage*, Policy Studies Institute, 1997

S. Moore, *Investigating Deviance*, Collins, 1991

S. Moore, *Social Welfare Alive*, Nelson Thornes, 1998

S. Moore *et al.*, *Sociology for AS-level*, Collins, 2001

J. Morris, *Independent Lives? Community Care and Disabled People*, Macmillan, 1993

L. Morris, *The Workings of the Household*, Polity, 1990

G.P. Murdock, *Social Structure*, Macmillan, 1949

C. Murray, 'Underclass', *Sunday Times* magazine, 26 November 1989

C. Murray, *The Emerging British Underclass*, Institute for Economic Affairs, 1990

C. Murray, *Underclass: The Crisis Deepens*, Institute for Economic Affairs, 1994

D. Myhill and S. Jones, 'She Doesn't Shout at No Girls: Pupils' Perceptions of Gender Equity in the Classroom', *Cambridge Journal of Education*, 36(1), 99–113, 2006

J. Nazroo, *The Health of London's Minorities*, Policy Studies Institute, 1997

A. Oakley, *Sex, Gender and Society*, Temple Smith, 1972

A. Oakley, *Housewife*, Allen Lane, 1974a

A. Oakley, *The Sociology of Housework*, Martin Robertson, 1974b

M. O'Donnell, *Race and Ethnicity*, Longman, 1991

A. Osler and H. Starkey, 'Learning for Cosmopolitan Citizenship: Theoretical Debates and Young People's Experiences', *Educational Review*, 55(3), 243–54, 2003

A. Osler and H. Starkey, *Changing Citizenship: Democracy and Inclusion in Education*, Open University Press, 2005

R.M. Page, 'New Labour and the Welfare State', in M. Holborn (ed.), *New Development in Sociology*, Causeway, 2002

R.M. Page, *Without a Song in their Heart: New Labour, the Welfare State and the Retreat from Democratic Socialism*, Cambridge University Press 2007

J. Pahl, *Money and Marriage*, Macmillan, 1989

S. Parker, 'Work and Leisure', in E. Butterworth and D. Wier (eds), *The Sociology of Leisure*, Allen and Unwin, 1976

T. Parsons, *The Social System*, Free Press, 1951

T. Parsons, 'The Social Structure of the Family', in R.N. Anshen (ed.), *The Family: Its Functions and Destiny*, Harper & Row, 1959

T. Parsons, 'The Sick Role and the Role of the Physician Reconsidered', *Millbank Memorial Fund Quarterly: Health and Society*, 53, 1975

T. Parsons, 'The School Class as a Social System', in A.H. Halsey, J. Floud and C.A. Anderson, *Education, Economy and Society*, The Free Press, 1961

T. Parsons, *The Social System*, Routledge, 1991

J. Patrick, *A Glasgow Gang Observed*, Eyre Methuen, 1973

M. Phillips, *The Sex-change Society: Feminised Britain and the Neutered Male*, Social Market Foundation, 1999

M. Phillips, 'The Feminisation of Education', *Daily Mail*, 19 August 2002

L. Platt, *Poverty and Ethnicity in the UK*, 2007, from www.jrf.org.uk/bookshop/eBooks/2006-ethnicity-poverty-UK.pdf

N. Postman, *The Disappearance of Childhood*, Vintage, 1994

M. Powell (ed.), *Understanding the Mixed Economy of Welfare*, Policy Press, 2007

S. Power, T. Edwards, G. Whitty and S. Wigfall, *Education and the Middle Class*, Open University Press, 2003

K. Pryce, *Endless Pressure: A Study of West Indian Life-styles in Bristol*, Penguin, 1979

R. Rapoport, 'Ideologies about Family Forms', in K. Boh, M. Bak, C. Clason, M. Pankratova, J. Qvortrup, G.B. Sqritta and K. Waerness (eds), *Changing Patterns of European Family Life*, Routledge, 1989

R. Rapoport and R. Rapoport, *Families in Britain*, Routledge & Kegan Paul, 1982

G. Ritzer, *Sociological Theory* (3rd edn), McGraw Hill, 1992

D. Rosenhan, 'On Being Sane in Insane Places', *Science*, 179, 250–8, 1973

R. Rosenthal and L. Jacobson, *Pygmalion in the Classroom*, Holt, Rinehart and Winston, 1968

R. Rosenthal and L. Jacobson, *Pygmalion in the Classroom: Teacher Expectation and Pupil's Intellectual Development*, Crown House, 2003

S. Rowntree and G. Lavers, *Poverty and the Welfare State*, Longman, 1951

D. Sainsbury, *Gender, Equality and Welfare States*, Cambridge University Press, 1996

T. Scheff, 'The Role of the Mentally Ill and the Dynamics of Mental Disorder', in S. Spitzer and N. Denzin (eds), *The Mental Patient*, McGraw-Hill, 1968

J. Scott, *A Matter of Record*, Polity Press, 1990

A. Scull, *Decarceration: Community Treatment and the Deviant – A Radical View*, Rutgers University Press, 1984

T. Sewell, *Black Masculinities and Schooling: How Black Boys Survive Modern Schooling*, Trentham, 1997

C. Shakeshaft, 'Reforming Science Education to Include Girls', *Theory into Practice*, 34(1), 74–9, 1995

T. Shakespeare (ed.), *The Disability Reader*, Cassell, 1998

T. Shakespeare, *Disability Rights and Wrongs*, Routledge, 2006

S. Sharpe, *Just Like a Girl: How Girls Learn to be Women*, Penguin 1976, 1994

M. Shaw, D. Dorling, D. Gordon and G. Davey Smith, *The Widening Gap: Health Inequalities and Policy in Britain*, Policy Press, 1999

J. Shepherd, *What Does Britain Expect*, 2007, from http://education.guardian.co.uk/schools/story/0,,2127671,00.html

T. Shultz, *Investment in Human Beings*, University of Chicago Press, 1962

D. Spender, *Invisible Women*, Woman's Press, 1983

M. Stanworth, *Gender and Schooling: A Study of Sexual Division in the Classroom*, Hutchinson, 1983

L. Steel and W. Kidd, *The Family*, Palgrave, 2001

P. Stephens *et al.*, *Think Sociology*, Stanley Thornes, 1998

B. Sugarman, *Social Class, Values and Behaviour*, Penguin, 1970

L. Sukhnandan, *An Investigation into Gender Differences in Achievement Phase 1: A Review of Recent Research and LEA Information on Provision*, NFER, 1999

T. Szasz, *The Myth of Mental Illness*, Harper & Row, 1974

P. Taylor *et al.*, *Sociology in Focus*, Causeway Press, 2002

S. Thornton, *Club Cultures*, Polity Press, 1995

P. Townsend, *Poverty in the United Kingdom*, Penguin, 1979

P. Townsend, D. Gordon, S. Nandy, C. Pantazis and S. Pemberton, 'Child Poverty in the Developing World', Townsend Centre for International Poverty Research, Policy Press, 2003

K. Trobe, *Revising AS Sociological Methods*, Lindisfarne Press, 2001

P. Trowler, *Investigating Health, Welfare and Poverty*, Collins Educational, 1995

G. Tuchmann, A. Kaplan Daniels and J. Benet (eds), *Hearth and Home: Images of Women in the Mass Media*, Oxford University Press, 1978

J. Tudor Hart, 'The Inverse Care Law', *Lancet*, 297(7696), 405–12, 1971

UCAS, Admissions Statistics, 2007, from www.ucas.ac.uk/figures/index.html

J. Urry, *The Tourist Gaze: Leisure and Travel in Contemporary Societies*, Sage, 1990

M. Walsh, *Research Made Real*, Nelson Thornes, 2001

M. Weaver-Highertower, 'The "Boy Turn" in Research on Gender and Education', *Review of Educational Research*, 72(4), 471–98, 2003

A. Whittaker, 'Qualitative Methods in General Practice Research: Experience from the Oceanpoint Study', *Family Practice* 13, 310–16, 1996

W.F. Whyte, *Street Corner Society*, University of Chicago Press, 1955

P.E. Willis, *Learning to Labour: How Working-class Kids Get Working-class Jobs*, Saxon House, 1977

D. Wilson, S. Burgess and A. Briggs, *The Dynamics of School Attainment of England's Ethnic Minorities*, Centre for Market and Public Organisation, 2005

N. Wolf, *The Beauty Myth: How Images of Beauty Are Used Against Women*, William Morrow and Co., 1991

P. Woods, *Schools and Deviance*, Open University Press, 1981

C. Wright, 'Black Students–White Teachers', in B. Troyna (ed.), *Racial Inequality in Education*, Tavistock, 1987

S. Yeandle, K. Escott, L. Grant and E. Batty, *Women and Men Talking About Poetry*, Equal Opportunities Commission, 2005

M. Young and P. Willmott, *The Sytmmetrical Family*, Penguin, 1973

Index